T0284829

AVID

READER

PRESS

THE TIGER SLAM

THE INSIDE STORY OF THE GREATEST GOLF EVER PLAYED

KEVIN COOK

AVID READER PRESS

NEW YORK   LONDON   TORONTO   SYDNEY   NEW DELHI

AVID READER PRESS
An Imprint of Simon & Schuster, LLC
1230 Avenue of the Americas
New York, NY 10020

First Avid Reader Press hardcover edition December 2024

AVID READER PRESS and colophon are trademarks of Simon & Schuster, LLC

Simon & Schuster: Celebrating 100 Years of Publishing in 2024

For information about special discounts for bulk purchases,
please contact Simon & Schuster Special Sales
at 1-866-506-1949 or business@simonandschuster.com.

The Simon & Schuster Speakers Bureau can bring authors to your live event.
For more information or to book an event, contact the Simon & Schuster Speakers Bureau
at 1-866-248-3049 or visit our website at www.simonspeakers.com.

Interior design by Ruth Lee-Mui

Manufactured in the United States of America

1   3   5   7   9   10   8   6   4   2

Library of Congress Cataloging-in-Publication Data has been applied for.

ISBN 978-1-6680-4364-6
ISBN 978-1-6680-4366-0 (ebook)

To Pamela,

my love

CONTENTS

CONTENTS

THE TIGER SLAM

PROLOGUE
GRAND OPENING

What was it all about?

For Eldrick Tont Woods, it wasn't enough to win trophies, tournaments, millions of dollars, the crowd's adulation, the whole world's attention. All of that was cool, he said, but he wanted more. He had always expected wealth, fame, and record-setting success, had *known* it was coming since he was a toddler hitting golf balls on national television. Growing up on hardscrabble public courses, he had learned the game from his father, who had nicknamed him "Tiger" to honor a fellow soldier who had saved his life in Vietnam. Soon young Tiger was beating players more than twice his age. He was signing autographs before he learned cursive writing. He broke 80 for the first time when he was eight and 70 when he was twelve. With every early victory he pictured himself older—all grown up, knocking drives out of sight, sinking putts, lifting trophies, smiling on TV.

That is exactly what happened. After winning three U.S. Amateur Championship titles to set a record that still stands, he turned professional in 1996. Within a year he was the youngest golfer ever to be ranked number one in the world. At twenty-one, he won the Masters by a dozen strokes. By then much of America was in thrall to "Tigermania." Crowds followed wherever he went. Fortune 500 companies threw endorsement money at him. Magazines from *Golf Digest* and *Sports Illustrated* to *Newsweek*, *People*, and *GQ* put him on their covers. Rappers name-checked him. "Tiger Woods transcends golf," Oprah Winfrey announced. "He is magical and mesmerizing."

Which led to a question few people ever face: What do you do after your dreams come true?

For Tiger, the answer was simple: Dream bigger.

Later years would diminish his magic and change the world's perception of him. A younger generation would know Tiger Woods as tabloid fodder, a balding, limping, middle-aged celebrity in recovery from sex addiction and car crashes that sent his life careening out of control. But all that is in the future. This story is set at the turn of the twenty-first century, the height of Tigermania, when the best player of his time set a challenge for himself.

He was already the most famous golfer in history, a charismatic young man looking for new ways to leave an indelible stamp on the ancient game. A handsome, charismatic young *Black* man dominating a sport known for its whiteness. In the late 1990s, not even one in fifty golfers was Black. You would have needed a crowd of more than two hundred golfers to put together a Black foursome, and that group would not have been welcome at many of America's best courses. Tiger knew how that felt. As a teenager he had been called "a little n——" and chased off a driving range. He was so familiar with the glare golfers of color often got at country clubs that he had a name for it: "the Look."

But here he was, not yet twenty-five, beating his supposed social superiors at their own game, making golf more popular than ever, and doing it with the crowd-pleasing style of a showman. When Tiger

Woods won, it was often by record-setting margins, with shots other players didn't dare try. What would he do next? His long-term goal was to surpass Jack Nicklaus's record of eighteen major championships, but that would take many years, even for him. In the late 1990s, he had something more immediate in mind.

A lifelong student of the game, Tiger knew that Bobby Jones had won golf's original Grand Slam in 1930. Jones, a gentleman lawyer who played in a dress shirt and tie, swept that year's U.S. Open, Great Britain's Open Championship, and two events reserved for nonprofessionals, the U.S. Amateur and British Amateur, to win the so-called impregnable quadrilateral. Thirty years later, Arnold Palmer opened the championship season by winning the 1960 Masters and U.S. Open. Amateur events had lost their luster, but there was talk that Palmer might achieve "a latter-day duplicate" of Jones's feat including the Masters, both Opens, and the PGA Championship. On the long flight to Scotland for the 1960 Open Championship, he discussed the idea with a reporter. "Why don't we create a new Grand Slam?" Palmer asked.

He went on to lose the Open Championship by a stroke, ending any Slam speculation for the year, but the seed was planted. Golf writers began describing a professional Grand Slam as the game's ultimate goal. Yet Palmer never won more than two majors in a row. Jack Nicklaus never won more than two in a row. Even today, no golfer since Ben Hogan in 1953 has won even three consecutive major championships.

With one exception.

On the night after his twelve-shot Masters victory in 1997, Tiger flew home to Florida with his friend and mentor PGA Tour veteran Mark O'Meara. As their Gulfstream II approached Orlando, Tiger brought up a short-term goal: "A Grand Slam. Do you think it's possible?"

O'Meara, eighteen years older, had played in fifty-four majors without finishing better than third. "No," he said. "It's unrealistic."

Tiger said, "I think it could be done."

ONE
WINNING STREAK

The sixteen months that changed golf forever began on December 30, 1999, when Tiger Woods celebrated his twenty-fourth birthday with family and friends at the Fairmont Scottsdale Princess Resort in Scottsdale, Arizona. A night later, on New Year's Eve, he hosted a fundraiser for the Tiger Woods Foundation in a Fairmont Scottsdale Princess ballroom. A deejay rocked the walls with Prince's *1999*. The evening's host joined several hundred paying guests in spectacular fashion, leading an entourage that included his parents, Earl and Kultida Woods; his girlfriend, Joanna Jagoda, a brilliant and beautiful law student; his friend Mark O'Meara; and several buddies from his college days at Stanford. As midnight approached, Natalie Cole sang "Unforgettable" to Tiger. Later they all toasted the new millennium with champagne and hors d'oeuvres, midnight hugs and kisses. And then it was the year 2000.

Later that week, he joined thirty other pros for the season-opening Mercedes Championships at the Kapalua Resort on Maui. Each

January, the previous year's PGA Tour winners gathered for sunshine and luaus for an event some of them still called by its traditional name, the Tournament of Champions. At the first tee, hula dancers crooned the golfers' names. Twenty-four of the players had qualified by winning a single PGA Tour title in 1999. Defending champion David Duval had topped all but one of the others with four wins, but that left him far behind the world's top-ranked golfer. Tiger had won the 1999 PGA Championship, his second major, before reeling off four straight victories to run his total for the year to eight, the most in more than half a century.

On Thursday, January 6, 2000, he teed up a 90-compression Titleist Professional ball and knocked it toward Moloka'i. It was like hitting your first drive of the year into a postcard. The Plantation Course at Kapalua snakes through seaside hills, long but toothless unless the island's trade winds kick up. They blew hard that week. Tiger traded three-hundred-yard drives and birdie putts with Ernie Els down the stretch on Sunday, when the first eagle-eagle finish in PGA Tour history sent them to sudden death.

They both birdied the first playoff hole. Tiger liked that. The higher the stakes and the tighter the fight, the more he enjoyed the game he felt he was born to play. On the second playoff hole he looked over a long birdie putt with his caddie, Steve Williams. It was a downhill forty-footer. The slope would make it slippery, but the grass between his ball and the hole was a dark shade of green rather than a shiny silver-green. That meant the putt would go against the grain. Earlier in the week, Tiger had watched Els miss the same putt. He told Williams, "It's going to break, but not as much as it looks."

Steve Williams was a jut-jawed New Zealander who raced cars on dirt tracks in his spare time and called his man "Tigah." He had replaced Mike "Fluff" Cowan on Tiger's bag after Cowan, a Falstaffian character with a bushy white mustache, got too famous for Tiger and Earl Woods, who didn't like seeing Fluff in TV commercials. Tiger had fired Cowan in 1999 and hired Williams, who served as Tiger's body man as well as his caddie, fending off fans, reporters, and photographers. The two of them sometimes bickered over club selections or putting lines, but they were usually on the same wavelength.

Now they studied Tiger's forty-foot putt. Later, watching a tape of the telecast, he would hear ESPN's Curtis Strange describe it as "not makeable." But what did Strange know? Three and a half years before, he had mocked Tour rookie Woods during an on-camera interview. When Tiger said he expected to win every event he played, Strange had laughed and said, "You'll learn!"

Williams tilted the flagstick over the cup, giving his man a target. He pulled the flag away as the putt broke two and a half feet, losing speed all the way. Turning over one last time, it fell in. Tiger threw a punch at the sky. His victory made him the first to win five tournaments in a row since Ben Hogan in 1948.

The runner-up was gracious as usual. Els, two inches taller and six years older than Tiger, was a former prodigy whose junior golf records had lasted until Tiger broke them. They had the same number of majors to their credit—Els the 1994 and 1997 U.S. Opens, Woods the 1997 Masters and 1999 PGA Championship—which didn't keep reporters from asking Ernie if it was exciting to play with Tiger. He nodded. "He's a legend in the making. He's probably going to be bigger than Elvis. Look at Nicklaus, look at Bobby Jones—I think Tiger is in the same group. He's going to be awfully tough to beat in the majors this year."

A month later, the Tour's annual West Coast Swing took them to Pebble Beach for one of Tiger's favorite tournaments. At the AT&T Pebble Beach Pro-Am, the world's best golfers teamed with celebrity hackers including Bill Murray, who clowned his way around the course, dancing with fans and tossing banana peels at the professionals. Tiger was well off the lead by Sunday, seven shots behind with seven holes to play. Then he lofted a pitching wedge that landed snow-flake soft and spun into the hole for an eagle deuce. He turned to a TV camera and crowed, "I'm back in it!"

Ballet legend Mikhail Baryshnikov, a bogey golfer who joined Murray, Kevin Costner, Jack Lemmon, and Alice Cooper in that week's amateur field, marveled at Tiger's sense of the moment. "This isn't my stage or my audience. My audience doesn't walk right up and gather around me," Baryshnikov said. "Tiger is amazing. There are people pressing all around him, standing just off his shoulder, and he can still dance."

Peter Ueberroth played in the same foursome that day. A former Major League Baseball commissioner and *Time*'s 1984 Man of the Year, Ueberroth watched Tiger barely miss holing another wedge for eagle at the sixteenth hole. "After a while," he said, "you're believing he can hole them all." Woods came from behind to win again, running his streak to six tournaments in a row.

A week after that, at the Buick Invitational, he trailed Phil Mick-elson by seven strokes with twelve holes left. Mickelson was another former teen phenom, a left-hander who could knock a drive out of sight or flip a flop shot into your pocket. Tiger caught him with a birdie at the thirteenth. Then the seemingly impossible happened again: he faltered, making back-to-back bogeys. "At least I made it interesting for Phil," he said. Asked about stopping his rival's winning streak, Mickelson said, "I didn't want to be the bad guy. I just wanted to win."

In February, Northern Ireland's Darren Clarke reached the million-dollar final at the Andersen Consulting Match Play Championship. So did Tiger. He had few friends among the other Tour pros, a cut-throat breed of independent contractors vying for the same pots of gold every week, but he liked Clarke, who could down a pint of Guin-ness in one lengthy quaff. They met for breakfast before their final match. Clarke, who carried a few extra pounds on his six-foot-two frame, had a warning: "If you hole a long snake and give one of those run-across-the-green fist pumps, I'm coming after you with a big Irish fist of my own."

"Give it your best shot," Tiger said. "You're so fat you couldn't catch me!"

He couldn't catch Clarke that day. He settled for second place and $500,000, then won the Bay Hill Invitational, an event he played as a favor to its host, Arnold Palmer. Woods had now won seven times in his last ten tries, with two second-place finishes. After another runner-up finish at the Players Championship, he skipped the Bell-South Classic to hone his game for the 2000 Masters.

The invitational that Bobby Jones founded in 1934 is the main event on golf's spring calendar, the first major of the year. Tiger spent more time preparing for the Masters than for any other tournament, spending much of the winter and early spring in long practice sessions with his swing coach, Butch Harmon, and his caddie, Williams, at his home course in the gated community of Isleworth, Florida, working on shots he would need at Augusta National Golf Club in April: a drive over the pines at the par-4 ninth; a sweeping draw around the dogleg at the thirteenth. He often finished with a high fade, the tee ball he planned to hit off the first tee at Augusta. If he struck it just right, he would turn on his heel and start for the parking lot, the driving-range version of a mic drop.

TWO
WELCOME TO THE CLUB

Every April, the sleepy riverside town of Augusta, Georgia, becomes golf's capital. The city's population more than doubles during Masters week. Traffic crawls on Washington Road, where in 2000 there were long waits for booths at the Howard Johnson's and the Waffle House across the road from Augusta National Golf Club.

On Tuesday, April 4, 2000, a select few golfers in courtesy cars turned off Washington Road onto Magnolia Lane and dined more grandly in Augusta National's white clapboard clubhouse.

Tiger stopped into the Champions Locker Room to pick up his jacket before dinner. The green jacket, symbolizing his runaway victory at the 1997 Masters, was a 42 regular. He looked forward to the annual Champions Dinner, one of his favorite Masters traditions. Each year, former winners gather in a second-floor banquet room for drinks and a multicourse meal. The previous year's winner selects the menu, which often features cuisine from his home country, and picks up the tab. "Just to be looking at the real Byron Nelson and the real Gene Sarazen," great players his father used to tell him about, had amazed the youngest member of the fraternity when he had hosted his first Champions Dinner in 1998. "I'm over here with Mr. Nelson on my left, Ben Crenshaw on my right, and here we are with dinner knives in our hands, demonstrating our grips." Nelson had been eighty-six years old that night. Sarazen, the celebrated "Squire" who had invented the sand wedge and won the second ever Masters in 1935, was ninety-six and not crazy about the menu the new champion chose that night: cheeseburgers, french fries, and milkshakes. "Cheeseburgers!" Sarazen said. "Who ever heard of a cheeseburger dinner?" Tiger vowed to do better if and when he won again.

In 2000, he was one of three dozen Masters winners enjoying pre-dinner drinks and defending champion José María Olazábal's four-course menu of chilled shrimp with salmon and mayonnaise, hake with pimientos, beef filets in red wine sauce, and vanilla ice cream with chocolate sauce. As usual, many of the international players sat with Gary Player. Tiger sat with O'Meara, who had won the 1998 Masters, and their friends Palmer and Nicklaus. Fred Couples, Raymond Floyd, and Tom Watson sat nearby. "Lord Byron" himself opened the festivities. Sarazen had died the year before, leaving the kindly, eighty-eight-year-old Nelson as the oldest of them. Looking around at Nicklaus, Palmer, Sam Snead, Watson, Player, Nick Faldo, and two dozen others, he said he had been delighted when reporters asked if Tiger might top his streak of eleven straight tournament victories in 1945.

"I want to thank Tiger Woods," Nelson said, "for making today's young people know what I did fifty-five years ago."

The green-jacketed champions applauded. One was 1979 Masters winner Fuzzy Zoeller. He and Sam Snead always sat together at the dinner, dueling to see which of them could tell the dirtiest joke while more high-minded champions tried not to laugh. Zoeller, a Hoosier quipster from New Albany, Indiana, had joked about the menu the

Tiger Woods played and practiced with his friend and mentor, Mark O'Meara.

day Tiger became the first Black Masters champion. "Tell him not to serve fried chicken next year," Zoeller told reporters, snapping his fingers, "or collard greens, or whatever the hell they serve." He soon apologized but lost endorsement deals with Adidas and Kmart. Tiger publicly forgave him, announcing, "We all make mistakes. I accept Fuzzy's apology." When the two of them met for lunch a month later, Zoeller apologized again. Tiger accepted that Zoeller "was trying to acknowledge that I had kicked everybody's ass that week." He forgave but didn't forget.

It was hard to forget race in Augusta, even if he wasn't as Black as people like Zoeller thought. Asked about his racial identity on *The Oprah Winfrey Show*, he described himself as "Cablinasian"—part Caucasian, part Black, part American Indian, part Asian. He was the American melting pot in one golfer, Black and Cherokee on his father's side and Thai, Chinese, and Dutch on his mother's. Still, the world saw him as Black. As Earl Woods put it, "The boy only has about two drops of Black blood in him, but in this country there are only two colors, white and nonwhite. And he ain't white."

Tiger and his father, who grew up in the segregated town of Manhattan, Kansas, knew all about Augusta National's fraught racial history. In the 1930s and '40s, the club's founders, Bobby Jones and the investment banker Clifford Roberts, had enjoyed "battle royal" boxing bouts, melees that pitted half a dozen blindfolded Black men against one another. Some were Augusta National caddies. They punched and brawled until only one was left standing. Wealthy white patrons flipped silver dollars into the ring for the winner to collect.

Roberts, who ran the Masters for forty years, claimed he had nothing against "our dark-complected friends." Even so, he insisted, "As long as I am alive, the caddies will be Black and the players will be white." No Black golfer was invited to the tournament until Lee Elder in 1975, the year Tiger Woods was born. Roberts was still alive, but not for long. One morning two years later the ailing eighty-three-year-old founder got a haircut in the club's barbershop. Then he walked out to Augusta National's par-3 course, sat down beside a pond, pulled a .38-caliber revolver from his pocket, and blew his brains out. It would be thirteen more years before the most exclusive club in golf admitted a Black member. Even after that, one scholarly study described Augusta National as golf's "epicenter of discrimination and exclusion." Tiger was more diplomatic, saying he had "developed a respect for the course and the Masters, but I would never refer to it as a 'cathedral in the pines'—the term you hear every April."

Earl Woods was more outspoken about race than his son was. One night, sipping champagne at one of Tiger's victory parties, he said, "How do you like this, Bobby Jones? A Black man is the best golfer who ever lived. Bobby Jones can kiss my son's Black ass."

In the year and a half after Tiger earned his green jacket in 1997, it was his hips that needed attention. They tended to fire too fast on his downswing, turning toward the target too quickly and forcing him to make handsy, last-instant corrections at impact. Working with swing guru Harmon, the Masters champion rebuilt what was already the best swing in the game, grooving a new move that synchronized the rotation of his upper body, hips, and legs. He did it by hitting thousands upon thousands of range balls in 1997 and 1998—"digging it out of the dirt," as Ben Hogan used to say—to forge the fearful symmetry that was now second nature. By the time he teed off on a breezy Thursday morning, he was such a prohibitive favorite to win the 2000 Masters that you could bet on him or take the same odds on the rest of the ninety-five-man field. The betting line made sense to Tom Watson, who had won eight major championships including the 1977 and 1981 Masters. "Tiger has better flexibility than anybody," he said. "He works out harder than anybody, hits the ball farther than anybody, putts better than anybody, and chips better than anybody."

But that day he played worse than thirty-eight players, including Olazábal, Els, Duval, and sixty-year-old Jack Nicklaus. After an even-par front nine, his approach shot at the long, downhill tenth plugged into a greenside bunker. He muscled his Titleist onto the green but three-putted for a double bogey. His 8-iron into a swirling breeze at the par-3 twelfth fell short and slipped back into Rae's Creek. After a penalty stroke, he pitched onto the green and three-putted from twelve feet for a triple bogey. The golfer with the multimillion-dollar smile looked like he had spent three hours sucking lemons. He rallied with a pair of late birdies but shot 75. A steady 72 on Friday got him to the weekend. He charged into contention with a front-nine 33 on Sunday but then fell short, six shots behind Vijay Singh.

"For some reason, the golfing gods weren't looking down on me," he said. His aim in retooling his swing had been to minimize the effects of swirling winds, biorhythms, and the strokes of good and bad luck golfers call the rub of the green, becoming so much better than anyone else that the gods could just sit back and watch him win. His fifth-place finish at the Masters proved that he wasn't there yet.

He skipped the next four tournaments. News reports had him "taking a month off," but that wasn't quite right. He was working on a secret project, testing a ball so new that it didn't yet have a name.

THREE
SPIN

One morning, Tiger was chipping balls around with Mark O'Meara. He watched O'Meara's chips nip the green and check up closer to the hole than his. After a while he asked, "How do you get the ball to do that?"

His buddy "Marko" was one of a few friends who could needle him. "Don't worry, T," he said. "You'll learn. It takes skill and maturity."

They kept it up with the same results until Tiger tried a few chips with the ball O'Meara was playing, a Top Flite Strata Tour with a solid core and a new-age polyurethane cover. In no time he was spinning and stopping chips as if they were on a string.

"It wasn't you. It's the ball!"

O'Meara nodded. "You're catching on," he said. "Let me explain something to you. You are playing an archaic golf ball." He wasn't pushing Top Flite in particular. In fact, a less prominent brand had hired some of the best golf ball designers in the industry. "Bridgestone could build a ball specifically for you, a ball that goes farther. It'll pierce the wind better. It'll be softer around the greens."

Tiger was intrigued. He had always brought an engineering approach to his profession, his equipment, even his swing. One thing he liked about living at Isleworth, seventy miles due west of Cape Canaveral, was watching space shuttles take off from the cape. He admired the NASA scientists who orchestrated the latest electronics, hardware, and the human element to send astronauts to space. In order to overcome gravity, a space shuttle—a 4.4-million-pound hulk with more than 2 million working parts—had to ride an enormous fuel tank full of liquid oxygen and hydrogen and a pair of booster rockets the size of grain silos. It had to be well armored to withstand the fires of reentry but nimble enough to glide to a landing like a passenger plane. As one of the astronauts he admired put it, designing such a flying machine was "like bolting a butterfly to a bullet." Compared to that, building a better golf ball ought to be easy.

It wasn't. But O'Meara convinced him that it was possible. After his fifth-place finish at the Masters, Tiger devoted a quiet "month off" to some of the most intense practice sessions of his life, testing a ball that was anything but archaic.

Golfers have been looking for a better ball since Tom Morris spent sweaty twelve-hour workdays sewing up featheries for his boss, Allan Robertson, almost two hundred years ago. The burly, mutton-chopped Robertson was the first full-time golf professional. Morris, known to history as "Old Tom," was his apprentice. In the 1830s, they fashioned four or five golf balls a day in Robertson's stone cottage on Pilmour Links Road in St. Andrews, Scotland. First they filled a top hat with boiled goose feathers. Tom then stuffed the wet, steaming feathers into a little leather pouch, then grabbed a needle and thread to sew it shut as fast as he could. As the feathers inside dried and expanded, the leather ball hardened. If not always perfectly round, it was ready for a round of golf.

Making featheries was hazardous labor. Workers like Tom Morris wore special harnesses and used iron pokers to pack the last few feathers into the ball. One ball maker broke a rib on the job. Another leaned on the feather poker so hard that his workbench broke and sent him to the floor in a clatter of knitting needles, saws, calipers, and cleeks.

All that labor made feather-filled balls so expensive that only well-to-do gentlemen could afford to play golf. In the 1840s, Morris became an early adopter of a new technology: the "gutty" ball, a solid sphere of gutta-percha, the sap of a Malaysian rubber tree. Gutties proved cheaper and more durable than feather-filled golf balls. Robertson called them "filth" and fired Morris for testing one on the links, so Old Tom decamped to Prestwick, a town on the other side of Scotland. It was there that he sold gutties and founded the Open Championship, the oldest of golf's major tournaments.

The game's next great innovation was the Haskell ball. Invented in 1898 by Cleveland businessman Coburn Haskell, it featured a round rubber core under a mantle of tightly wound rubber threads and a thin cover of gutta-percha. It carried far longer off the tee than the gutty and was superior in every way. For the next century, every professional from Harry Vardon to Bobby Jones to Palmer, Nicklaus, and Woods would tee off with a ball constructed pretty much the same way. The gleaming white Titleist Professional that Tiger and most other Tour pros maneuvered from tee to green in the spring of 2000 had a mantle of tightly wound rubber bands under a skin of balata, the sap of a rubber tree that grows in Central and South America. Balata is similar to gutta-percha but a little softer. The other main difference between Haskells in 1900 and the Titleists of a century later was in the ball's core.

The Haskell had a solid rubber core. Twentieth-century Titleists featured a liquid center the size of a grape in a thin rubber shell. According to a popular myth, their liquid centers held a deadly poison. Young golfers cut the balls open and dared each other to taste the goo they found inside. But the liquid in the balls' cores wasn't deadly. It was a mixture of water and corn syrup. Why? Because water and corn syrup made them cheap to mass-produce.

Tiger spent months testing a different design, a prototype similar to O'Meara's Top Flite Strata. Made in Japan by Bridgestone, funded by Nike, the new ball had a solid core, a mantle made of polybutadiene, the synthetic rubber that made Super Balls bounce so high, and a cover of urethane, a polymer used to make floor wax, bowling balls, and traffic cones. As one golf ball designer put it, a ball's cover "is its steering wheel, but the core is its engine." Compared to a liquid core wrapped in rubber bands, the prototype's core and mantle transferred more energy from the club to the ball, which spun less and flew farther. Its urethane coating had next to no effect on shots struck at driver speeds but felt soft and added grab on short-iron and wedge shots.

Tiger had planned to spend several more months if not the rest of the year experimenting with various versions of the new design, like a Formula 1 driver testing a new engine. He wasn't the type to introduce a variable that was still in beta, but he loved the way the Bridgestone prototype came off his driver. And there was a business reason to expedite his switch to a new ball.

Titleist was paying him $4 million a year to play its ball. But he was also a "head to toe" Nike endorser, paid to wear the company's clothing. The year before, he'd been filming a Nike commercial, killing time on the range between setups, when ad executive Chuck McBride saw him juggling a ball with his wedge. Tiger had been amusing himself and his friends with driving-range tricks for years. He could keep the ball going hacky-sack style for minutes at a time, switching the club from his right hand to his left, between his legs, and behind his back. Sometimes he would finish by flipping the ball belt high, turning sideways, and using a baseball swing to slam it out of sight.

With McBride egging him on, he tried it on camera. But not even Tiger could pull it off every time. He'd keep the ball in the air for fifteen or twenty seconds, only to drop it when he switched hands or whiff on the baseball swing. They were running out of daylight when a crew member who happened to be a gambling man pulled a $100 bill from his wallet. "Bet you can't do it on the next try," he said, placing the money on top of the camera.

"So Tiger starts juggling again," McBride recalled. *Bounce bounce bounce* went the ball as he shifted the club between his left and right hands, between his legs, behind his back, until they reached the half-minute mark and McBride cued him for the baseball-swing finale. "I give him the cue, and he just smacked it." Tiger swung his wedge and fungoed the ball out of sight. "Everyone stood there like 'Shit, he did it!' Tiger reaches down, grabs the hundred-dollar bill and walks off."

The commercial made news. Many viewers were sure there had to be special effects involved. When *Sports Illustrated* editors screened the ad at the magazine's headquarters in New York, one said, "Nobody can do that—not even him."

It seemed that the only people who didn't like the "Hacky Sack" commercial worked for Titleist. The number one ball maker was paying Woods millions of dollars to play its liquid core ball, the 90-compression Titleist Professional he was bouncing in the ads. But with no close-ups on the ball and Nike's swoosh filling the screen at the end, viewers might well have thought he was juggling the sponsor's ball. Within a month, Titleist sued Nike for false advertising.

That gave Phil Knight, Nike's combative CEO, a chance to pry the game's top endorser away from its top golf ball maker. He promptly offered to double Woods's endorsement deal to more than $17 million a year, plus a cut of the company's profits.

Tiger listened. Titleist's policy was to spread its endorsement money around, enriching him and many more of the world's leading players, but Woods already *was* Nike Golf. His role as the company's "next Michael Jordan" had only grown since 1996, when Knight and Nike had signed him to a five-year, $40 million deal the day he turned pro, introducing him with a now-famous ad in which he spoke of the prejudice he faced as a minority golfer and saying "Hello, world." With that, he became the face of golf and Nike's successor to Jordan. The company was planning a new Tiger Woods Building on its Beaverton, Oregon, campus, one that would be nearly twice the size of its Michael Jordan Building.

For Tiger, switching to a Nike ball might kill three birds with one Space Age prototype. It could teach Titleist and other sponsors not to take Tiger Woods for granted. It could reward Nike for its loyalty to him. And it could give him an edge on every Tour golfer who was still playing an archaic ball full of rubber bands.

But only if the prototype performed better than the Titleist Professional he'd been playing.

That spring, after his fifth-place finish at the Masters, he picked up the pace of his work with Nike's prototype.

Kel Devlin, the son of the Australian tour pro Bruce Devlin, was Nike's point man on the project. A scratch golfer who traveled with an early model of a launch monitor, Devlin was awed by Woods's feel for the technical aspects of his game. Tiger would say, "I'm going to hit a cut here, so my spin rate will be four hundred RPMs more than if I hit a draw." When Devlin checked the monitor, the number was never more than a few RPMs off. Or Tiger would say, "My swing speed was one twenty-eight. I'm going to crank it up, give it five more miles an hour." Devlin checked, and there it was: 133. Sometimes Devlin's team would test him by slipping a different ball into the mix. Tiger wasn't fooled. "What kind of ball was that? It felt harder."

In mid-May, he flew to Texas for the Byron Nelson Classic. Still hitting his 90-compression Titleist Professional, he missed a playoff by a stroke.

Devlin's phone rang the next day. "With the new ball I would have won by five," Tiger said. "Can you meet me in Germany on Tuesday morning?"

Devlin booked a flight and called Hideyuki "Rock" Ishii, the chief scientist at Bridgestone, a second-tier ballmaker based in Japan. Under Ishii's direction, Japanese chemists and technicians had produced the balls Woods had been testing. (It would be months before news leaked that Nike farmed out its golf ball manufacturing to another company.) Ishii packed a suitcase full of prototypes and caught a flight out of Tokyo.

On the morning of Tuesday, May 16, Ishii met Devlin at Gut Kaden Golf und Land Club near Hamburg, where Tiger was set to tee off in a European Tour event in forty-eight hours. Steve Williams spotted them on the driving range. An expert caddie but no diplomat, the pugnacious Williams asked, "What the fuck are you idiots doing here?"

Tiger began by knocking balls into a left-to-right wind. Some were Titleists. Some were Nike prototypes with slight differences among them. He tried a drive with his natural draw. He tried a stinger sneaking under the breeze. He tried a high fade with a Titleist Professional and watched the wind carry it fifteen yards to the right, enough to send a tee ball into the rough during a tournament. Then he put the same swing on one of Ishii's solid-core balls. The wind took that one to the right by less than half as much.

The difference was due to what golf ball designers call "spin separation." When an expert player smacks a three-hundred-yard drive with a fast-spinning ball, any gust of wind can carry it far offline. That makes high spin rates a problem when Tour pros hit driver. Yet spin is crucial to iron shots, which need to bite and stop on the putting green.

Ballmaker Ishii's goal was to find a golden mean: to create a ball that reduced spin off the driver, for more distance, while maintaining it on lofted shots for control near the green, and he was getting closer. His prototypes spun less at driver velocity, making them fly straighter than any Titleist did, while their urethane cover provided what golfers call feel on wedge shots. Like balata, the urethane cover brought a high coefficient of friction at impact, meaning that the ball stayed on the clubface microseconds longer. Along with the grooves on the clubface of a wedge, that friction coefficient added spin for shot-stopping control on approach shots.

Tiger liked the result. He felt the difference in his hands and saw it in the way the new balls flew. His Titleist, with its century-old design, spun similarly when hit with a driver or a wedge. Ishii's prototypes seemed to know what an elite player wanted them to do.

Ishii would never forget their day on the range in Germany. He remembered Tiger's hitting one of his prototypes and instantly rejecting it. "Sounds wrong." The designer could barely hide his pleasure at working with a test subject he considered more technologically advanced than Iron Byron, the ball-driving robot (named after Nelson) that the United States Golf Association employed to test clubs and balls at its headquarters in Far Hills, New Jersey. "He's so sensitive to sound. And also trajectory. His eye is much better than anybody else's," Ishii said.

When they were finished, Tiger selected his favorite prototype. Ishii had a box of samples rushed from Japan to Germany, where Tiger put the new ball in play at the European Tour's Deutsche Bank–SAP Open. He stayed near the lead until the back nine on Sunday, when he airmailed a 7-iron into a pond beyond the sixteenth green.

That shot worried Ishii. "I thought he might stop using the ball after that." But despite finishing third that week, Woods said he was ready to switch balls. He figured he could adjust to being straighter off the tee and five yards longer with his 7-iron. He wanted a couple hundred of the new balls as fast as Bridgestone could make them.

• • •

Back in Isleworth, he phoned O'Meara. "Marko, get over here."

Hearing the excitement in his voice, O'Meara jumped in his car and sped to Tiger's Spanish-style mansion on Greens Drive. As soon as he went inside, Tiger showed him two plain white boxes. Each contained a dozen golf balls. He was grinning. "We gotta go play."

FOUR
HOME ON THE RANGE

On Thursday, May 26, he teed up a multilayered ball with a plain black swoosh over the number 1 and TIGER stamped on its equator. Made in Japan by Ishii's Bridgestone team, the ball would be marketed as the Nike Tour Accuracy. Its American debut came at the 2000 Memorial Tournament in Dublin, Ohio, hosted by Jack Nicklaus. Tiger was the defending champion. He always made a point of playing in Arnold Palmer's Bay Hill Invitational in March and Nicklaus's tournament in May. That was one way he honored his friendships with the heroes of his dad's generation—and pleased Palmer and Nicklaus by doubling the attendance at their tournaments.

Tiger prized his friendships with his elders in golf's pantheon. Like almost everyone who spent any time with Palmer, he sparked to Arnie's genuine warmth. Sometimes he'd zip from Isleworth to Bay Hill in his white Porsche to spend an hour with the seventy-year-old Palmer in his workshop—just a couple of golf gearheads talking about the clubheads

Arnie fashioned there in clouds of steam and sparks and the two thousand–plus putters in his personal collection, not one of them quite good enough. When they parted, Palmer would hug him.

Nicklaus wasn't a hugger, but even he saw Tiger as something special: a golfer who might be better than he was.

They had first met on a sunny morning in 1991, when a scrawny teenager with a high-powered swing attended a clinic Nicklaus held at the ultra-exclusive Bel-Air Country Club in Los Angeles. At that point, fifteen-year-old Tiger Woods was already playing off a handicap of +2. Nicklaus asked him to hit some balls. After watching the kid drill a few drives into the distance, Nicklaus said, "Tiger, when I grow up, I hope my swing is as pretty as yours."

Tiger never forgot that compliment from the Golden Bear. Nor was he awed by it. As a high school and college golfer, he filled out dozens of tournament applications and questionnaires over the years, some asking about entrants' school studies, hobbies, and heroes. When a form asked players to name their golf heroes, Tiger's answer was always the same: "None."

If he had a hero, it was his father. He liked to tell an old story about the way Earl used to outsmart him in long-drive contests on their last hole of a round. His dad would "hit his little 230 down the middle," recalled Tiger, who proceeded to knock his ball forty or fifty yards farther to claim the long drive. "And he'd say, 'No, you don't. You've got to be in the fairway.'" Earl stressed keeping the ball in play above all.

At a press conference at the 2000 Memorial, Tiger was asked about rumors that he was ditching the Titleist Professional he had played since the day he turned pro. Which ball was in his bag that week?

"Nike ball," he said. "I'm just testing it out, to get the feel of the golf ball. The only way to do that is to test it in competition."

Asked about his narrow miss at the Byron Nelson Classic two

Earl Woods believed his son was destined for greatness.

weeks before, where he had settled for a fourth-place prize of $176,000, he said he still expected to win every tournament he entered. Some players might be satisfied with lucrative top-ten finishes, but he wasn't one of them.

A reporter followed up: "Are there guys who are just looking to cash in?"

Tiger nodded. "Uh-huh."

"Does that bother you?"

He shook his head. "No. I like it."

His new ball held its line in the wind and bit Nicklaus's greens in the first two rounds of the 2000 Memorial Tournament. On Friday, he made four front-nine birdies in a row. He chipped in for another at the sixteenth. His 9-iron from 164 yards at the next hole dropped and stopped a foot from the flagstick. He had made up nine strokes on the first-round leader, Harrison Frazar, in twenty-four hours.

Tiger's 7-iron approach at the long eighteenth carried over the top of the flagstick and landed twenty feet past. He watched his brand-new Nike ball check up with just the right spin and creep backward as a record crowd cheered it toward the cup. Was he really going to finish with an eagle deuce at the last hole?

Almost. He tapped in for birdie, a one-shot lead over Frazar, and a 63 that he called the best round of his three and a half years as a pro. Saturday's third round with the new ball was almost as good. After four front-nine birdies and an eagle, he had played twenty-two holes fifteen under par. And his last tournament before the upcoming U.S. Open was just kicking into gear. On the back nine he lashed a 220-yard 5-iron that awed his playing partner, Frazar, who said, "He's hitting shots no other human can hit." Woods's 65 put him half a dozen strokes ahead of everyone else.

Ernie Els, ten shots behind, was asked if he or anyone else could catch Tiger. "What do you want me to say?" he asked. "It's over."

The new ball "has done pretty good so far," Tiger said. "Obviously, it feels different." The three-piece ball flew "not necessarily higher or lower, but there's a different arc." With lower spin off the driver, his tee shots "tend to be a little more flat."

He never liked the press conferences that were mandatory for Tour players. There was no upside to them. For the better part of a century, flawed sports heroes from Babe Ruth and Mickey Mantle to Michael Jordan and Lance Armstrong had relied on friendly newsmen to burnish their images. Arnold Palmer, a man of great warmth and kindness who gave millions of dollars to charity, was also a prodigious philanderer—a fact that his friends in the media kept to themselves for decades. Reporters got access to sports stars; the sports stars got to keep their foibles under wraps. But the equation was changing. By the late 1990s, corporate sponsors spent millions of dollars promoting their clients in carefully controlled combinations of commercials, ad campaigns, and choreographed public appearances. In the new mediasphere, beat reporters were nosy nuisances at best. At worst, they were threats to an athlete's carefully managed public image.

Reporters could still make news by exposing sports heroes' flaws. Tiger had learned that lesson the hard way. Three years before, he had told *GQ*'s Charles Pierce a couple of his favorite dirty jokes. "Why do two lesbians get where they're going faster than two gay guys? Because the lesbians are always going sixty-nine." Another one involved Buckwheat, the Black member of the old "Little Rascals" comedy troupe, who had a speech impediment and a catchphrase: "O-tay!" The way Tiger told the story, a schoolteacher asks Buckwheat to use the word "dictate" in a sentence. He points to a little girl and says, "Hey Darla, how's my dick ta'te?"

One way to react to his jokes would be to see the young Tiger as a kid with a puerile sense of humor, a twenty-one-year-old who cracked up when his buddies had "Heywood Jablomi" paged at a five-star hotel. Instead, the GQ piece made news, stirring up his first nation-wide scandal. He weathered it, but the scandal taught him that there was little upside to being open with the media. He had no intention of getting burned again. And so, like Derek Jeter, Tom Brady, and other perceptive athletes, he learned to talk at length in interviews and press scrums without saying much.

Eldrick Woods was brainy and inquisitive, a high school honor student who had majored in economics and studied calculus, civics, and Intro to Buddhism in his two years at Stanford. But like many pro golfers other than Mickelson, who soaked up any sort of attention, he loathed press conferences. Swamped with media obligations, he came to view them as an occupational hazard. His own agent called him "arguably the worst interview in golf." That week at the Memorial, Tiger's answers to reporters' questions ranged from guarded to rote. "I hit a great shot on six from the first cut of rough," he said after his third-round 65. "At seven I hit my drive in the right rough. Had a great lie. Hit three-wood, went for the front bunker. Blasted out of there to about twelve feet and made the putt. At fifteen, three-wood off the tee, three-iron to the left of the green, chipped to about a foot and a half, tapped in for birdie. At seventeen I hit a nine-iron to about a foot and a half." Some of his rote recitation was simply to help reporters with their accounts of his round. It was also a way to avoid saying anything meaningful, like Nuke LaLoosh learning his clichés in *Bull Durham*.

Golf writers took down every word while he stared into the distance. Sometimes his own quotes seemed to bore him—but every so often he said what he was thinking. That Sunday, after cruising to a five-stroke win at Nicklaus's tournament, sitting through another press conference that left him literally yawning, he perked up when a reporter asked about the state of his game going into the U.S. Open at Pebble Beach.

"Every area of my game can get better. That's the great thing about golf. You try to find things that will take you up to that next notch, whether it's a swing change, a putting posture, a new putter, new clubs, or a new ball." Recalling a 7-iron he'd rocketed over a green that day, he rolled his eyes. "I mistimed it and delofted it, and *see ya*." But his drives had been ten yards longer than before. His playing partner, Justin Leonard, who finished second, had watched in amazement as one of Tiger's drives climbed over the top branches of a tall, stately oak 280 yards from the tee. Despite the occasional "See ya," he was learning to tame the new ball.

"Golf is a game of control. Right now, with my A game, I know exactly what number the ball is going to fly." If a shot called for a 132-yard wedge, he said, "I'm going to fly it 132. Not 135. Not 130. One thirty-two."

Nicklaus paid the winner a compliment by comparing Tiger to himself. "I always felt like if I was hitting the ball the way I wanted to, everybody else was playing for second. He's the same way. He hits the ball farther, but equipment has something to do with that. He manages his game well. I managed my game well. He probably plays better right to left than I did." Nicklaus preferred a high fade off the tee, a more controllable shot than Woods's natural draw. But Tiger could hit a fade as well as Jack ever had. "And he's got a far better short game than I ever had."

Neither of them was ever satisfied. Moments after lifting the 2000 Memorial's cut-crystal trophy, Tiger told reporters he had "stuff to work on." With the United States Golf Association growing shin-high rough at Pebble Beach, he was going to need precision more than power.

Over the next ten days, he spent intensive hours on the range with swing coach Butch Harmon. Tiger often hit five hundred to six hundred balls a day, a typical total for a Tour pro. If he was working on a swing tweak, he might hit a thousand. Harmon swore that his prize pupil "hits more balls than anybody on the planet." Tiger's callused hands weren't always up to so many reps. His father had taught him that five of a right-handed golfer's ten fingers control the club during the swing: the bottom three on the left hand and the middle two on the right. "Those five fingers get trashed when I practice a lot," Tiger said. His glove protected the three on his left hand, but during heavy-duty practice the callus on his right middle finger tended to split open and bleed. He would tape the bottom joint of that finger and tee up another ball.

Some Tour pros hated to hit balls on the driving range. Bruce Lietzke, the winner of thirteen Tour events and more than $6 million, liked to say he preferred eating burgers at Steak 'n Shake to spending hours on the range. After the last Tour event one fall, Lietzke said he was worn out. He told his caddie to put his clubs away for the winter. The caddie was sure he'd relent and slip out for at least a few swings. As a joke, he slipped a banana under the cover of Lietzke's driver—and found black banana goo the next spring.

Thirty years later, Brooks Koepka would claim that he, too, hated hitting range balls. "I practice before the majors. Regular tournaments, I don't. If you see me on TV, that's when I play golf," he said. But it wasn't true. "I was just fucking with you," he told reporters later. In fact, Koepka was a range rat like every other pro who joined the Tour after Tiger took the job to a higher level.

For Tiger, every hour hitting balls on the range was an escape from fans, reporters, phone calls, autographs, business meetings, and a hundred other tasks that had nothing to do with hitting a golf ball better than anyone else. As one friend put it, "The range is his church." Tiger copped to being "addicted" to beating balls, giving each shot his best effort, evaluating the feedback from his hands, his ears, and the flight of the ball.

Harmon kept up a running commentary during their practice

sessions. If he praised one—"There it is, a beauty"—Tiger would reach out with his club, rake another Tour Accuracy off the foot-tall pyramid of balls at Harmon's feet, and try to hit the next one better. They made a recognizable pair of silhouettes on the range, the lean six-footer drilling balls and the five-foot-seven coach watching with his arms crossed, nodding, suggesting tweaks so slight that most players would need a slow-motion camera to detect them.

Claude "Butch" Harmon was a balding, graying Vietnam veteran with a bit of a paunch over his belt. Unlike Tiger, Harmon had a golf pedigree. His father, Claude Sr., had won the 1948 Masters and spent decades as head professional at two of the sport's most exclusive country clubs, Winged Foot Golf Club in New York's Westchester County and Seminole Golf Club in Juno Beach, Florida. The last club pro ever to win the Masters, the elder Harmon was a no-nonsense teacher who had once served as personal tutor to King Hassan II of Morocco. Before their first lesson, eyeing the diplomats and servants who accompanied Hassan to the tee, he said, "Your Majesty, before we get started, I want you to know one thing: that ball and that club don't know you're the King of Morocco." Years later, he rolled his eyes after a movie star flew east for a lesson and arrived at the practice range in a limousine. Claude listened patiently while Mr. Hollywood lectured him about the golf swing. Again and again, the man insisted that Jack Nicklaus's swing proved that all power in the golf swing comes from the legs. At last Claude took a driver, got down on his knees, and slugged a ball 250 yards. He stood up, handed over the club and said, "Why don't you stick that up your rear end and see if you can hit it that far by swiveling your legs?"

As a boy, Butch Harmon caddied for his old man in friendly rounds with Sam Snead and Ben Hogan. He became a championship-level golfer and eventually turned pro, but he never made a living on the PGA tour. His father, an honored guest at the Masters Champions

Tiger's mother, Kultida, often dressed in tiger stripes.

Dinner every spring, used to lord it over Butch and his three brothers, who all became golf pros. "I've got a green jacket," Claude Sr. would tell them. "Where's yours?"

His eldest son, Butch, had a temper. Again and again he would play fourteen or fifteen holes under par, then hook a drive out of bounds and snap the club over his knee. He broke one set of clubs into pieces and flung them into a pond. He got into bar fights and once punched a priest. In 1963, after a falling-out with his father, Butch joined the army. Shipped out to Vietnam, he saw combat so horrific he would keep the details to himself for the next fifty years. "I lost friends," he recalled, "and saw things that no man should ever see."

One day, Sergeant Harmon stepped on a land mine and knew he was dead. By sheerest luck, the mine didn't go off. Feeling gifted with a second chance at life, he came home with a calmer disposition. The Masters champion's son toiled on golf course construction crews, taught lessons, and spent twenty years climbing through the teaching ranks. He worked with Tour pro Steve Elkington and then, starting in 1991, with Greg Norman, who rose to number one in the world with Harmon's help.

Harmon's work with Norman caught the attention of Earl Woods. Tiger's father was another Vietnam vet, one who had far outranked Harmon. Lieutenant Colonel Woods had served as a Green Beret, fighting the Viet Cong beside Nguyen Phong, a South Vietnamese soldier who had saved his life during a firefight. The man was so fierce that Earl called him "Tiger" Phong.

Years later, Earl married Kultida Punsawad, a young woman he met on a tour of duty in Thailand. They named their son Eldrick, an invented name that began with an *E* for Earl and ended with a *K* for Kultida. Earl nicknamed him "Tiger" in tribute to the soldier who had saved his life.

Tiger Woods was seventeen in 1993, the year Earl had him

demonstrate his swing for Harmon, by then one of the top teachers in the game. The swing coach had never seen such raw talent. Later he compared the moment to "seeing a teenage Mozart at the piano."

They made a good match, the teen prodigy and the coach who could break a one-second golf swing into a dozen or more interacting components. But Harmon was wary at first. He didn't want Tiger's headstrong father pulling rank on him. "If I work with your son and you dispute what I am saying, it probably won't work," he told Earl.

"I'll make a deal with you," Earl said. "I won't try to be his golf coach if you don't try to be his dad."

With that, Harmon signed on to Team Tiger. By 2000, that core group included Woods's parents; his girlfriend, Joanna Jagoda; his school friends Jerry Chang and Bryon Bell; and Nike liaison Greg Nared; as well as Harmon; his caddie, Steve Williams; and his agent, Mark Steinberg. Tiger called the last three "Butchie," "Stevie," and "Steinie," chummy nicknames that signaled his favor. He and Harmon traded notes in person or on the phone after every Tour round Tiger played. When it came to what mattered most—his swing—not even Earl had his ear the way Harmon did.

Player and swing guru both felt they were on the brink of something: not only a way to play golf better than anyone had played it in the game's five-hundred-year history, but something still more ambitious: a way to play it better than anyone else imagined. Even before the Nike ball added a last piece to the puzzle, Harmon suspected that his prize pupil might be about to take golf to a higher level. He had hinted at such a thing that February, when Tiger faced another Harmon client, Davis Love III, in the semifinals of the Tour's annual Match Play Championship. After Tiger smashed a 330-yard drive past Love's ball, a fan yelled, "Hey, Butch, what are you feeding him?"

Harmon said, "Davis, today."

Woods had cruised past Love at the Match Play. By the end of

May, he had played half a dozen Tour events without finishing worse than fifth, winning twice while adjusting to a new ball.

By early June, all systems were go. Tiger hit thousands of balls at Isleworth Country Club and at Harmon's palatial range at Rio Secco Golf Club in Las Vegas. He was "laser focused," Harmon recalled, working mostly on accuracy. To win the U.S. Open, he would need to hit the Nike ball straighter than he had driven his Titleist at Pebble Beach during the West Coast Swing, when he had stormed to a come-back victory at the AT&T. The fairways would be tighter and faster in June. In the run-up to the Open, he worked on "shallowing out my arc at impact," keeping his downswing slightly flatter than his back-swing—a move that helped him fling the face of his driver to impact at up to 130 miles per hour while keeping the ball from "ballooning" too high.

Practicing with Harmon, chatting about Kobe Bryant, Shaquille O'Neal, and the rest of his beloved Los Angeles Lakers, Tiger spent hours making range balls do his bidding. Here's a three-hundred-yard drive that draws twenty yards. Here's one that draws fifteen yards. Here's a high Nicklaus fade. Here's a 2-iron stinger that stays under the wind.

The week before the U.S. Open, he flew to Las Vegas to drill down on a few last details at Harmon's Rio Secco facility. Between practice sessions he played a round with Adam Scott, then a nineteen-year-old Australian prodigy who was thinking about turning pro. With the wind howling out of the desert, Scott shot an even-par 72. Harmon called it "a hell of a score" considering the weather. Meanwhile, Tiger shot 63 to set a new course record. Scott said, "Boy, I have a hell of a lot of work to do."

Looking back years later, after winning the 2013 Masters (and serving Moreton Bay lobster and Australian Wagyu beef at the next Champions Dinner), Scott described his first ever round with Tiger as an "eye-opener . . . a complete ass-whipping." He left the course "reconsidering if I should actually worry about a career in golf."

Harmon had a different reaction: that evening he drove to a casino and bet on Tiger Woods to win the U.S. Open.

The new Rio Secco record holder gave Harmon a smile before they flew to California for the tournament. "You know," he said, "the way I feel about my game right now, I just might blow everybody away."

FIVE
PEBBLE BEACH

By the time Tiger motored down 17-Mile Drive and pulled up to the gate at Pebble Beach Golf Links, the weather forecast on the radio called for sunny days with temperatures to match the scores the best players were expected to shoot: high sixties and low seventies. Experts predicted that the dreaded U.S. Open rough would keep the winning score around par. A mild, wetter than usual spring on the Monterey Peninsula had been ideal for growing the course's *Poa annua* and ryegrass, which left the rough higher and visibly thicker than when Tiger had won the AT&T Pebble Beach Pro-Am there in February. The narrow strips of primary rough lining the course's emerald fairways reached players' shoe tops. The denser second cut stood five inches high.

Seen from above, Pebble Beach Golf Links is an oasis of green between blue Carmel Bay and miles of sprawling housing developments. Locals like to call it "the greatest meeting of land and water in the world." Gulls dot the gray rocks in the bay. Whitecaps lap onto the beach below the nine seaside holes. The course, a true links, follows the shore south as far as the tenth green near Pescadero Canyon, then doubles back to where it starts, near the Lodge at Pebble Beach, which overlooks the first and final holes.

Tiger could hardly wait to get out there.

The one hundredth U.S. Open would be his one hundredth tournament as a professional. He liked the thought of shooting for his third major at one of his three or four favorite courses on Earth. Its ocean vistas, rugged cliffs, and gnarled cypresses made it one of the sport's showplaces, familiar to anyone who followed the game on TV, played video golf, or bought one of countless Pebble Beach calendars and posters. The United States Golf Association, which runs what it calls America's national championship, had been planning its centennial Open since Tiger was a high schooler in Orange County, 350 miles south. He had first played there as a thirteen-year-old junior phenom who stood five foot three and weighed a hundred pounds if he had coins and a few golf balls in his pockets. The course's beauty dazzled him. Its lengthy carries beat him up. "The golf course was so-o-o long!" he said. Five years later, making his way around the same links at the 1994 California Amateur Championship, he was surprised at how much the course had shrunk. "The fact that I'd added six inches in height might have helped."

He won the California Amateur that year and defended his title as a nineteen-year-old Stanford sophomore in 1995, the year before he turned professional. Five summers later, the three-to-one betting favorite called the U.S. Open venue "one of the courses I truly love. The beauty of Pebble Beach still awes me."

The USGA saw one of its missions as "defending par" against a field made up mostly of touring pros who seemed to hit the ball farther and shoot lower scores every year. That meant making U.S. Open courses as punishing as possible. The organization's blue-jacketed officials claimed that their goal was "not to humiliate the best players in the world, but to identify them." To do that, they turned their marquee event into the most grueling test in golf.

"It does more to make a man out of you than any other tournament," Jack Nicklaus said.

Pundits expected a winning score around even par, depending on wind and weather. "Pebble Beach will hurt some feelings this week," the *New York Times* predicted. Along with pinched fairways and ankle-deep rough, players would need to negotiate Pebble's small, notoriously bumpy *Poa annua* greens. A strain of bluegrass that thrives in humid, temperate climates, *Poa* can wilt in warm weather. It can shrivel under the wear and tear of a tournament, particularly late in a day featuring nine or ten hours of being trampled by more than 150 players and their caddies. That added a variable Tiger factored into his thinking that week. One way to limit the effects that the gnarly *Poa* had on putts would be to fire a few risky approach shots at flagsticks, leaving shorter putts. "Hopefully," he said. But warm, sunny weather might bake the greens and make that even riskier. An 8-iron that had stuck like a dart in the first week of February might bound off the green in mid-June. He planned to keep one thought in mind: land every iron shot below the hole.

Nicklaus was making his forty-fourth and farewell U.S. Open appearance with fanfare that week. Team Tiger liked to joke that Eldrick Woods had been negative thirteen years old when the Golden Bear had won his first major, the 1962 U.S. Open, and negative three in 1972, when Nicklaus had struck a legendary 1-iron at Pebble Beach's par-3 seventeenth hole in the 1983 U.S. Open, a 219-yard bullet that clanged off the flagstick and stopped two inches from the hole, clinching the third of his four U.S. Open titles. Tiger knew those shots by heart. His father had steeped him in the game's modern history since Eldrick was in diapers. Earl had held him in his lap while they watched staticky videos of Palmer charging, Lee Trevino at Merion, Johnny Miller at Oakmont, Nicklaus everywhere.

In the early 1980s, Tiger had grown from toddler to junior golfer, tacking *Star Wars* and sports car posters to his bedroom walls. But it was Nicklaus who loomed over him when he went to sleep at night and woke up in the morning. A poster of the Golden Bear overlooked his bed—not because Nicklaus was his hero but because he was the game's gold standard. Tiger always wanted to be his own hero. He taped a *Golf Digest* list of Nicklaus's achievements beside his Golden Bear poster. It showed Nicklaus's career milestones in chronological order.

Nicklaus had first broken 50 for nine holes when he was nine years old. Tiger did it at age three. Nicklaus had first broken 80 in a full round when he was twelve. Tiger did the same when he was eight. Nicklaus had broken 70 when he was thirteen. Tiger did it at twelve.

Other items on the taped-up list served as goals for the game's best junior golfer. Nicklaus had won his first U.S. Amateur at nineteen. Tiger went on to win his first at eighteen. Nicklaus had won his first major, the 1962 U.S. Open, when he was twenty-two. Tiger won the Masters when he was twenty-one. But three years later, in June 2000, he was falling a little behind. Nicklaus had won his third major, the 1963 PGA Championship, at age twenty-three. Tiger was a year older, still seeking his third.

He was one of the few Tour pros who had watched and re-watched Nicklaus's greatest hits often enough to tell you that Jack birdied the seventeenth at Pebble Beach after his 1-iron bullet and went on to win the 1972 U.S. Open with a score of two over par. Tiger thought he could do better.

He was more than a little miffed that the USGA had chosen that particular tournament to start calling Pebble's par-5 second hole a par 4. At 484 yards, the hole was rugged enough for scratch golfers and entrants in every tournament ever held there. But the Tour pros who came through once or twice a year routinely birdied it, so the pooh-bahs in their blue jackets had changed the scorecard. For Open week only, one of the world's iconic courses would play to a par of 71 rather than 72. That struck Tiger as the wrong way to defend par. It offended his sense of history. It was like saying that Michael Jordan could commit only four fouls. "We've always played this golf course as a par seventy-two," he said, "and all of a sudden it's a seventy-one? I don't think that's right." Suppose he or Els or Duval challenged the tournament record for strokes under par—they would have to make four extra birdies to match Vardon, Francis Ouimet, Sarazen, Jones, Nelson, Hogan, Palmer, Player, Casper, Trevino, Miller, and Watson, all U.S. Open champions whose name his dad could reel off as if they were the twelve apostles.

He wasn't yet one of the greats, but he was working on it. Before tournament rounds he would meet Williams at the practice range an hour and twenty minutes before his tee time. On other days he liked to hit balls at what he called "dawn-thirty," half an hour after sunup. Early that week he was striking the ball so purely, with a sound that made other players stop, watch, and listen, that Williams thought he might be peaking too soon.

On the morning before the tournament began, Tiger played a practice round with O'Meara and Tour pro Paul Goydos. At the twelfth hole, a 202-yard par 3, Goydos hit a 4-iron that came in too hot and bounced over the green. Tiger stepped up and struck a towering tee ball that carried the front bunker, dropped, and stopped four feet from the hole.

Goydos asked, "What did you hit?" It is illegal to ask another player about his club choice in competition, but practice rounds are more casual. Given the shot's trajectory—so high that the ball "had reentry burns on the way down," Goydos joked—he figured Tiger had smoked a 7-iron as far as he'd hit his 4.

"Four-iron," Tiger said. A 7 might have spun too much. He had swung under the ball, lofting his 4-iron high enough to take twenty yards off its usual flight.

They both hit solid drives at the par-5 eighteenth. Both had about 230 yards to the flag. Goydos reached the green with a 3-wood, Tiger with an iron shot. Again Goydos asked, "What did you hit?"

"Four-iron," Tiger said, looking poker-faced while Goydos tried to keep his jaw from dropping. With the same club, Tiger had lofted an approach that came down like a 7-iron on one hole, then drilled the same club thirty yards farther when he needed more distance. Goydos told him, "That's not even fair."

That same day, twenty Tour pros joined Mike Hicks, Payne Stewart's longtime caddie, for a "twenty-one-gun salute" on the eighteenth fairway. Stewart was one of golf's most colorful characters, a two-time U.S. Open winner known for playing in retro knickers and tam o'shanter caps. He would have been the defending champion had he not been killed in a plane crash the previous fall. On October 25, 1999, four months after winning his second U.S. Open, Stewart and three friends took a charter flight from Orlando to Texas for the season-ending Tour Championship. Early in the flight a sudden depressurization sucked the air out of the plane. Within minutes, everyone on board was either unconscious or dead. The Learjet continued on autopilot. Military F-16s swooped around it, reporting no signs of life. TV networks tracked the plane's path over Georgia, Alabama, Tennessee, Missouri, and Iowa. There was a rumor that Tiger Woods was on the flight. Finally, after almost four hours, Stewart's so-called ghost flight, a thousand miles off course, ran out of fuel and crashed in a cattle pasture near Aberdeen, South Dakota.

Eight months later at Pebble Beach, Hicks and twenty golfers including Phil Mickelson, David Duval, Davis Love III, Paul Azinger, and Sergio García gathered to remember the 1999 U.S. Open champion.

Eighty-eight-year-old Byron Nelson, the tournament's oldest living champion, used a cane to hobble across the eighteenth fairway and hug Stewart's widow, Tracey. Moments later, Hicks and the others drove twenty-one balls into the Pacific. García wore knickers. His drive was one of the worst. He was weeping.

Tiger Woods skipped the ceremony. He and Stewart had been fishing and drinking buddies, angling for salmon and trout on trips to Scotland and Ireland, downing pints together. Stewart "will be sorely missed," he told reporters. Even so, "I can't be thinking about Payne right now. If I do that, I'll transport myself back to some pub late at night in County Down where he's singing a drinking song. And I can't afford to be there right now. I have to put that out of my mind and focus on what I'm going to do."

On Thursday he teed off in brilliant sunshine with Jim Furyk and Jesper Parnevik. The course was dewy, the greens softer than the USGA would have liked. Tiger wore black slacks and a short-sleeved shirt with sleeves baggy enough to show off his biceps. He hated the feel of tight sleeves. He was not as muscled as he would be later in his career but still strong enough to swing at 90 percent and outdrive Furyk and Parnevik on the fly. He liked to keep some power in reserve for when he needed it.

His 4 at the second hole would have been a birdie any other year but left him even par for his first half hour on the course. He got into red numbers by playing the short par-4 fourth perfectly: a 2-iron off the tee within a yard of his target, a sprinkler head at the bellybutton of the fairway; a 60-degree wedge that stopped a foot below the hole; a tap-in. At two under par at the ninth hole, with a chance to make the turn in 32, he got too aggressive and ran a birdie putt nine feet past the cup. Caddie Williams averted his eyes. Tiger gave his ball a dirty look before settling over it, taking a long breath, and sinking the comebacker. After four back-nine birdies he signed for a bogey-free 65, the lowest score ever shot in a U.S. Open at Pebble Beach.

His playing partners couldn't remember seeing such command of every shot. "If the pin was on the right side of the green, he'd start it in the middle and cut it toward the pin," said Furyk. "If the pin was on the left side, he started it in the middle and drew it."

Parnevik added, "He putted like a god." Tiger had worked his way around Pebble's pimply greens with six two-putts and a dozen one-putts including five par savers that meant as much to him as birdies. Recounting his round that evening, he remembered the par putts: "A nine-footer, an eight-footer, a twelve-footer, a six-footer, a ten-footer." To him, each of them felt as good as a birdie.

By then, John Daly was long gone. The thirty-four-year-old Daly had won two majors, the same as Tiger and Els. A bulky bleach blond whose motto was "Grip it and rip it," he had led the Tour in driving distance every year since 1995. He was Tiger's opposite in many ways, overweight and undisciplined, packing Marlboros and candy in his golf bag. Daly hit driver every chance he got, which was why he would go on to lead the 2000 PGA Tour in driving distance with an average of 301.4 yards, three yards ahead of second-place Tiger Woods, who often hit 2-irons to tight fairways. Three over par as he waggled his driver at the last tee on Thursday, Daly needed a par at the eighteenth and a decent round the next day to make the cut. But his drive sailed sideways and bounced out of bounds. Now lying two on the tee, the driving distance king demonstrated how hard golf can be. He proceeded to pump two drives into Carmel Bay before smacking one to dry land. Ten angry minutes later, after laying up near the spot where Payne Stewart's friends had hit twenty-one drives into the surf, he was lying seven. From there he pulled a wedge shot that drifted left and joined those ceremonial balls in the water. Ten minutes later, he two-putted for a 14. The opposite of a grinder, Daly signed for an 83, withdrew from the tournament, and peeled out of the parking lot.

A fog bank rolled in that afternoon. Half the field was still on the course when play was suspended. Tiger was pumping iron in the gym by then.

Fitness was one way he boosted his edge on players like Daly, who was known to munch half a dozen packs of peanut M&M's during a tournament round. Tiger had packed thirty pounds of muscle onto his six-foot frame since his college days. He did it with intensive workouts like this one, often lasting two to three hours. He worked out six days a week including tournament weeks. Under the watchful eye of his trainer, Keith Kleven, he emphasized strengthening his back, shoulders, legs, and chest. Explosive moves with heavy weights helped him develop fast-twitch muscle fibers. As he put it, "Fast-twitch muscles helped me really tear through the ball from the top of my backswing." So did sprints, while his frequent six-mile runs helped build endurance. During roadwork, as on the range or in the gym, he often reached a meditative state. The repetition of steps, swings, or reps could bring an inner solitude he prized almost as much as winning. In those times he could mind his business without answering questions or signing autographs. Scuba diving, another recent passion, cast the same spell. Four years later, when he bought a $20 million yacht, he would name it *Privacy*.

SIX
OPEN ROUGH

There is a particular sound a golf ball makes when a PGA Tour player strikes it. If you are twenty or thirty yards downrange, you can hear the ball hiss as it zips through the air. But there was a different sound when Tiger Woods hit a golf ball: the percussion of near-perfect contact. Even at majors, other pros heard the sound and stopped practicing to watch him.

The second day of the U.S. Open began that way. Tiger slept in past dawn-thirty that morning, then hit balls on the range while some of the seventy-five golfers who had been on the course when the fog rolled in completed their first rounds. His first-round 65 held up to make him the early leader, with Miguel Ángel Jiménez a shot behind and John Huston another shot back. As usual, some other players took a few moments to watch Tiger warm up. The swing they saw was as powerful as the one they had admired when he lapped the field at the 1997 Masters, but tighter. Despite his dominance at Augusta that year, he knew that Augusta, with its wide fairways and barely-there rough, was uniquely suited to his freewheeling power game. But there were three other majors he was determined to win. The U.S. Open in particular called for drives that steered clear of rough the USGA had grown so high and thick that landing in it was as bad as or worse than driving into a bunker. That was one reason he had spent a year and a half risking his career to remake his swing.

To win majors, he told Butch Harmon in 1997, "I need a better swing."

Harmon admired him for it. To mark the occasion, he showed Tiger a vintage photo of Ben Hogan swinging a club. The black-and-white photo still hangs in Harmon's office at Rio Secco. It shows Hogan at the instant of impact, his weight shifted to his left side, his left wrist bowed toward the target.

Tiger didn't have heroes, but like Harmon he considered Hogan the best ball striker the game had ever seen. He liked hearing his coach tell old family stories about Bantam Ben, the five-foot, eight-inch immortal who was known as much for his competitive fire as for the purity of his swing. One oft-told tale had to do with the 1947 Masters, in which Hogan was paired with Butch's father. At Augusta's tricky par-3 twelfth, Hogan banged his tee shot three feet from the flag. Claude Harmon followed with a 7-iron that bounced once and jumped into the hole for the first ace in Masters history. Claude Harmon hugged his caddie. Patrons went bananas. A minute or two later, after Hogan sank his birdie putt, he said, "You know, Claude, I think that's the first time I've birdied that hole. What did you have?"

"I had a one, Ben."

Half a century later, Butch Harmon saw a similar intensity in Tiger Woods. When they began rebuilding Tiger's swing in 1997, "I said we should make incremental changes. It would take years, but that way it wouldn't cause a major disruption in his game."

Tiger disagreed. "Let's do it all at once," he said.

"All at once" turned out to take eighteen months. Fighting his

Along with swing coach Butch Harmon, Tiger rebuilt his swing to win more majors.

swing, cursing himself, Tiger won only once in 1998, while David Duval led the money list and rose to number one in the world. "Tiger didn't care," Harmon remembered. "He wasn't looking for a quick fix. That's who he is. When he decides to do something, he goes all in."

Teaching pros like Harmon will tell you that even the best golfers have bad habits. Hogan fought a tendency to hook the ball, a flaw he fought his whole career. "I hate a hook. I could vomit when I see one," he said. "It's like a rattlesnake in your pocket."

Tiger's Achilles' heel was "getting stuck" on the downswing. As Harmon described it, "He generated so much speed by firing his lower body on the downswing that his arms couldn't catch up." As his lower body rotated toward the target, his upper body lagged behind. He was gifted enough to compensate by flipping his hands at the bottom of the swing, just in time to bring the clubhead square at impact—most of the time. But if he made that last move a fraction of a second too late, he blocked the ball offline to the right. If he was a hair early, he pulled the ball or hooked it. On good days he made enough adjustments to win with the swing he had, but in his own opinion, "I was still too handsy and flashy through the ball. The shaft was pointed far right of my target, which forced me to dump my hands a little under" on the downswing.

He had a more foolproof move in mind, one that worked almost as well on his worst days as on his best. "I don't want to rent my swing," he told Harmon. "I want to own it."

They both knew that fractional errors hurt Tiger more than they hurt other players because he generated more force. At a swing speed of 120 miles per hour, a speed he often topped, the ball is in contact with a driver for one two-hundredth of a second before launching at more than 180 miles an hour. As Harmon put it, "A tenth of a degree of variance in the position of his clubface or the path of the swing meant the difference between finding the fairway and having to yell 'Fore!'"

The photo he showed Tiger captured Hogan at the moment of impact, his left wrist bent forward at impact. A bowed left wrist can keep the clubface square to the target milliseconds longer. But emulating Hogan would take muscle as well as technique. To match Hogan's near-perfect strike, Tiger would have to get stronger.

So he started lifting weights. He swore off his beloved McDonald's and Arby's in favor of grilled chicken and yogurt. Only three years before, when he had weighed 155 pounds and worn glasses, his Stanford buddies had teased him by calling him "Urkel" for his resemblance to the nerdy, bespectacled star of the sitcom *Family Matters*. Now he went on long runs and enjoyed them. A typical day might start with a four-mile run, two to three hours in the gym, and two hours on the range. Then he would have lunch. In the afternoon he'd often play eighteen holes, work on his short game, and run four more miles before dinner. Such a regimen was a far cry from the habits of older players like Fuzzy Zoeller, who tended to confine workouts to their post-round wrist curls with tumblers of scotch. When the first fitness trailer appeared at PGA Tour events in the 1980s, one Tour pro had wandered in, carrying a beer, and asked, "What's going on in here?"

A new generation of players was coming, with Tiger Woods leading the way. After 1999, after LASIK eye surgery, countless workouts, sprints, and endurance runs, he looked like his earlier self's tougher big brother. His abs rippled. His pecs and biceps bulged. Old-timers marveled at the sight of a player who was as lean as Gary Player and as muscly as Frank Stranahan. In less than five years, Urkel had morphed into a 185-pound athlete who could bench-press three hundred.

Here was a level of fitness other golfers could not match. From now on, players like Daly and Zoeller would need to rely more on hot streaks and hot weeks to compete with him—the rare four rounds when all the bounces went their way.

One benefit of Tiger's muscle was the power he kept in reserve.

Caddie Steve Williams (*left*) joined Harmon and Team Tiger in 1999.

In 1999, "Wild Thing" Daly led the Tour in driving distance with an average of 305.6 yards. Tiger came in third at 293.1. Daly would lead again in 2000 with an average drive of 301.4, while runner-up Woods averaged 298. Of course, Daly often hit driver while Tiger opted for a 2-iron on the same hole. For all his power, the new, improved Woods never once led the PGA Tour in driving distance—because he didn't need to. By the spring of 2000, he didn't have to swing all out to carry the ball three hundred yards. He could outdrive Daly if he had to, but he didn't care about winning the driving distance title. He was out to win majors.

On Friday afternoon, he rejoined Furyk and Parnevik at the first tee. With the golfers ahead of them fighting for pars, the pace of play was glacial. He birdied the third hole to get into red numbers for the day. At the par-3 fifth, they waited twenty minutes before Tiger flared an 8-iron into a greenside bunker. His first bogey of the tournament left him six under par.

His next full swing was another mistake. At the tee on Pebble's sixth, a reachable par 5, he got sticky if not fully stuck on the downswing. A degree or two of variance at impact sent his 322-yard drive sailing to the right, where it settled into heavy rough two hundred yards from the hole.

His caddie wasn't worried. Par was a safe bet: pitch the ball back to the fairway, knock a wedge onto the green, and two-putt.

Instead, Tiger reached for his 7-iron. To Williams's surprise, his man was going for the green.

It was a shot hardly anyone else would consider, uphill over a sprawling thirty-foot Monterey pine and then a cliff, and from shin-high rough. The risk seemed ten times greater than the possible reward. He could easily make double bogey if his ball hit the tree. A scratch golfer taking the same line might make 8 or 9. But as Tiger explained later, he figured he could "catch a flier, a hot one, if I came down steep enough."

A flier from the rough carries farther than a similar shot from the fairway because blades of grass get between the clubface and the ball, decreasing the ball's spin. Catching a flier can send a 7-iron that might normally go 180 yards twenty yards farther. But that was what he wanted from such a rotten lie: a 7-iron flier that would clear the tree and carry as far as it could go.

He swung all out, slashing almost straight down, leaning sideways with the force of his follow-through. Williams would call it "a shot that took *strength*," the kind of gym-built muscle few players had in 2000.

The all-out 7-iron cleared the tree, carrying almost two hundred yards and kicking forward to the green, fifteen feet from the flag. Williams shouldered Tiger's golf bag and started uphill, shaking his head at his player's strength and another quality he admired: the kind of balls that aren't coated with urethane.

Tiger's daring approach set up a two-putt birdie that got him back to red numbers on a day that beat up most of the field. He birdied the eleventh to go to eight under for the tournament. By then the marine layer off the Pacific was blocking the sun. Much of the course was in shadow. Play was still crawling, so Tiger took a moment to eat the peanut-butter-and-banana sandwich Williams had stashed in the bag. The sandwich was a tradition; Tiger usually ate one on the seventh tee and saved another for the thirteenth hole, but they usually reached the thirteenth in less than three hours. With the sun sinking, there wouldn't be enough light to play much longer.

Phil Mickelson's group finally cleared the green. Tiger laced his tee shot to the safe side, thirty-five feet from the hole. His threesome was heading for the green when a deer sprang through the gallery. They let the deer go through. It was after eight o'clock when a horn finally sounded, calling the golfers back to the clubhouse. The rest of the second round would be played the next day. The rules gave players two options if they were still on the course when the horn blew: they could either mark their balls and resume their rounds from that spot the next morning or finish playing the hole they were on.

Tiger wanted to finish. He had a feel for the pace of the greens, which could change after the grounds crew mowed and rolled them before another day's play. At the same time, reading such a long putt in near-darkness was like trying to read a book in a closet.

Depth perception gets hazy in half-light. Williams held the flagstick over the hole to give him a visible target. Tiger went into his pre-putt routine, which never varied. Settling his feet until they felt precisely balanced, he took two practice strokes. Next, he placed the head of his putter behind the ball and shifted his feet forward into putting position, his eyes directly over the ball. He turned his gaze to the hole, then back to the ball. After a breath he looked up to check the line one last time. Then he pulled his putter back—*tick*—and with a smooth, slightly inside-to-out stroke—*tock*—sent the ball on its way.

He was just trying to get it close. Two putts here, then he could start thinking about playing twenty-four holes on Saturday. Williams pulled the flag away as Tiger's putt began rolling.

Ten feet from the cup, it looked like it had a chance.

Two feet away, it looked dead center, only to slide an inch to the right as it died.

On its last rotation, the ball fell in.

His roller in the gloaming put him at nine under par, three up on the field. All that stood between the leader and a good night's sleep were the press duties he saw as the worst part of his profession.

According to Harmon, "The biggest pressure Tiger faced was media pressure. Getting asked the same questions over and over gets old—especially, I think, if you have an active mind. He was always very,

very smart, very verbal, but he'd learned not to say much. He learned to be guarded."

Some who knew him said Tiger could be lively company, with a goofy, bawdy, sometimes juvenile sense of humor. Golf-beat reporters blamed his standoffishness on the 1997 *GQ* exposé that had regaled millions of readers with his dirty jokes. After that, he was wary of anyone carrying a notepad or microcassette recorder—the complete opposite of Phil Mickelson, who might have been a glad-handing phony, some said, but at least Phil would look you in the eye and give you a quote worth writing down. One member of the press corps joked that Tiger was the world's most famous introvert, a line that wasn't far from the truth. Tiger had long since overcome a stutter that had made him afraid to be called on in grade school, but he still claimed to be shy by nature. He still hung back in many social situations. According to one story golf writers liked to tell, he had gone clubbing one night in New York with his older, savvier buddies Michael Jordan and Derek Jeter. After watching them chat up the women who flocked around the three of them, Tiger reverted to Urkel mode.

"How do you talk to girls?" he asked, sending Jordan and Jeter into fits of laughter.

"Tell 'em you're Tiger Woods!" they said.

At Pebble Beach, he fell back on clichés. "I've always felt I'd rather have the lead than try to catch up," he said when asked about strategy. As for Jack Nicklaus's farewell appearance after forty-four U.S. Opens dating back to 1962, when Nicklaus won the first of his eighteen majors, Tiger said, "Jack has obviously set the bar up pretty high for everyone to chase after. To win as many majors as he has is very remarkable. Unbelievable, if you think about it." Asked about his goals in the years ahead, he surprised reporters by bristling. "My long-term goals are known to me and my team."

After several more clichés about hitting fairways, keeping the ball below the hole, and remembering that there was a long way to go before Sunday, he surprised the gathered reporters by returning, unprompted, to the subject of goals, admitting to one that made him smile.

"I'd like to hit the perfect shot," he said.

But first he was aiming for a good night's sleep. He was scheduled to finish his second round early the next morning and then, weather permitting, play the whole third round that afternoon. With all that coming up on Saturday, he said he was going to try to "sleep fast."

SEVEN
PRICKLY PAIR

He spent part of Friday night practicing putting on the carpet in his room at the Lodge at Pebble Beach. Asleep by midnight, he woke early on Saturday to meet Harmon and Williams on the range at 5:00 a.m., leaving a few balls in the room. It was sweater weather. At first, the light was worse than when the second round was called on account of darkness, but it improved as the sun rose over the range.

NBC pre-empted Saturday-morning cartoons and the Saturday edition of the *Today* show for unscheduled "bonus coverage" of golf beginning at 6:30, Tiger Woods's tee time. NBC Sports chief Dick Ebersol said there was no coincidence behind the schedule change. "In the TV age there have been two people who have attracted viewers beyond their sport, Muhammad Ali and Michael Jordan," Ebersol said. "Tiger Woods is clearly the third." He wasn't concerned about losing viewers if the leader blew the field away. Tiger's twelve-shot victory at the 1997 Masters was (and still is) the highest-rated golf telecast of all time.

With only two balls left at the 2000 U.S. Open, Tiger hooked his drive into the Pacific.

It was going to be more than a two-peanut-butter-and-banana-sandwich sort of day. Before teeing off for what promised to be a marathon of a third round, he had to play Pebble's last six holes without giving strokes back to the field. He and Williams met Jim Furyk, Jesper Parnevik, and their caddies at the thirteenth tee. While the players loosened up with a few final practice swings, Williams reached into Tiger's golf bag for a ball and didn't like what he found there.

There were only three Nike Tour Accuracys in the pouch that held them. Williams checked other pouches and found nothing but tees, sandwiches, and a raincoat. Tiger had left three balls, half their supply, in his hotel room.

No worries, Williams told himself. Three balls would be plenty to play the last six holes of the second round. It would probably leave them with two extra. Williams wasn't overly worried when Tiger pulled his first drive of the morning into the rough and slashed out, leaving a scuff mark on his brand-new Nike ball, and tossed the ball to a little boy in the gallery. Now they were down to two. Williams thought about asking the boy to give the ball back but didn't want to make a scene on international TV. "It wouldn't be a good look if Tiger Woods's caddie took a ball off a happy kid," he recalled. "There would be tears."

He kept his thoughts to himself as his player reached the eighteenth tee leading the tournament at nine under par. Then Hogan's rattlesnake struck. After two and a half days of piercing fairways, Tiger launched a hook "halfway to Hawaii," as he put it later. He cursed himself: *"Goddamn you, fucking prick!"* An NBC microphone caught every syllable. Within minutes, viewers were phoning the network to complain about his language.

The same mic caught Tiger's next word. Turning to Williams he stuck out his hand and said, "Ball."

It was Williams's worst moment. The broad-shouldered Kiwi was perhaps the fittest, toughest caddie on Earth as well as the most famous, a distinction that went to whoever carried Tiger's bag. He raced dirt-track cars back home in New Zealand and kept pace with the player he called "Tigah" on their frequent morning runs. Williams had laughed off car crashes, blisters, shin splints, and even the chaos of following around the most visible golfer on the planet, but here was a more private discomfort. "I have never, ever been that nervous," he recalled. "I am standing there with my backside trembling. My butt cheeks were absolutely clamoring. I don't want to tell him it's our last golf ball!"

Tiger was in no mood to stand there waiting. "Give me another fucking ball."

Williams had found his way into a caddie's nightmare. One part of his job was checking their supply of balls before every round. He had done it before the second round began but had forgotten to check through the bag before they resumed play on the back nine that morning. Now he was afraid he might get his player disqualified in the middle of the U.S. Open. Tiger, who knew the Rules of Golf as well as anyone, could have told him that the situation wasn't necessarily so desperate. But it was complicated. The Rules of Golf allow a player who runs out of balls to borrow one from another golfer, provided it is the same make and model. That clause might have saved Williams's backside a month before, when Tiger was teeing up the same Titleist so many other players used, but it was no help now. Only one player in the field had even one Bridgestone-make Nike ball. Under the rules, a player who borrows and uses a different model of ball incurs a two-stroke penalty. Another option would be for Williams to run to the clubhouse and buy more balls, but the Tour Accuracy wasn't on sale in pro shops. Or he could sprint to Tiger's hotel room to grab the three balls he had left behind, but he'd never make it back in time to avoid a two-stroke penalty for slow play. So they were looking at two strokes either way.

Tiger knew none of that. Williams wasn't about to tell him that if he hooked another one to the beach, he would lie four on the tee at Pebble's eighteenth hole after two lost balls and two penalty strokes. Add another penalty for using one of Furyk's or Parnevik's Titleists— now he'd be lying six. Not even he would be able to knock a 543-yard drive from the tee into the cup for a double bogey. In that scenario, after lying six on the tee, he would need to "birdie" the hole in order to make a quintuple-bogey 10. There goes most, if not all, of the biggest lead in U.S. Open history, with Williams to blame for the biggest screw-up in caddying history.

He put Tiger's driver back into the bag, silently willing him to play safer with a 3-wood off the tee this time. But Tiger was determined to swing the big stick. He reached for the driver.

"Take your fucking hand off that," said Williams.

"Give me the fucking driver!"

Williams handed it over. He watched and worried while Tiger belted a drive to the right-hand side of the fairway. He was lying three with a tree, the lone cypress that stood in the middle of the fairway, blocking his way to the green. From there, a layup to the left was the sensible play. He could still save his 6 with a wedge and a putt that way. "But he wants to hit a big cut out over the ocean," remembered Williams, who still didn't admit they were down to one ball. Lips zipped, he watched his man open the clubface of his 3-wood and bang a long, looping left-to-right approach that flirted with disaster all the way to the green. As it curled back over the savior bunker between the beach and the last hundred yards of the fairway, Williams felt his backside relax. "My heart rate didn't return to normal until he'd reached the green and made bogey."

Even after dropping a shot on a birdie hole, Tiger led by six strokes through two rounds. No one had ever held such a commanding lead at the midway point of a U.S. Open. Later that morning, the field was trimmed to the customary top sixty players plus ties plus anyone else within ten shots of the lead. Tiger was so far ahead that the "within ten shots" provision didn't help anybody. Only seventeen of the sixty-three golfers who survived to play the last two rounds were within ten shots of him.

Tour pros accustomed to raving about Tiger's power now praised his versatility. "He hit it high, low, right, left," said his playing partner, Parnevik, who along with his wife, Mia, would soon hire a Swedish nanny named Elin Nordegren and introduce her to Tiger. "Every shot was pretty much different from the shot before."

Tiger napped between rounds. Williams made sure to put plenty of balls into the bag before the third round began that afternoon, along with a fresh peanut-butter-and-banana sandwich.

A marine wind whistled off the Pacific that afternoon, greeting the players who had made the cut. Pebble's bumpy greens were getting harder and quicker. The same wedge shot that had stopped under the flagstick during the AT&T in January might bound to parts unknown in June. But the second-round leader thought the weather might work in his favor. Tiger disliked surprises, believing that quirky hops and sudden shifts of wind introduced random factors that could upset his planning and his game. At the same time, he figured that bad conditions favor the player with the most control of himself and his game, and everyone knew who that was.

He made a birdie 3 at the long second hole, a score that would have been an eagle any other year (take that, USGA), and had a chance to build his lead at the third hole, where one of golf's surprises struck. His second shot ballooned in a gust of wind. A Titleist, with its higher spin rate, might have ballooned a bit more and dropped well short of the green, leaving a pitch and a putt for par. His new ball, engineered to resist the wind, carried far enough to plunge into thick rough beside a greenside bunker. The ball was barely visible, looking like a pearl onion at the bottom of a salad bowl. He considered taking a penalty drop. After a minute of weighing his options, all bad, he decided to punch it sideways to the fairway.

He chopped at the ball, but it barely noticed. It moved less than a yard. Lying three, he hacked a pitch that fell short of the green. Now lying four on one of the easiest par 4s on the course, he chipped on and had an eight-foot putt for double bogey.

Woods almost always made the putts he had to make. This one fell off to the right. He stared at it. Here was golf at its most mercurial, the world's best player looking like a weekend duffer, taking six shots to go 130 yards. Tapping in for a triple-bogey 7, he fell from nine under par to six under. The field was back in the tournament.

That's when he did something that shocked his caddie: he laughed.

"Normally, Tiger gets quite temperamental," Williams explained later. "If it had been another event, the putter would have been thrown, the ball would have been thrown, the ball would have been kicked, the bag would have been ripped. But he knew how unlucky he'd been on that hole!"

Instead of getting mad, Tiger set himself a new short-term goal: to get back to even. "*Somehow, some way,*" he later recalled, "I thought, *I'll figure out a way to get back to even par for the round.*"

At the sixth, where he'd struck his already famous 7-iron from the rough the day before, a shot from within a few yards of the same spot veered into rough ringing a fairway bunker. He had to stand in the sand below the ball, choking up on his wedge. "He's got to hit it off his navel," Johnny Miller told TV viewers. Testing his footing, Tiger nearly toppled over into the sand. He tried again, building a stance with one foot in the bunker and the other on the lip. After three tentative practice swings, he punched the ball sixty-five yards to the front of the green. It rolled to a stop near the flagstick while his gallery whooped, hollered, and chanted his name.

His seven-foot birdie putt looked as slippery as a ski run. "Bury it," Williams said.

He did. Tiger's unlikely up-and-down got him to one over par for the third round, seven under for the tournament. With the wind howling and Pebble's toughest holes ahead, his latest short-term plan was simple: "Keep my head down and keep grinding away."

He pushed an approach shot at the tenth, flaring it so far into the gallery below the green that he had to jump to see the top of the flag. To add a degree of difficulty, his ball was lying against a rock. He swung harder than he would have otherwise, sending ball and rock flying and etching a nick in his wedge. Floating like a knuckleball, the ball carried most of the way to the flag, close enough for him to get down in two as the wind, five-inch rough, and manhole-cover greens abused the rest of the field.

Ernie Els, playing an hour ahead of Tiger, had the shot of the day, a sand wedge that hopped into the cup for a deuce at the short par-4 fourth. Els's eagle contributed to a third-round 68 that was Saturday's best by three strokes and got him into the final pairing for Sunday's final round. Els regarded his 68 one of the best rounds he'd ever played in a major, "considering the weather." And where did that leave him? "I've got half a chance." At thirty, the tall South African considered Tiger a friend. Not a close friend, but unlike millions of weekend golfers who play a clunkier version of the same sport, the two former junior phenoms had a keen sense of how onion-skin-thin the pro game gets at its highest levels, with a new generation of players vying for the top spot every twenty years or so. "In the sixties you had Palmer," Els said. "In the seventies it was Nicklaus. Now it's Tiger Woods. He's probably the most recognizable sportsman on the planet. And he's good for us. Good for me—he brings in sponsors, a lot of media. Golf has really taken off thanks to him." But Els hoped to help make the game more compelling, starting as soon as the following day. The professional game would get even more interesting, he said, "if someone could step up and play with him."

The last pairing was still on the course when Els finished his round. Tiger's third-round playing partner, Sweden's Thomas Bjørn, who had shared second place that morning, was on his way to shooting 82 in flagstick-bending winds. "I just tried to stay out of his way," Bjørn said of Tiger. "If he's six shots ahead, he wants to be seven ahead. He plays every shot like his life depended on it."

Tiger finished with an even-par 71, the number he'd been aiming for since his triple at the third hole. It would have been 70 if a long putt from the front of the eighteenth green hadn't died six inches from the hole, a shortcoming that left him leaning backward, giving the sky an accusing look. Still he would take a ten-shot lead to the last day. Saturday's carnage was such that Vijay Singh stayed on the leaderboard despite shooting 80. Furyk's 84 featured eight consecutive bogeys. Darren Clarke, who had pipped Tiger at the Match Play Championship in February, carded an 83 and headed for the nineteenth hole. Scotland's Colin Montgomerie, third ranked in the world behind Woods and Duval, shot 79. Informed that he still led the tournament in hitting fairways, Montgomerie said, "That's great. They should put the holes in the fairways."

Els's 68 turned out to be the only subpar score of the day. Tiger had been a Stanford undergrad watching on TV when Els won the 1994 U.S. Open at Oakmont in a playoff with Montgomerie and Loren Roberts. Ernie had been the game's young lion then, a twenty-four-year-old with a rhythmic swing that was the envy of the Tour. Three years later, when Tiger was a PGA Tour rookie, Els again edged the long-suffering Montgomerie at Congressional Country Club in Bethesda, Maryland, another tough track, to win his second U.S. Open. But he hadn't won a major since, and he was getting almost as tired of answering questions about Tiger Woods as Tiger was.

EIGHT
"NO BOGEYS"

When Pebble Beach Golf Links hosted its first tournament on February 22, 1919, the anniversary of George Washington's birthday, fifty golfers gathered around a newly planted cherry tree and recited an oath: "We pledge ourselves by our faith in the cherry tree to turn in honest scorecards."

Designed by Jack Neville and Douglas Grant, a pair of amateur champions who had never built a course before, Pebble Beach was an instant classic. Course designers including Alister MacKenzie and Jack Nicklaus improved the original layout, with Nicklaus adding a new fifth hole in 1998. Over the years, the course played host to four major championships, including three U.S. Opens. It was here that Arnold Palmer entertained fans by knocking balls into Stillwater Cove during a rare snow delay in 1962. Jack Nicklaus drilled his 1-iron off the flagstick at the seventeenth in 1972. Tom Watson chipped in on the same hole and topped Nicklaus in 1982. Two years after that, during the Bing Crosby Pro-Am, Hale Irwin hooked his drive at the eighteenth halfway to Hawaii and might have called himself a few choice names if his ball hadn't struck a rock on the beach and caromed right back to the fairway.

Tiger Woods pegged his tee into the ground at 3:40 in the afternoon on Sunday, June 18. He wore black shoes with steel spikes and a spit-polish shine, pleated black slacks, a blood-red Nike golf shirt, and a black cap with a white swoosh. Red shirts on tournament Sundays were a college tradition at Stanford, but there was more to his favorite color than that. As he explained, wearing red for a final round was "a superstition that started with my mom." According to Thai tradition, each day of the week is represented by a color. Red is for Sunday. In his amateur days he had sworn to his mother that he could win in any color he wanted. After losing three times while wearing blue on Sundays, he switched back.

Tiger also liked red because it is the color of subpar numbers on golf scoreboards. As the fourth round of the 2000 U.S. Open began, woods was the only name with a red number beside it.

Until then, no player since 1933 had led a U.S. Open by as many as five strokes after fifty-four holes. His margin on Els, his playing partner, was twice that. Over the tournament's first sixty-seven years, the average lead going into the final round had been 1.4 strokes. Now Phil Mickelson, tied for fifth at +4—often a competitive score in a U.S. Open—was a dozen shots behind. Paul Azinger, eighteen strokes back, joked that the only way to catch Woods would be to kneecap him: "We might need Tonya Harding."

Tiger had felt off-kilter that morning on the range until Harmon suggested a tweak: "Square your shoulders. They're a little open." After he shifted his left shoulder a degree toward the ball at address, his next shot took off like a bullet.

"That's it," he said. "Let's go."

His first two swings of the day were flawless, but he missed a twelve-footer for birdie. At the long par-4 second, he socked his tee ball past Els's 285-yard drive on the fly. His approach came in a degree too hot and skipped past the flagstick, a slight error that left him a slippery downhiller for birdie. All week his goal had been to leave iron shots below the hole on Pebble's small, bumpy greens. He stalked the putt from every angle, giving it his usual circumspection, then watched it skin the edge of the cup. Another tap-in par.

A safe drive at the third left him 122 yards from the flag. The day before, from within a few yards of the same spot, he had chopped his way to a triple-bogey 7. This time, with no sudden gust to knock the ball down, his wedge shot dropped twenty feet from the pin. Again he stalked the putt from every angle before giving it a rap. This one was dead center, only to quit a quarter inch short of the lip. He dropped to his knees. This brinksmanship was killing him. No thanks to the golf gods, he had missed three birdies by a grand total of two or three inches. He was still ten up on Els, who had carded three pars of his own. Ten shots behind, Ernie was already starting to run out of holes.

Tiger's five-footer for par at the fifth sparked a wide, toothy grin. Some par saves feel even better than birdies. Meanwhile, Els was bogeying his way into a second-place tie with Spain's handsy, mustachioed Miguel Ángel Jiménez, while Pádraig Harrington was on a birdie run that got him to within eight shots of the lead.

The leader found a new way to cause himself trouble at the par-5 sixth, the site of his miraculous uphill 7-iron on Friday. From a similar spot, his 5-iron approach burrowed into thick rough beside a fairway bunker. He'd made birdie from a lousy lie on the same hole on Saturday, inventing a stance and improvising a recovery shot. Now, with his left leg bent on the bunker's lip, he choked up all the way to the steel shaft of his sand wedge, punched downward, and caught a mini-flier that flew the green. He and Williams trudged after his ball and found it in rough up to their shins. Bogey or even double bogey was likely until a chip with a jeweler's touch left Tiger a six-footer for par.

Again, he went into his pre-putt routine. He stood behind the ball,

looking over his line to the cup. Then he walked to the hole and sur-
veyed the line from the other side before leaning down for a close
look at the turf around the cup. Seeing no spike marks, pebbles, or
bugs there, he paced back to his ball and crouched behind it, deciding
precisely what line he would take. Only then did he take two practice
strokes, settle his feet, and begin the smooth *tick-tock* of bringing his
cavity-backed Scotty Cameron Newport 2 putter to the ball.

Down it went. Another par saved, another ovation. Another step
closer to the trophy.

At the seventh, Els got a merciful round of applause for a long
putt to match Tiger's par. At the eighth, a cautious iron off the tee left
Tiger 225 yards to the steeply sloped green, a daunting carry over a
cleft in the shoreline that the course guide described as "a deep oceanic
chasm." Nicklaus called the second shot at Pebble's eighth hole his favorite approach in the world for its beauty as well as the fact that the
mere thought of it might turn lesser golfers' stomachs.

Tiger's 6-iron approach was still going up as it cleared the chasm.
Squinting to follow its flight, he said, "Be the right club, baby. Come
on!" It was. It did. He went on to two-putt for his eighth consecutive par.

At the ninth, a 329-yard drive set him up for another textbook par.
Els could only shake his head. If Tiger did nothing more dramatic than
keep making pars on the inward nine, Ernie would need six birdies
and three eagles to tie.

As it turned out, that wouldn't be enough.

The tenth at Pebble Beach, where the course reaches its south-
ernmost point before turning back the other way, is a 446-yard par 4
with a fairway that tilts toward Carmel Beach. It is the most difficult
hole on the course, a dangerous drive and long iron or fairway wood
to a cliffside green for ordinary golfers. Tiger's 321-yard drive left
him a flip-wedge approach, and this time the birdie putt fell. The only
player in red numbers was nine under par. He had a chance to get to

–10 at the twelfth, a 202-yard par 3 where his majestic 5-iron climbed toward the MetLife blimp and nose-dived to a stop eighteen feet from the hole.

He and Williams gave the putt a long look. "About a ball left," Tiger said. He settled his feet, took two practice strokes, sent a dagger to the heart of the hole. The gallery whooped. He gave Williams a nod. With the tournament as good as won, he was willing to strike his putts a little harder. At –10 he was only the second player in the tournament's 105-year history to reach double figures under par. (The first, Gil Morgan, had gotten as far as twelve under at the 1992 U.S. Open at Pebble Beach before collapsing with a final-round 81 to finish thirteenth. You never know when and where Pebble might bite.) For the par-defending USGA, the only consolation was that nobody else was in red numbers.

With a good lie in the rough at the thirteenth, Tiger opened the face of his sand wedge until it glinted in the late-afternoon sun. Sliding it knifelike under the ball, he sent a high, lazy-looking pitch that rose along with the crowd's voice, then fell, hopped once, and gave the hole a scare.

A tap-in birdie got him to eleven under. After cementing his lead with nine pars on the front nine, the leader was stepping on the gas, threatening to lap the field the way he had done at the '97 Masters. Looking back later on their round together, Els marveled at "the ball flight and the velocity of the ball off the club. I've never seen anything like it. He was at his best, and I just tried to enjoy the walk with him."

The 573-yard fourteenth is the longest hole on the course. Teeing his ball inches from the left tee marker to optimize the angle of the high fade he intended to hit, Tiger swung almost all out. Holding his finish, he watched his drive with his tongue sticking out between his teeth—not a Michael Jordan tongue, just a little bit—a sign that he liked what he saw. Narrating a slow motion replay of the swing later, Johnny Miller said, "Notice how he synchronizes his fast body move with a fast arm move, all synchronized so it *works*." It was the powerful, repeatable swing he and Harmon had spent a year and a half refining.

"It wasn't perfect," Harmon said later, "because perfect doesn't happen in golf. But he got pretty close."

Two shots later, Tiger floated an eighty-four-yard lob wedge to spitting distance from the pin. A minute after that, taking his putting stance over the ball, he tugged on his left sleeve—a habit thousands of junior golfers would add to their pre-putt routines, the same way a generation of Little Leaguers would start holding up their hands to the umpire, Derek Jeter style, when they stepped into the batter's box. Tiger proceeded to knock in the putt for his fourth birdie in five holes. So much for near misses and cautious pars. He was treating the rest of the field the way his father had always told him to. "Be a cold-blooded assassin," Earl used to say.

Tiger's mother had put the same thought another way. "Step on their throat," she said.

Kultida Woods, 56, was walking along with Tiger's gallery that day. The original "Tiger mom" had on her usual sun hat and sunglasses and a Sunday-red shirt of her own, a crimson blouse embossed with a golden tiger. Less visible and less verbose than her husband, she was often left out of accounts of her son's youth—but anyone familiar with the Woods family knew that Tida, as she was known, had had as much to do with molding his character as Earl had.

Kultida Punsawad had grown up in Thailand, the well-educated daughter of a prosperous architect. In 1967, at the height of the Vietnam War, she was working as a receptionist at a Bangkok employment office when a pair of US Army officers stopped in, looking for Thai workers to help with construction projects. Twenty-two-year-old Tida asked the white soldier, "May I help you, sir?" She was embarrassed when the man introduced his boss, Lieutenant Colonel Earl Woods, but Earl thought the mix-up was funny. On his way out he told his aide, the white officer, "I'm going to go and talk to that fine little thing."

Lieutenant Colonel Woods was smitten. He was also married, with a wife and three children back home in the States. He dated Tida for months without once mentioning his family. A year later, after his deployment in Thailand was over, he flew her to America and arranged a legal separation from Barbara Woods, his wife of thirteen years. Earl told Tida he was divorced, but the divorce wasn't finalized until 1972, three years after he married Tida in New York. In a self-published memoir, Barbara called him an all-caps BIGAMIST who had considered her and her kids a "practice family." According to Barbara, he broke the news to their children, Earl Jr., Kevin, and Royce, "and tried unsuccessfully to get them to stop crying. Earl then walked out."

Later that year, during a stint as an ROTC coordinator and military science professor at City College of New York, Earl was stationed at Fort Hamilton, which happened to be across the street from Brooklyn's Dyker Beach Golf Course. Had the army sent him anywhere else, Ernie Els and Phil Mickelson might now be remembered as the dominant golfers of their time. Lieutenant Colonel Woods took up the game in his free time and was quickly hooked. A good athlete who had played varsity baseball at Kansas State College, he soon worked his handicap into the low single figures. After he and Tida moved to southern California, where he worked for the defense contractor McDonnell Douglas, they settled into a bungalow in Orange County. Earl played the nearby Navy Golf Course and hit thousands upon thousands of balls into a net he built in the garage. His children from his first marriage visited and lived with Earl and Tida from time to time, but the couple's home life soon revolved around Eldrick Tont Woods, born at Long Beach Memorial Hospital on the second-to-last day of 1975. "Tont" is Thai for "beginning." Earl soon dubbed him "Tiger" after Tiger Phong, the fierce fighter who had saved his life. Even then, Lieutenant Colonel Woods had a sense that there was something special about the son he called "the chosen one."

As a tot, Tiger would sit in a high chair in the garage, watching his dad hit ball after ball. Recent studies in neuroscience suggest that those hours may have served as his first golf practice. Brain cells known as mirror neurons enable primates, including humans, to picture themselves doing what they see others do. Mirror neurons explain why infants a few hours old stick out their tongues at adults who do the same to them. According to Dr. Marco Iacoboni of UCLA, "Such behavior is a key to human learning. We are mimicking machines." In golf, Phil Mickelson was an even more extreme example than Tiger Woods. Like Tiger, Mickelson had spent many hours as a tyke in a high chair, watching his father hit golf balls, picturing himself doing the same thing. When he began swinging a club himself, he did it left-handed, literally mirroring his right-handed dad's swing. Mickelson would become world-famous as "Lefty" despite being right-handed in everything but golf.

After the two-year-old Tiger began swinging a cut-down club, he made his first ace at the age of six, and he beat his father over eighteen holes for the first time when he was eleven. That was one of many firsts including three consecutive U.S. Junior Amateur Championships and three straight U.S. Amateurs. Soon he was winning professional majors, with his mother cheering and clapping for "my boy." She liked to give golf writers a good idea for their ledes: "My boy wins again."

Tiger's parents separated in 1996, the year he turned pro and bought his mother a home of her own, a $700,000 five-bedroom, six-bath mini-mansion in Tustin, twenty minutes from the Cypress bungalow where he had grown up. As Earl explained the separation to friends and reporters, "My wife likes a big-ass house and I like a small house." After the separation, their only child did his best to acknowledge both parents' contributions. When Oprah Winfrey asked if he was Black, he said no, he was "Cablinasian," a mix of the ingredients in his personal melting pot. The term would be roundly mocked, with Talib Kweli rapping "My facts more than make up for what you lack in imagination / You more confused than Tiger Woods when he made up Cablinasian." *Sports Illustrated* joked, "It's tough to be a minority, but did you know the average Cablinasian earns more than $20 million a year?" When pressed about race, Tiger stuck to his guns, saying he was proud to be Black but not only Black, determined to honor his mother as well as his father. She was the disciplinarian in the family, he said, the steely one who had taught him to be friendly only *after* he won.

At Pebble Beach, Tida Woods applauded her son's conservative 3-iron off the sixteenth tee. Fans were bowing and chanting his name as he passed. By then he could have used his putter on every shot and still won. NBC's Gary Hallberg told TV viewers that Tiger's sense of history was one of his advantages. "I've heard he has a lot of footage of old major championships," he said, "and actually watches them to see what the great players used to do and how they used to do it."

Hallberg was close. In fact, Tiger often prepped for major tournaments at the Golf Channel's headquarters in Orlando, where he would sit alone in a cubicle, fast-forwarding and rewinding footage of previous majors, looking for something he didn't already know: a bounce, a club selection, a subtle break on a putt he might face when he played the same hole. His knowledge of major-championship history was one reason he wasn't particularly invested in the U.S. Open scoring record. Nicklaus and Lee Janzen had set it, shooting 272 in 1980 and 1993, respectively. They had done it at Baltusrol Golf Club in New Jersey, where par was only 70. And Baltusrol was a pushover compared to Pebble Beach when the wind blew. That was why the number 272 meant less to Tiger than a goal he had set for himself that morning. "People were thinking 'You've got a chance to break the scoring record.' But I could not have cared less." He had a different goal that Sunday at Pebble. "For me, it was about not making a bogey."

His approach from the rough at the sixteenth hole caught another flier he called "a nuker, a real heater." The ball carried over the flag as he pleaded with it: "Aww, *bite!*" But it disobeyed, hopping into the rough behind the green. From there, he took a full swing at a delicate, dead-handed pitch, "trying to undercut it a lot. I didn't realize the ground was hard underneath." His wedge bounced into the ball and sent it fifteen feet past the hole.

Surveying his par putt from every angle, he decided it would break four inches left. He took his stance over the ball, breathed, and rolled it in. "I got a big kick out of making that putt."

Tida applauded as her son pumped his fist. The gallery hooted and hollered. Tiger fished his ball from the cup and shot Steve Williams a look other golfers called his "death stare." Why so serious? "Because I was saying to myself, 'No bogeys,'" he said later. With the tournament won, he needed something to shoot for. He told Williams, "I'm not making a bogey today."

The seventeenth at Pebble Beach is the windswept par 3 where Nicklaus rifled a 1-iron off the flagstick in 1972. Nicklaus, who counted four U.S. Opens among his eighteen majors, had missed the cut that week in his farewell U.S. Open appearance. One fan waved a sign that read THANKS JACK. LONG LIVE TIGER. Another wore a head-to-toe tiger costume worthy of a Broadway production of *Cats*.

Nicklaus had hit a 219-yard 1-iron at the seventeenth in 1972. A generation later, Tiger hit a 4-iron, aiming for the bunker guarding the green. It was the right choice for a player determined to stay bogey free. He would have an easier time making 3 from the bunker than from the rough ringing the hole's firm, narrow green. But he found himself looking over another lousy lie. With his feet above the ball, he took just enough sand to send a soft, video game–perfect shot that stopped three inches from paydirt. After tapping in for par, he led the tournament by fourteen strokes.

"Not a lot of fear in this guy," Johnny Miller told TV viewers.

"It's been rumored that the only fear he has is marriage and kids." Miller expected Tiger to hit driver at the eighteenth. "He wants the record." The scoring record. Tiger surprised him by banging a 4-iron to the center of the fairway. From there, rather than trying to bend a fairway-wood approach over the surf as he'd done with his last ball the day before, he laid up with a 7-iron short of the green while one witless fan howled, "Get in the hole!" Tiger set off toward his ball, picturing his third shot to the green and feeling what he would remember as an eerie calm. While the crowd surged forward behind him, "I felt very peaceful inside."

He and Els waited for Jiménez and Harrington to finish. Jiménez bogeyed, adding a fifteenth stroke to Tiger's lead. No one else in the 140-year history of major-championship golf had held such a lead.

Els, needing a birdie to finish second, tried to reach the green in two. His fairway metal from 246 yards conked the cypress tree short of the green and hopped into the rough. Tiger's cautious wedge came down safely on the eighteenth green. He strode forward to a thunderous ovation with Williams making a point to stay a step behind. As they reached the green, Tiger offered his caddie a triumphant fist bump. This being golf, it turned out to be one of the year's most awkward fist bumps. With Williams holding up his open hand, expecting a high-five, Tiger almost missed it. He wound up fist-bumping Stevie's wrist.

Tida waited behind the green, beaming. It was Father's Day, but Earl had stayed home to watch his son on TV. "I wanted to give him space to perform and be himself," he said. "It was all part of the plan."

With his gallery jumping, Tiger ran his last birdie putt of the week four feet past the hole. He could fourteen-putt from there and still win, but the miss irked him. "I was so pissed," he said later. "I fought so hard all day. Now I'm thinking I could three-putt and end my U.S. Open on a bogey, and it would ruin the day."

As ever, he took his stance over the putt with his weight balanced just so. He eyed the hole, turned his gaze back to the ball, took a breath, and sank the putt. The crowd erupted. He hugged Williams, took his cap off, and shook hands with Els. Coming off the green, he embraced Butch Harmon, who thumped him on the back.

Tiger was hugging his mother when runner-up Jiménez tapped Harmon on the shoulder. "Butch, excuse me," he said. "When does the playoff start—between Ernie and me for second place?" Jiménez and Els had finished at +3, a number that might have won the U.S. Open if not for a player who was fifteen strokes better.

With his mother beside him, the winner waved to the crowd. NBC's Jimmy Roberts held a mic to his face for the usual post-round comments, which went out over loudspeakers behind the eighteenth green. Roberts asked Tiger if he had ever imagined winning the U.S. Open. "Well, yeah," he said. "That's what I had in mind."

The crowd laughed. He grinned and said, "Well, I'm honest!"

Asked if he had a message for Earl, he smiled and said yeah. "Not too bad of a Father's Day present!"

He had led wire to wire, becoming the fifth U.S. Open champion to do so. He had hit an iron off the last tee, laid up, and still tied the tournament's scoring record, finishing at 272, twelve under par, while Els and Jiménez had tied for second at three over, fifteen strokes behind. David Duval and Vijay Singh, nineteen strokes behind, finished in the top ten. Tiger's fifteen-shot margin eclipsed Willie Smith's eleven-shot victory at the 1899 U.S. Open, a record that had stood for 101 years. It surpassed Old Tom Morris's thirteen-shot margin at the 1862 Open Championship for the widest margin in major-championship history. And as *Sports Illustrated*'s Rick Reilly quipped, "Old Tom beat three sheep and two shepherds." Tiger's first-prize check for $800,000 made him the PGA Tour's all-time leading money winner at the age of twenty-four. He had led the tournament in driving distance by almost ten yards, averaging 299 to Duval's 290 and Els's 287. While contending with fierce winds, fog, and two weather delays, he had played

Pebble Beach's par-3 holes four under par, its par 4s four under par despite a triple bogey, and its par 5s four under par despite a hook that went halfway to Oahu. But his week's most remarkable stat was zero. On greens fourth-place finisher John Huston called "the bumpiest I've ever seen," the winner had zero three-putts. Year after year, Tour pros sink about 55 percent of their eight-foot putts and fewer than half of their nine-footers; Tiger had played seventy-two holes on Pebble Beach's tricky, sometimes illegible greens without missing a single putt of ten feet or less.

Els said it had been "a privilege" to play with him. "Whatever I say is going to be an understatement. If I played out of my mind, I probably would have lost by five, six, seven shots." Calling Tiger "the Michael Jordan of golf," he said, "I considered tackling him, but that wouldn't work, because on top of everything else, he gets stronger every day."

Titleist endorser Mickelson tied for sixteenth, twenty-one shots off the lead. Curious about Nike's new ball, he buttonholed Wally Uihlein, the CEO of Acushnet, Titleist's parent company, to ask if Acushnet's golf ball designers had anything in the works to help him keep up with the guided missile Tiger Woods was hitting. Uihlein apparently got the message. Titleist fast-tracked production of a ball that would be called the Pro V1.

While Tiger spent an hour on hugs, handshakes, and interviews, Williams cleaned his clubs and stuck them into the boot of their courtesy car, then found a leather-seated chair in the Tap Room, Pebble Beach's nineteenth hole. He was knackered. The majors were even more of a grind than a typical Tour event, considering the flop sweat and butt clenching along with carrying a forty-five-pound bag more than six miles a day, all while doubling as a player's adviser, cheerleader, and chief psychologist. On a hot day a caddie could burn more calories than a boot camp trainee. But after surviving Saturday's lost ball scare and seeing his man cruise to a victory that meant far more than the first-place check for $800,000, of which Williams would get 10 percent, he wasn't complaining.

Finally Tiger came into the Tap Room. Seeing Williams, he pointed at him and smiled. "It's on to St. Andrews," he said.

But first he had a favor to do for a friend. His next on-course appearance came on the Wednesday after the U.S. Open, when he slipped through a sparse crowd to stand beside the second fairway during a qualifying event for a little-known USGA tournament, the U.S. Amateur Public Links, at Black Mountain Golf & Country Club in Henderson, Nevada. He was there to support Jerry Chang, a Stanford teammate who was playing in the qualifier. To avoid making a scene, Tiger waited on the second hole, dressed in shorts and sunglasses, while Chang played the first hole. Then he sneaked out and shouldered his buddy's golf bag. Chang didn't advance to the 2000 Public Links' main event in Oregon, but for one day he had a distinction no other player could match: for seventeen holes in 100-degree heat, Jerry Chang had the world's best golfer as his caddie.

NINE
THE OLD COURSE

Butch Harmon was back in his office at Rio Secco when he received a package. Inside he found a bright yellow flag, a pin flag from the U.S. Open, signed and inscribed by the champion. "Butchie," it read, "they said I couldn't win one of these."

Tiger's few critics had claimed that he might never bag a U.S. Open because he didn't drive the ball straight enough. "He always responded when someone said he couldn't do something," Harmon recalled. After their year and a half of work rebuilding his swing, Tiger was the longest straight driver in the game, just as Harmon's client Greg Norman had been, but thirty to forty yards longer off the tee than Norman ever was.

The TV ratings for his romp at Pebble Beach had been the tournament's highest in twenty-five years. One of the millions tuning in that week was an eleven-year-old from Northern Ireland named Rory McIlroy, who watched between rounds of a junior-golf tournament. "I idolized him," McIlroy remembered, calling Tiger's fifteen-stroke victory "a once-in-a-lifetime performance. I don't think something like that will ever happen again." Another viewer was two-time U.S. Open winner Curtis Strange, who had scoffed at Tour rookie Woods for saying he expected to win every tournament he entered, saying "You'll learn!" But it was Strange who had learned a lesson. He called Tiger's performance at Pebble "by far the best seventy-two holes ever played in the history of the game."

Sports Illustrated put Tiger on its cover under the headline "ANY QUESTIONS? TIGER WOODS DELIVERS THE GREATEST PERFORMANCE IN GOLF HISTORY." Meanwhile, a few staffers at the weekly *Golf World*, still buzzing about his "fucking prick" outburst at the last hole on Saturday, mocked up a spoof cover headed PRICK WINS U.S. OPEN. After Tiger found out about that, he got two copies.

There were four events on the PGA Tour schedule between the U.S. Open and the upcoming Open Championship in Scotland. Tiger skipped three of them. His Stanford teammate Notah Begay III won the first two to leap from sixty-first in the world to twenty-fourth. During that time, Tiger finished arrangements to buy a lakefront mansion at Isleworth for $2,475,000. O'Meara lived nearby. So did Arnold Palmer, Shaquille O'Neal, baseball's Ken Griffey, Jr., the actor Wesley Snipes, Planet Hollywood founder Robert Earl, and Tottenham Hotspur's billionaire owner, Joe Lewis. Fairly modest by Isleworth standards, Tiger's new home featured seven bedrooms, a swimming pool and Jacuzzi, a four-car garage, a game room, and a movie theater. He practiced scuba diving in the pool and soon graduated to diving in the Atlantic, enjoying the privacy he found underwater. In time he became a master scuba diver, capable of holding his breath for four minutes during training.

Two weeks before the 2000 Open Championship—the oldest major, which many Americans call the British Open—Tiger tied for twenty-third at the Advil Western Open in suburban Chicago, where he was the defending champion. He blamed his putting. "I need a seeing-eye dog out there. I'm putting so bad it's a joke." Steve Williams thought he knew why. His man wasn't focused on winning—at least not on winning the tournament he was in that week. Instead, he was working on shots he would need two weeks later at St. Andrews. That meant hitting drives low enough to burrow under the winds he was likely to encounter at the 129th Open Championship. It meant grooving a shallower downswing because the turf in Scotland is harder than cushy American fairways, which explained why he took shallower than usual divots at the Western Open. As he swung the club at Cog Hill Golf and Country Club in Lemont, Illinois, he was picturing himself at the Old Course at St. Andrews, thinking, *Stand tall.* Dropping his head even a half inch at address would steepen his downswing and deepen his divots. According to Harmon, Tiger focused so exclusively on majors that he often hit "inappropriate shots" in nonmajors like the Western Open, "shots that might not be right for the tournament he was playing in." A no-divot 9-iron picked off the turf at Cog Hill, for instance. "It looked like he was missing shots, and nobody knew why." He was practicing for the Open Championship and didn't want to confine his practice to the range. "Everything's different in a tournament. He wanted to try those shots in competition."

He finished twenty-third at the Western Open. Then it was on to St. Andrews.

The Old Course at St. Andrews was not the first golf course, but it is the most important. Its original twenty-two holes were trimmed by four in 1764, setting the standard for a round of golf at eighteen holes. Almost a century later, Allan Robertson, the first golf professional, bossed his apprentice, Tom Morris, around while they fashioned clubs and feather-filled balls for the wealthy gentlemen of the Royal and Ancient Golf Club of St. Andrews. After they feuded over the new gutta-percha ball, Morris moved to Prestwick, where he founded the Open

Championship in 1860. In those days the Open was seen as a minor event, far less important than the annual club championships played by red-coated, claret-sipping gentlemen of leisure. Professional golfers were club makers and caddies, looked down upon by their social superiors as uncouth, uneducated whisky drinkers, though not all of them were uncouth. Their clothes were so ragged that the first tournament's sponsor, the Earl of Eglinton, donated lumbermen's jackets for the players to wear—the same plaid coats that laborers on his estate wore.

There were only eight players in the 1860 Open Championship at Prestwick, golf's first major. Tom Morris, the host and tournament organizer, teed off first. He foozled the shot but had an excuse: he was starting his swing when the wind blew his tie up into his face. He went on to win four Opens before his son, Tom Morris, Jr., known as Tommy, won four in a row from 1868 to 1872. Tommy Morris, the Tiger Woods of his time, made the game's first recorded ace on his way to an eleven-stroke victory in 1869. He won again the following year, stoking what British newspapers called "golfomania" and spurring the game's growth as a spectator sport. But only twenty golfers participated in the 1870 Open, which Tommy Morris won by a dozen strokes. Only seven had joined his father in the third-ever Open in 1862, which Old Tom won by thirteen, a major-championship margin of victory that stood for 138 years until Tiger drubbed a field of 156 players to win the 2000 U.S. Open by fifteen.

Another of Tom Morris's lasting contributions had to do with the holes in his putting greens. In his time, long before wooden tees were invented, golfers would reach into the hole to pull out a dollop of sandy dirt that they used to make a "sand tee" for their drives on the next hole. Their digging, combined with frequent rains, could make holes fall in on themselves. Nobody wanted to putt at a muddy blot, so Old Tom repurposed drainpipes as the game's first cup liners. The drainpipes used at St. Andrews in his day happened to be four and a quarter inches in diameter. If not for an accident of Scottish plumbing, millions of golfers might have made millions more putts in the past century and a half.

To his countrymen's chagrin, the original major lost much of its luster in the twentieth century. American pros routinely skipped it. In 1946, Sam Snead, two years out of the US Navy, made his first trip to Scotland for the Open. Riding the train into St. Andrews, he looked out the window at patchy grass and heather and wondered where the golf course was. "It looks like an old, abandoned kind of place," he said.

Snead's rival Ben Hogan won the 1953 Masters and U.S. Open before flying to Scotland for the Open Championship, where Scottish fans dubbed the steely-eyed five-foot-eight Texan "the wee ice mon." Hogan won that year's Open at Carnoustie but had no chance to add the PGA to his historic sweep because he couldn't be in two places at once. Seven years before Arnold Palmer and his friends in the press hatched the idea of a modern Grand Slam, the 1953 Open Championship and PGA Championship were played the same week.

Palmer fell short of three straight modern majors when he lost by a stroke at St. Andrews in 1960. Soon Jack Nicklaus, ten years younger, arrived to steal Arnie's thunder. Palmer would settle for seven career victories in the modern "big four" he invented, while Nicklaus went on to win eighteen.

Eighteen majors was Tiger's long-term goal, the record he intended to beat. "Twenty was his number," Williams revealed in a 2022 podcast, *Chasing Majors*. "His aim in life was to better Jack's record in the majors." Tiger talked so much about winning twenty majors that Williams would goad him, saying "C'mon, man, why not twenty-one?" He challenged his boss by using a Sharpie to write the number on Tiger's golf glove: 21. A tall order in light of the fact that by July 2000, Tiger had won three.

• • •

On the Tuesday before the 2000 Open Championship, Nicklaus joined Gary Player, Lee Trevino, Seve Ballesteros, Nick Faldo, and sixteen others in the posh clubhouse of the Royal and Ancient Golf Club of St. Andrews for claret, conversation, and the first ever dinner for former Open champions. The R&A was creating a new tradition by copying the Masters. That night Snead, the 1946 winner, now eighty-eight, reminisced about the days when he and his fellow touring pros had driven back roads between tournaments that might pay the winner a thousand dollars. "We'd party all night and then play hungover," said the Slammer, who could no longer win bar bets by leaping to touch chandeliers with his foot but was still spry enough to kick off tournament week by doing a tap dance across the centuries-old Swilcan Bridge between the first and last fairways on the Old Course.

Tiger wanted to join Snead, Nicklaus, and the others at the next year's dinner. Steeped in golf lore by his history-minded father, he called St. Andrews "the coolest place on Earth." An Open victory would give him another historic distinction. He would be the youngest ever to complete a career Grand Slam by winning all four modern majors. Nicklaus had been two years older when he had held off Player, Doug Sanders, and Bruce Devlin—the father of Tiger's Nike liaison, Kel Devlin—to do so in 1966.

Tiger was the oddsmakers' prohibitive favorite at two to one with nobody else close. During practice rounds on the Old Course's sandy, bumpy turf, he smacked 3- and 4-irons while Williams wrote down how far each shot carried and rolled. At St. Andrews, where the fairways can be faster than the greens, the last thing they wanted was for a cautious iron off the tee to roll seventy or eighty yards into one of Tom Morris's pot bunkers, which were more like oversized manholes than the shallow sand traps on American courses. Scottish links golf is about mastering the game's subtlest skills—spin, trajectory, imagination—while avoiding the trouble lurking in spots like the cavernous Hell Bunker on the fourteenth hole.

Tiger's pre-round practice sessions were consistent: He would start with a few easy swings with a sand wedge, loosening up. Next he would hit 8-irons. On the Old Course, landing the ball on a precise spot could be the difference between a birdie putt and Hell. "The ball's going to take one decent bounce," Williams reminded him, "then check up a little bit and roll out." When Tiger was satisfied with his 8-iron flight, he went to his 4-iron, then his 3-wood, and finally his driver, a steel-shafted, titanium-headed 7.5-degree Titleist 975D. His last swing on the range was always the shot he planned to hit off the first tee that day—in this case a smooth stinger.

Tickets were selling like oatcakes. Long before Thursday's first round, it was clear that the Millennium Open would break attendance records. Ernie Els, smoothing long irons of his own down the range from Tiger, felt good about his chances. "I am one of only a few players who could beat Tiger," he told reporters.

Fans filled the temporary bleachers behind the driving range to get a glimpse of Tiger, but not everyone was pulling for him. "I am not backing Tiger Woods," a *Guardian* columnist wrote that week. "He is an arrogant, ethnic fellow." Twenty-one years after Lee Elder broke the color line at the 1979 Open Championship, a Black golfer in Scotland was still a rare sight.

"I never saw a more jittery Tiger," Harmon remembered. "He was focused. Fired up. But nervous!"

Tiger looked calm enough on Thursday morning, July 20, rolling balls on the practice green. Called to the tee, he used his cavity-back Scotty Cameron putter to pick up his ball. With a flick of the putter he flipped the ball into the air and, without looking, caught it behind his back.

The weather was balmy for summer in Scotland. The *St. Andrews Citizen* predicted a high of 20 degrees. Of course, that was Celsius. It was 60 degrees Fahrenheit when Tiger teed off under bright skies carrying pillowy clouds across the Firth of Tay toward Dundee. Dressed in a black Nike cap, short-sleeved gray shirt, black sweater-vest, and gray slacks, golf's most fashionable player reported to the tee beside the R&A clubhouse and knocked a 3-iron stinger safely short of Swilcan Burn, the stream that guards the Old Course's first green. A stinger called for control as well as the wrist and forearm strength he had built in the gym. He teed the ball low, played it back in his stance, bent his knees a bit more than usual, and took a long, shallow arc to the ball. *Bang!* The ball rolled out to wedge distance. He parred Tom Morris's first hole and the next seven, playing carefully, the way he'd started his Sunday round at Pebble Beach. "He was in that trancelike mood again," Williams recalled.

A pitching-wedge approach at the ninth left a twelve-footer for birdie. He sank it to polite applause to make the turn in 35. His gallery was six and seven deep as usual but quieter than American crowds. "If he had made that birdie at the Masters, the roar would have shaken Augusta National's cathedral pines," the *New York Times*'s Dave Anderson reported. "If he had made that birdie at the recent United States Open at Pebble Beach, the roar would have rolled across Carmel Bay like the surf." But there were no Scottish fans yelling "You da man!" One spectator went so far as to say, "All right, Tiger!"

His drive at the par-4 tenth, a hole named Bobby Jones after the first Grand Slam winner, rolled out to 330 yards. He had forty-nine yards to the flag. He could have flipped a wedge, but that would bring the wind and a ripply green's unpredictable bounces into play. He decided to putt from a distance of 147 feet. "He'd practiced that shot," Williams said later. "The idea was to run the ball along the contours of the fairway. If you hit it in the air, it could land on an upslope and stop dead or catch a downslope and spring forward. Putting was the best option."

Tiger's long putt rolled over the undulating turf to the green and parked beside the hole for a tap-in. This was the opposite of American-style "target golf" that saw pros lofting high, spinning floaters onto soft, receptive greens. This was links golf at its best, as no one knew better than the Scottish fans who gave Tiger's putt from the fairway their loudest cheer so far.

"They *know*," Tiger said later. "They understood and appreciated a good putt."

He drove the green at the short par-4 twelfth and two-putted for birdie. Two holes later, at the 581-yard fourteenth, known simply as Long, a drive of more than three hundred yards left him within sight of the Hell Bunker. St. Andreans sometimes made a solemn sign of the cross before descending ten feet into Hell, hoping to get out in one shot. The bunker covers 2,700 square feet, the size of a good-sized house. During the 1995 Open, Nicklaus took five slashes to escape Hell on his way to a quintuple-bogey 10. Five summers later, Tiger walloped a 3-wood over the bunker and over the green a hundred yards beyond. His eighty-yard chip for eagle shaved the edge of the hole. After a tap-in birdie he hit driver, 9-iron, and a ten-foot putt for yet another birdie at the fifteenth. But nobody's perfect. With the first-round lead in sight, he yanked his drive into thick heather at the seventeenth, the notorious Road Hole that Seve Ballesteros called "the hardest hole in the world." A bogey or worse looked likely. Sportswriter Tim Rosaforte, a few yards away, would say that Tiger needed "a sickle" to have much chance of advancing the ball.

But his lie was no worse than the one he'd had at Pebble's uphill sixth a month before. He gave it a steep slash, "trying to hit it hard with my right hand and hold on with my left," he said later. A weaker player's left hand would twist, closing the clubface and sending the ball squirting sideways. Tiger's swing scythed through the heather as he kept the clubface open, swinging so hard that his right leg came off the ground on his follow-through as the ball carried to the green. He birdied and went on to shoot 67. He thought that might hold up and make him the first-round leader, but dozens of players had yet to tee off. Ernie Els was one of them. Tiger was back in his suite at the

He slashed a shot on the Road Hole during the Open Championship at St. Andrews.

hulking Old Course Hotel, with its views of the finishing holes, by the time Els played the back nine. By then Notah Begay was Road Hole roadkill. Begay, the hottest golfer on Tour during Tiger's weeks off, held the first-round lead before driving into the heather near the spot where Tiger had muscled his ball out. He squirted his second shot to another nasty lie, then bounced a 9-iron into Swilcan Burn. The Road Hole "had me by the tail," he admitted afterward. "One thing led to another. Before I knew it, I was getting wet." Still, Begay called his zigzag adventure "fun." He got a decent lie in the burn, with his ball in two or three inches of water. "Once I got in here and my feet were not totally immersed, I knew I could get it out. That was a lot more entertaining than taking a boring drop." He splashed his ball out and sank a putt for triple bogey.

The Road Hole was taking its customary toll. By sunset the 157-man field would record four birdies there along with fifty-six pars, seventy bogeys, twenty-one double bogeys, and seven triples or worse. One of the birdies belonged to Els, whose three-hundred-yard drive, deadeye approach, and birdie putt gave him the first-round lead, one shot ahead of Tiger and Steve Flesch. Asked if his 66 made him Tiger Woods's greatest rival, Els said no. "Whoever wins this week is probably the next rival—if it's not him."

Flesch, meanwhile, took a different approach, pretending not to know who else was on the leaderboard. Asked how it felt to be tied for second place with Tiger Woods, he asked, "Who? Has anybody ever heard of him?"

TEN
CHASING LEGENDS

Long before it became the world's capital of golf, the thousand-year-old town of St. Andrews was known for religion and violence. Throughout the Middle Ages, pilgrims flocked to the seat of Scottish Catholicism, where the cathedral was said to hold a tooth, a kneecap, and three finger bones of Saint Andrew the apostle. In the sixteenth century, Cardinal James Beaton, the archbishop of St. Andrews, would lean out the window of his grand castle next door, clapping his hands as Protestant "heretics" were burned at the stake below. One day seven spies slipped into the castle. They stabbed Beaton, gutted him, and threw his body over the ramparts, inviting local Catholics to "see their God." In 1559, after a fiery sermon by the reformer John Knox, townspeople tore into the four-hundred-year-old cathedral with sledgehammers and pickaxes, tearing most of it down. They used chunks of the cathedral to build the town's stone pier. In 1567, Mary, Queen of Scots, knocked a ball around the links shortly after her husband, Lord Darnley, was murdered, making her the first golf widow.

Today's pilgrims flock to the Royal and Ancient Golf Club of St. Andrews, which administers the game everywhere but in the United States and Mexico. A select few are allowed into the R&A's gray sandstone clubhouse, where relics include the Open Championship's original trophy, the red leather Challenge Belt that Tommy Morris first won in 1868, and the Claret Jug that replaced it after the young Morris made the belt his own by performing the game's first Grand Slam–like feat, winning three Opens in a row. Less privileged visitors are welcome in souvenir shops up and down North Street and Market Street, where they can buy miniature Claret Jugs and Swilcan Bridges, caps, tam-o'-shanters, divot tools, cuff links, and golf ball–shaped mints and whisky stones. In 2000, many American fans were pleased to find that they could place golf bets at the local Ladbrokes betting shop, where £10 on Tiger Woods would get you £20 if he won. Ernie Els was next at seven to one, David Duval at eight to one, Sergio García at twelve to one.

Els took an easy practice swing under the steady gaze of Old Tom Morris, who peers toward the first tee box from his bas-relief bust halfway up the west wall of the clubhouse. After teeing off in weather that was almost Floridian, Els struck full shots as fluidly as ever but came down with a case of what some golfers call liprosy. He missed a five-footer. He lipped out from two feet. He fell back while Sergio García hunted flagsticks. Two hours into a sunny second round, the towering yellow leaderboard over the bleachers beside the first fairway showed García and David Toms on top at –8, with left-hander Flesch a shot behind.

The player most of the crowd wanted to see had yet to appear. Tiger Woods was just leaving his suite in the Old Course Hotel, making sure not to leave any of his precious Tour Accuracy balls behind. When he emerged with his girlfriend, Joanna Jagoda, as well as three security guards hired by Nike and a contingent of local police, more than a thousand fans lined his path to the practice putting green. Tiger was rolling practice putts when a full-throated cheer went up from the grandstand. Jack Nicklaus was striding up the last fairway. The Open Championship was the second leg of the sixty-year-old Nicklaus's farewell tour of the majors. Now sometimes called the Olden Bear, he had no chance to make the cut after a first-round 77, but Scottish golf fans loved Nicklaus, whose mother had been born in Scotland, as much as any American since Jones. In thirty-six Open appearances, he had won the Claret Jug three times. He had also taken home seven of the filigreed silver platters that go to the runner-up. To a history buff like Tiger, those silver platters and Nicklaus's dozen other second-place finishes in the majors were worth remembering along with his eighteen victories.

Both of them believed that the point of playing the first three rounds of any tournament was to be "in the mix"—to have a chance to win on Sunday, when other players started to sweat. Tiger was such a golf nerd that he knew another Jack stat: from 1961, when he turned professional, to 1986, when he won the Masters at the age of forty-six, Nicklaus had played in one hundred majors and finished in the top five in more than half of them: fifty-four. In Tiger's four years as a pro, he had played in fourteen majors and finished in the top five six times. So he still had some work to do. He stopped putting long enough to watch Nicklaus for a moment.

After a few more minutes on the practice green, he climbed into a white R&A van for the two-minute ride to the range, where spectators cheered his arrival. He started with wedges, then moved to 8-irons. As he loosened up he graduated to his 4-irons, his 15-degree 3-wood, and finally his driver. After half an hour on the range, he struck the long, low iron shot he would use at the Old Course's first hole.

As with his driving range warm-ups and pre-putt ritual, Tiger's pre-shot routine on the tee seldom varied. Much of it would soon be standard for golfers all over the world who followed his lead. After a couple smooth practice swings, he moved behind the ball, looking beyond it toward his target, picturing the shot he planned to hit. Then he returned to the ball and took his stance beside it, adjusting his feet until he felt balanced. After a couple waggles and a last look at an intermediate point on his target line, he leaned into his backswing.

You could tell he liked the low stinger he struck off the first tee by the way he spun the club as his ball sailed toward Swilcan Burn. A sand wedge from Old Tom Morris's hard, sandy first fairway left him a ten-foot putt for birdie. He pushed it, but it was a fraction better than Els's lip-outs that morning. It caught the right lip and dropped in. He was six under par, already closing in on García and Toms with seventeen of the Old Course's puzzles waiting to be solved. He birdied the fourth, named Ginger Beer for a concession stand where caddie "Old Daw" Anderson had sold refreshments from a wicker basket in the 1800s, adding a dram of whisky for players he liked. Tiger then birdied the fifth, the long Hole O'Cross, then the longest in major-championship history at 568 yards. At the ninth, after a Port-a-Potty break (with TV cameras covering his entrance and exit), he holed a twelve-footer to take a one-shot lead.

The tenth at the Old Course is named for Bobby Jones, who won the Open in 1926, 1927, and 1930. That was a more fitting choice than naming the next hole after him, for it was at the eleventh that the nineteen-year-old Jones, playing in his first Open Championship in 1921, took four swings trying to escape a pot bunker, tore up his scorecard, and stormed off the course.

Tiger's drive at the Bobby Jones hole was headed for trouble, taking a beeline toward a pot bunker. He got a lucky bounce, his ball hopping past the bunker to a clean lie just short of the green. He smiled, a little embarrassed to get away with a miss, and made 4 instead of 5 or 6. That was links golf, a quirkier, less predictable game than the aerial target practice that went on every week on the PGA Tour. Links golf "demands resourcefulness," he said. "I like that." Not to mention the occasional good hop when you need one. After a pair of textbook birdies, he reached the tee at the seventeenth in first place at –11.

Even for him, the 455-yard Road Hole at the Old Course played as a par four and a half. His approach shot landed safely but rolled through the green to a grassy berm between the green and the stony road behind it. With no way to pitch or flop his third shot from there, Tiger improvised: playing the ball back in his stance, he punched a low chip that barely cleared the berm, raced past the hole, rolled up the greenside edge of the Road Hole Bunker on the other side of the green, and curled back toward the flag. A clever play, but he hadn't saved four yet. His eight-foot par putt was a delicate double breaker. It bent left and then right and then dropped into the cup, a perfectly executed putt to capitalize on the best Road Hole chip of the day. He clenched his fist and tipped his cap to the cheering crowd.

The Old Course's last hole, called Tom Morris, is a short par 4 that takes golfers back toward town. Its eponym had built the green on a mound of dirt over a communal grave that held the victims of an 1832 cholera epidemic. By 2000, it was a 357-yard birdie hole, reachable by the most daring, powerful professionals. The second-round leader hit a cautious tee ball and a wedge to Old Tom's green. He two-putted for a three-stroke edge on David Toms, with García, Flesch, and deadeye putter Loren Roberts another shot back.

Nick Price was standing behind the green as Tiger putted out. "Those guys behind him better pray for the wind to blow," said Price, who called Tiger's 66 "as close as I've ever seen to someone playing links golf to perfection." Price, a three-time major champion who had won the 1994 Open at Turnberry, said, "The par fives are par fours for him." The short par-4 tenth named for Bobby Jones was "a par three for him. With the right wind, the eighteenth is a par three."

Dating back to his third round at Pebble Beach, Tiger Woods had played sixty-two holes of major-championship golf without making a bogey.

Nicklaus praised him, too. "The fact that Tiger is coming along doesn't bother me," he said. "If it's Tiger or somebody else who comes along to challenge my record of eighteen majors, I think it would be good for golf. I have not really watched Tiger play that much, but every time I turn on the television, he holes a putt." Like Jack, who had blasted 270- and 280-yard drives with persimmon-headed woods, Tiger demoralized opponents with his power, but he had a more complete game than anyone before him. "He's longer than I was because of equipment," Nicklaus said before adding, "He definitely has a better short game than I had."

Tiger said he was "comfortable" with his play that day but not satisfied with his three-stroke lead. Before dinner that evening, he went back to the range. "I always loved it when he told the media he was 'comfortable,' or 'happy' with a round," Harmon recalled years later. "Then he'd tell *me* he wasn't a bit happy with his swing and say, 'We're not leaving the range till we get it right.'"

Tiger seldom felt more comfortable in his skin than when he was hitting balls on the range. He and his friend Duval, the second-ranked player in the world, particularly enjoyed a lighthearted duel they staged at the Open. "David and I were the only ones out on the practice range as night approached," he remembered. "The fans sitting in the stands were asking us to have some fun, maybe put on a trick show of sorts. So David and I said sure, what the heck. We hit shots simultaneously—I'd hit a hook and David would hit a slice, or vice versa. The balls crisscrossed in flight. We were a couple of golfers enjoying ourselves, having some fun."

ELEVEN

CATCH ME IF YOU CAN

Looking out at the links from his suite in the Old Course Hotel, Tiger could see why Sam Snead had wondered "Where's the golf course?" There are no trees on the old village green between the R&A clubhouse and the River Eden, few greenside bunkers, and certainly none of the ponds with fountains found at some of America's showier courses. Scottish links defend par with wind, weather, pot bunkers scattered seemingly at random, thornbushes that the rest of the world calls gorse but the locals call whins, and sly undulations that make local knowledge a must. In early-morning or late-day light, the rolling turf resembles unsteady seas. The ancient seaside game's quirks combine to offer players different ways to go from the tee to the hole. That was what Tiger liked most about links golf: it gave him "the opportunity to be creative." As opposed to American-style target golf, which can resemble precision dart throwing, it sometimes felt more like croquet. "Links golf is about controlling the ball on the ground," he said. He claimed that he had never hit a perfect shot, but some of his recent favorites, like the punched chip at the Road Hole the day before, shooting past the flag before running up a slope and curling back, were "pretty darn good." Conceiving and executing a shot like that gave him "just pure joy."

He knew more than most golfers about the zigzag story that led the professional game back to Scotland's east coast in the summer of 2000. In the late 1800s, a sport played on the village green and always open to the public became an American pastime due to a Scottish diaspora of course designers including Donald Ross, Charles Blair Macdonald, Alister MacKenzie, and Albert Tillinghast. All disciples of Old Tom Morris, they carried the game to the United States along with scores of Scottish caddies and club makers. They arrived during the Gilded Age, a time when the country's social and financial elite sought a respite from urban hurly-burly. And so the American country club was born. Those who could afford country club memberships escaped from city streets piled with horse manure and trash snuffled by pigs to a setting resembling a British country estate. But a person can play only so many hands of whist before looking for something more active to do. Polo was difficult and dangerous, while croquet and shuffleboard proved less compelling than the sport the rough-hewn Scots brought with them. Golf caught on quickly as a game for the upper crust. In 1894, the not coincidentally named Saint Andrew's Golf Club in New York's Westchester County joined the Chicago Golf Club; the Country Club in Brookline, Massachusetts; the Newport Country Club in Rhode Island; and Shinnecock Hills Golf Club on Long Island to form the United States Golf Association. American golf's reputation as a businessman's pursuit was sealed twenty miles from Manhattan at Westchester County's Saint Andrew's, where the Scottish-born steel baron Andrew Carnegie, an avid golfer, met Charles Schwab in the clubhouse in 1901. With Schwab acting as middleman, Carnegie agreed to sell his company to investors led by J. P. Morgan in a

$480 million deal that created U.S. Steel. As golfing billionaires Bill Gates, Warren Buffett, and Donald Trump might say, $480 million was a lot of money in those days.

Newspapers sometimes ridiculed the "howling swells" knocking balls around meadows. President Theodore Roosevelt, a burly equestrian, wrestler, and boxer, mocked golf as a snooty sport, but by then the game was a favorite of a new American elite. Roosevelt's successor, William Howard Taft, was a passionate duffer. Since Taft set the precedent, seventeen of twenty US presidents have been golfers, including Trump and Joe Biden.

A century into American golf's evolution, Tiger Woods was a public-course golfer in a mostly white country-club sport. At the Navy Golf Course in Long Beach, where he often played with his father, he was hitting balls on the range one day when some older white golfers began goofing off, knocking balls at a house across the road. The homeowner wasn't pleased. As Tiger remembered, "He phoned the pro and said, 'This little n—— was hitting balls at my house.' And the pro comes screaming out, accusing me." Playing country-club courses during his amateur days, he learned to ignore "the Look" that club members often gave a golfer of color. Not even the majors were immune to the sport's institutional racism. Augusta National was well known for its decades-long resistance to integrating the Masters field. In 1990, Hall Thompson, an Augusta National club member and the founder of the exclusive Shoal Creek Club in Alabama, site of that year's PGA Championship, boasted that his club did not discriminate against Jews, women, or anyone else, "except the Blacks."

Now a Black player was drawing record crowds to the Old Course, which like Pebble Beach was open to all, if bloody expensive. The game's most discerning fans came out not because he was the best Black, white, or Cablinasian golfer but because he was one of the best in the long history of the Scottish game.

• • •

At 2:40 in the afternoon of July 22, starter Ivor Robson, the longtime "Voice of the Open," introduced the leader in his usual squeaky voice: "On the tee, from USA, Tiger Woods." Saturday's sunshine promised low scores in the third round. Tiger was paired with David Toms, a former junior phenom from Louisiana. As the penultimate pairing of Steve Flesch and Loren Roberts crossed the stone bridge on the way to the first green, Tiger moved into his pre-swing routine, standing behind the ball and eyeing his target, a spot short of a gorse bush just to the right of the bridge. He began his third round with his usual stinger, playing for position. The ball's low flight and long rollout set up a wedge and a ten-foot putt. He knocked it in to get to a dozen under par, only to three-putt the giant double green at the second—his first bogey in sixty-three holes of major-championship golf dating back to the third round at Pebble Beach.

He birdied the third with a near-perfect approach and sank a short putt to get back to –12. But level par for the round wouldn't be enough to hold off his pursuers. Clarke, who had bested him at the Andersen Consulting Match Play Championship in February, went on to fire a front-nine 33. Ernie Els made five birdies to climb into contention before driving into a thicket of gorse and making a double-bogey 6 at the twelfth. That dropped him off the leaderboard, but Els kept his chin up. As Steve Williams put it, "Ernie makes keeping the lid on his frustrations look easy."

Twenty-year-old Sergio García, the only contender younger than Tiger, made a run at the leaders. Then he missed five short birdie putts. At the fifteenth, his eighteen-inch putt spun off the cup. Unlike Els, Spain's biggest golf star since José María Olazábal and Seve Ballesteros made keeping a lid on his frustrations look impossible. He swooned and smacked his forehead. After double-bogeying the Road Hole, he signed for a 73 that could have been a 68, then composed himself. "The difference between number one in the world and number fifteen," he said, referring to his current world ranking, "is making putts. Tiger makes the putts, and I don't." He would learn that there was more to it than that.

At the fifth hole, David Toms, Tiger's playing partner, made an only-in-Scotland blunder. Taking dead aim, he struck a pure 8-iron at a flag. The wrong flag. "I thought I'd hit a great shot," he recalled. He was pleased with himself until his caddie, Scott Gneiser, sputtered, "What are you doing?" Toms had aimed at the flag for the thirteenth hole, which shares a double green with the fifth. That enormous green measures 38,000 square feet, nearly an acre, making it more than seven times the size of the largest green at Pebble Beach. "My caddie was like, 'You hit it fifty yards left of where we're trying to go!'"

Toms fell back while David Duval drew many of the day's loudest cheers. With birdies at the fourth, fifth, eighth, and ninth, Duval carded a 32 on the outward nine. His back was hurting—he did cautious knee bends to pick his ball from the hole—but his full swing looked as good as it had the year before, when he had spent three months atop the Official World Golf Ranking. At the 430-yard thirteenth, he lofted an 8-iron to ten feet and rolled in the putt. After another ten-footer at the last hole, he signed for a 66, which would be the best round of the day.

Tiger's back nine featured a risky pitch from thirty yards at the twelfth. Here was one of the links-golf choices he liked. He could putt over roller-coaster turf to the green or loft a pitch shot that might bounce too far. This time he chose the aerial approach—a three-hopper that crept to tap-in distance. The locals gave it a warm round of applause. He ran in a twenty-footer at the thirteenth to gain another stroke. He was fifteen under par. At the 581-yard fourteenth, called simply Long, a 309-yard drive left him 272 yards from the flag, with a tight lie and a left-to-right wind with out of bounds to the right. After talking with caddie Williams about his target for the next shot, a TV crane in the distance over the Hell Bunker, Tiger took a breath and a last look at the TV crane, then swung his 3-wood almost as hard as he could. The shot was barely on its way when he turned to Williams.

"*That* the one you're talking about?" he asked with a smile.

"That's the one right there," Williams said as the ball carried 260 yards and kicked left to the green.

If that fairway wood wasn't the first perfect shot of Tiger's life, it would do for the moment. (Years later, looking back on the 2000 Open Championship at St. Andrews, he would call it the one shot of the year that "turned out exactly as I had planned.") Two putts for a third straight birdie put him six strokes up on the field. He bogeyed the Road Hole but got that stroke back with a left-to-right breaker at the eighteenth to finish the third round at sixteen under par.

Tom Lehman, who had been the world's number one golfer in 1996, Tiger's rookie year, was in seventh place, eight shots behind. "I'm getting lapped," Lehman said.

Tiger was nervous about Sunday's final round despite his six-shot lead. "The bigger the lead, the more pressure you feel," he said. With no rain, sleet, or gale-force winds in the forecast, "You know you're going to have to make some birdies" on the Old Course. "All I can ask of myself is to give myself chances."

Duval liked his chances despite a six-shot deficit. After firing Saturday's best round, he would join his friend in Sunday's final twosome. It would be the first time he and Tiger were paired in a major. "It will be a circus, a slugfest," he said.

He had fought his way to this moment. As a nine-year-old boy growing up in Florida, Duval had endured an excruciating surgical procedure, donating bone marrow to his twelve-year-old brother, Brent, who had a potentially lethal case of aplastic anemia. But the transplant didn't take, and Brent died before his thirteenth birthday. Fifth grader David blamed himself, thinking his bone marrow wasn't good enough. He learned to keep his feelings under wraps.

He had learned the game on a Donald Ross–designed course at Timuquana Country Club in Jacksonville, where his father was a teaching pro. Soon he was a junior golf star, right up there with Ernie Els and Phil Mickelson. A four-time All-American at Georgia Tech, he teamed with Mickelson on the United States' victorious Walker Cup team in 1991. Tiger Woods, four years younger, was a freshman on the golf team at Western High School in Anaheim that year.

Duval had a bit of a belly during his first years on the PGA Tour, but after Tiger turned pro and they became friends he devoted himself to workouts that rivaled Tiger's. Leaner, stronger, and longer off the tee, he reached number one in the world while Tiger was retooling his swing in 1999. That was the year Duval shot a final-round 59 at the Bob Hope Chrysler Classic, tying the record for the best round in Tour history. Respected by his peers, who admired his swing, he often looked grim on the course, his eyes hidden behind wraparound shades.

"Tiger had great respect for David," Steve Williams said. "I think he had more respect for David Duval than for any other player in their prime at that time. He thought his demeanor and ability were somewhat similar to himself, and he saw him as an absolute threat. Tiger knew this was a guy who could beat him." But by the summer of 2000, the Tigerish workouts that added yards to his drives may have backfired on Duval. While other players sat behind the mic for their press conferences after the third round, he stood to keep from bending his sore back. Physical therapist Tom Boers, who had helped Mickelson, Fred Couples, and tennis's Steffi Graf return to form after spinal miseries, flew to Scotland that week to work on Duval between rounds. Tour pros called Boers the world's best back man. "He doesn't use ice, heat, or machines," Brad Faxon said. "He straightens your joints with his hands."

Boers liked to say that swinging a golf club could be hazardous to a golfer's career. Like an NFL running back's knee or a baseball pitcher's elbow, a golfer's back is subject to unnatural demands. The force and torque a Tour pro repeats under pressure can push the lower back to its limits. According to Boers, "Each player has a finite number of healthy swings." With his help, Duval hoped to make it through Saturday's press conference and Sunday's final round without crumpling in pain.

Was he looking forward to his first last-round pairing with Tiger? "Yes," he said. "You get to look him in the eye."

Would it mean something extra for Duval to win his first major by beating Tiger? "Absolutely. It would mean more to beat him. It's like 'I want you to know that when you're at your best, I can beat you.' That may sound cocky, but it's simply wanting to compete at the highest level. So, yes, I'm excited. How could I not be?"

When there were no more questions, he turned stiffly and made his careful way from the press tent to his hotel room, where he could lie down.

TWELVE
THE CLARET JUG

A little after noon on Sundays, congregants stream out of Holy Trinity Church, a gray stone hulk on St. Andrews's South Street. Tom Morris once served as an elder at Holy Trinity, passing around the black bag that served as a collection plate and hearing parishioners' confessions. An occasional sinner would confess to playing golf on the Sabbath, which Old Tom frowned on. He closed the Old Course on Sundays, keeping the Lord's day safe from the players' and caddies' customary turf slashing, spitting, and cursing. "Even if the golfers don't need a rest," he said, "the course does." The ban on Sabbath golf still stands, with only a few exceptions: a pair of annual amateur tournaments, the European Tour's Alfred Dunhill Links Championship, and, every five years, the Open.

Normally, Holy Trinity's parishioners make their way home after services. But Open week is different. On the fourth Sunday of July 2000, many went straight from church to the links, where the last round's play was underway. The town would empty out the following day, but now its narrow cobblestoned streets and much of the village green that holds the Old Course were jammed with tourists and locals. They crowded into the grandstand under the giant yellow leaderboard, and stood six deep along the first and last fairways, and filled the bleachers behind the nearby practice range, where Tiger Woods and David Duval were warming up side by side.

Duval was feeling looser than usual after a training-table session with Boers, who had flown first-class to Edinburgh to muscle his lower back into fighting shape. On the range, Woods and Duval exchanged glances and laughs between swings. There was nothing feigned about the warmth between them. Tiger was always respectful to older immortals like Nicklaus and Palmer, cordial with Els, friendly with contemporaries including Darren Clarke, Fred Couples, and Steve Stricker, and still tight with his Stanford pals Notah Begay and Jerry Chang, but other than O'Meara, his honorary big brother, no one on Tour but Duval was in his inner circle. They were close enough that Tiger had hung a nickname on him: "Double D." Duval and his girlfriend, Julie McArthur, had recently spent a weekend in Vegas with Tiger and Joanna Jagoda. They were frequent guests on the private jet Team Tiger called TWA for "Tiger Woods Airlines." Duval had flown TWA with Tiger from Orlando for the Open. But once a white R&A van ferried them the quarter mile from the range to the course, their camaraderie was put on hold. Taking their last warm-up swings under the bust of Old Tom in the clubhouse wall, both players looked as stone-faced as the gargoyles on the gables of Holy Trinity.

Duval, seeking his first major after seven top-ten finishes in his five years on the Tour, stood stiffly in black slacks and a white shirt buttoned up to his Adam's apple. His black Titleist cap and Oakley M Frame sunglasses shielded his eyes. Tiger wore black slacks and a subdued burgundy shirt under a red sweater-vest. The weather was sunny and cool. The leaders knew there were birdies out there today. Els, playing three groups ahead of them, was in the process of climbing within five strokes of Tiger's lead with four birdies in his first five holes. Clarke, Paul Azinger, and Tom Lehman were almost as hot.

Peering toward the first green 376 yards away, Tiger barely acknowledged the friend standing next to him. As Steve Williams put it later, "He wanted to stamp some domination" on Duval. "Despite having a sizable lead, Tiger saw David as a threat."

He opened with cautious pars, as he'd done at Pebble Beach. Duval, six strokes behind as they began, birdied four of the first seven holes to pull within three. Ahead of them, Els lipped out a point-blank par putt at the eleventh, effectively ending his chances. Midway through a summer of three-hundred-yard drives, pitch-perfect wedges, and too many flubs with the putter, the mild-mannered South African kept his composure. With the slightest shake of his head, Els muttered, "Damn."

Woods and Duval finished their first nine at −17 and −14. David Toms, two holes ahead of them, was still alive at −13 until he missed a three-footer at the eleventh. As almost everyone had expected, the Open was coming down to Tiger and Duval.

Duval had another chance at the 379-yard tenth, the hole named after Bobby Jones. He rifled a drive that skipped over a yawning bunker by inches and then faced a short pitch to the double green the Bobby Jones hole shared with the eighth hole. Tiger drove the green but would need to negotiate an approach putt covering the better part of an acre. After Duval's pitch kicked forward and rolled to a spot eleven feet from the pin, Tiger's putt curled sideways and stopped a foot closer. Now the challenger could hope for a two-stroke swing. If he sank his putt and Tiger missed, Duval would be within two strokes of the lead with eight holes to play.

A breeze stirred the heather behind the green while he settled over his putt, white glove sticking out of his back pocket. He took a practice stroke, then turned his head to look at the cup, drew back his Scotty Cameron Pro Platinum Newport putter, and sent the ball on its way.

He had judged the line just right. He was walking after it, expecting to pick his Titleist out of the cup, when the ball slowed down half a second too soon. Had he misread the grain? It died two inches short. Duval tapped in for par.

Tiger had spent the last few minutes repeatedly blowing his nose, taking care not to do it when Duval was putting. If nothing else, his summertime allergies proved he wasn't superhuman. He had spent parts of all four rounds fighting hay fever that may have been worsened by the yellow blooms of Scottish gorse. He took his stance over his Bridgestone-made Nike ball, which would soon be the hottest new product in golf, shifted his weight from his left foot to his right and back until he felt perfectly balanced, and rolled in his birdie putt. As so often happened, make-miss had worked in his favor and not his opponent's. Instead of pulling within two, Duval fell four shots behind with seven holes to play.

With the sun dipping toward Perth, Duval put on a black sweater. He was dressed all in black except for the very top of his golf shirt, a white ring that resembled a clerical collar. But the gods seemed to favor Tiger, who drove the twelfth green and two-putted for another birdie while Duval three-putted to bogey the shortest par 4 on the course. Suddenly he was six behind, right where he'd started the day.

Tiger signaled to Williams. He wanted a towel. Between shots he used the towel to clean specks of dirt off his shoes. He was starting to think of how he should look coming up the eighteenth fairway.

With the wind whistling from the left, he tried drawing a 3-wood at the bunker-pocked thirteenth, the inward Hole O'Cross, and double-crossed himself. "Lost it straight right," he remembered. His ball arrowed toward a bunker and skipped safely past. Duval took the same line off the tee, but his ball plunged into the bunker.

Tiger missed a long, double-curling eagle putt at the fourteenth, settling for another birdie. He was no longer playing only to win. With victory assured, he was playing for history, and he wanted to finish the right way.

Tiger had the honor at the Road Hole.

Even in summery weather, major-championship golf's cruelest par 4 held its own that week. The 455-yard dogleg-right hole the *New York Times* called an "outdoor torture chamber" had given up only thirteen birdies along with thirteen triple bogeys or worse. Some of the pros joked that it was "the hardest par 5 on the course." That week, attacked by 158 of the world's best golfers, the par-4 Road Hole played to an average of 4.7.

After booming his drive over the OLD COURSE HOTEL sign to the fairway, Tiger tried a punch-and-run approach to the green. Setting up with the ball even with his back foot, he chopped down hard and botched the shot, leaving his ball short of the notorious Road Hole Bunker. From there he had next to no chance to get his third shot near the hole, but that was better than being in the bunker—where his playing partner wound up after shooting for the flag. Duval's approach fell just short of the green, diving to an ugly lie in the sand.

Tiger was away. Forty yards from the green with little chance to save par, he took his medicine. He putted his ball around the Road Hole Bunker to the green. Now lying three, he could two-putt for bogey and still lead by half a dozen strokes.

Duval's options were worse. He could aim for the flag and try to save par, but that would call for a nearly vertical sand shot to clear the bunker's steep, beveled face. Or he could wedge out sideways and try to get up and down for bogey. Japan's Tommy Nakajima had taken four swings from near the same spot during the 1978 Open, leading to a quintuple-bogey 9 and a new nickname for the Road Hole Bunker: "the Sands of Nakajima."

Like Nakajima, Duval chose the direct route. Swinging hard, he dug under the ball and sent it almost straight up. His ball kissed the lip of the bunker. It could have kicked forward but instead it bounced straight up and fell back to his feet. He was now lying three, his ball sitting beside the gouge he'd just made in the sand. Duval could have chipped out sideways and lived to fight another day. Instead he tried the direct route again, aiming straight up at the flag. This one caromed off the face of the bunker and dripped back to an even worse lie. Lying four with no hope of advancing the ball, he turned his wedge around and backhanded the ball a few feet to the middle of the bunker. From there, he pitched his sixth shot onto the green to polite applause. After spending four strokes and five of the longest minutes of his life in the bunker, he two-putted for a snowman in July.

"I felt bad for him," Tiger recalled. "He worked so hard all day, and I wanted him to finish second."

Alex Harvey, the engraver who inscribed winners' names on the Claret Jug, began etching TIGER on the silver band that would add the new winner's name to the trophy. Harvey's policy was to wait for final scores before starting his work, a sensible choice after Jean van de Velde's meltdown at Carnoustie the year before, when he had blown a three-shot lead on the last hole. But with Duval out of the picture and a single hole to play, it was safe to add TIGER WOODS to the list of Open champions that had begun with THOS. MORRIS JR. in 1872.

The new champion needed a par at the short eighteenth to break Nick Faldo's Open scoring record of 270, set at St. Andrews in 1990. Now forty-three, Faldo had finished at a respectable one under par, eighteen shots off the lead. "I don't like it a bit," he said. "I'll just have to go and play in Tiger-less tournaments."

Teeing off at Tom Morris's short finishing hole, the leader aimed for the first tee. That was the safe play. His drive left him a short pitch to the green. He and Williams crossed the Swilcan Bridge to the fairway, followed by a horde of spectators. The fans overwhelmed the marshals and bobbies trying to keep them at bay. Some leaped over narrow Swilcan Burn, chanting "Tiger, Tiger!" A few missed the jump

Tiger consoled David Duval after his friend made an 8 at the Road Hole.

and fell into the burn, then clambered out and chased him toward the green.

One spectator took a more daring approach. Jacqui Salmond, an exotic dancer from Edinburgh, stripped off her clothes and dashed onto the eighteenth green wearing nothing but her reading glasses. *Sports Illustrated* described her as "a comprehensively tanned woman" who "gamboled from the gallery to the green, where she grabbed the flag and danced around it as if it were a maypole."

"Tiger was at the eighteenth hole," Salmond remembered. "I pushed to the front of the crowd, crouched down and slipped the strap of my dress off my shoulders. Fresh air blasted my naked body. It was now or never. I burst through the cordon and legged it toward the eighteenth hole, arms in the air and as naked as the day I was born."

Caddie Williams could barely believe his eyes. "The crowd was going berserk," he recalled. Security guards corralled Salmond and led her off the green while the worldwide telecast cut to commercial. Once order was restored, Tiger flipped a wedge to the back of the eighteenth green. His mother, standing beside the green with Joanna Jagoda, wearing a Sunday-red visor with a black bow on top to match Tiger's outfit, applauded. Kultida Punsawad Woods had followed her son through hundreds of golf tournaments without shedding a tear, but now she wept, daubing her eyes with a tissue as Tiger stepped onto the green, tipping his cap to the cheering town.

He left his putt five feet short, a minor annoyance. With his ball five feet from the hole, he could take seven from there and still win. But as at Pebble Beach, he didn't want to end with a bogey.

Duval putted out, clearing the stage. He finished with a back-nine 43 to come in eleventh, a dozen shots behind.

Tiger knocked in his five-footer to break Faldo's scoring record. As they left the green, he gave his friend a hug. "You're a true champion," he told Duval. "Walk off like a champion."

Ernie Els had cobbled together a final-round 69 to tie Thomas

Bjørn for second place. That made Els the only player ever to finish second in three consecutive majors. The pro game was "at a different level now. I'm thirty years old, going against a guy who's fearless and with so much confidence it's tough to beat him." How could Els compete? "Go back to the drawing board," he said. "Maybe make the holes bigger for us and a little smaller for him."

After avoiding three-putts on Pebble Beach's bumpy greens to win the U.S. Open, Tiger had used a different strategy in Scotland, tacking his way from tee to green without hitting into a single one of the Old Course's 112 bunkers. "Some of it is just karma," he said. "You need some lucky bounces."

Nicklaus had a different view. "You don't get lucky bounces for four straight days," he said.

That night, Team Tiger celebrated its man's second straight major at the Old Course Hotel. Butch Harmon called Tiger's performance "the greatest ball-striking exhibition I've ever seen and perhaps the greatest in history." Caddie Williams marveled at the precision that had left a 2.1-inch tee intact all week. Through seventy-two holes of some of the best golf ever played in Scotland or anywhere else, Tiger had used only one tee. "His lucky charm," Williams called it. From that day on, Tiger would keep that tee in a leather pouch in his golf bag with his wallet and his watch.

That night, with the Claret Jug under one arm, Tiger dropped in on the tournament committee. He didn't want to leave town without saying thanks. He smiled and posed for pictures while flustered committee members fumbled with their cameras and lined up for autographs. Finally the Champion Golfer of the Year raised a flute of champagne. "A toast," he said. "To St. Andrews!"

And then he was gone. Tiger led an entourage including Jagoda, Williams, Tour pro Stuart Appleby, Duval, and Julie McArthur to an

RAF air base three miles up the coast, where his Gulfstream V was waiting. One of his suitcases featured a sticker showing Cartman, his favorite foul-mouthed *South Park* character. Another carry-on was the 137-year-old Claret Jug, which they filled with champagne and passed around during the eight-hour flight home to Orlando. Even Duval had a sip.

Tiger's victory made him the youngest ever to record a career Grand Slam by winning all four majors. Ben Hogan was forty when he flew to Scotland to add the 1953 Open Championship to his eight American majors. Gene Sarazen was thirty-three when he won the 1935 Masters to complete a career Slam including two U.S. Opens, three PGA Championships, and the 1932 Open Championship. Gary Player was twenty-nine when he won the 1965 U.S. Open to notch his career Grand Slam. Nicklaus was twenty-six when he flew to Scotland to win his first Open Championship in 1966, joining Hogan, Sarazen, and Player as one of four players to sweep the modern majors at one time or another. Thirty-four years had passed before twenty-four-year-old Tiger turned their career Grand Slam foursome into a fivesome, and he was starting to think about a different sort of Slam, one that didn't yet have a name.

THIRTEEN
VALHALLA

Tiger's run of victories brought attention of a thousand different kinds. The Golf Channel's Scott Van Pelt pronounced Tiger Woods "the new Michael Jordan, *the* singular force in sports." Other commentators reacted differently after Tiger's win in Scotland, playing the race card to cringeworthy effect.

"Golf has gone strictly black-Thai," *Sports Illustrated* quipped. ". . . With Woods having won the PGA, the U.S. Open and the British Open and Vijay Singh having won the Masters, it has been more than a year since a white guy won a major championship." According to the *Washington Post*'s Tom Callahan, "Counting Fijian Vijay Singh's victory at the Masters, all of this year's loving cups are in black hands."

Tiger ignored those and other printed versions of "the Look." He had another major to think about. He skipped the next three Tour events but made an early-August scouting trip to the site of the upcoming PGA Championship, Valhalla Golf Club in Louisville, Kentucky.

He would be the defending champion in the 2000 PGA Championship, having outdueled Sergio García at the 1999 PGA at Medinah Country Club near Chicago. Butch Harmon flew in from Vegas to join him for a practice round at Valhalla. Tiger seldom went twenty-four hours without hitting practice balls, getting antsy if outside obligations or opportunities kept him off the range, but after his record-setting victories at Pebble Beach and St. Andrews, he had taken a few days off. There was less need to fix flaws in a swing that wasn't broke. At Valhalla, as always, he worked his way back from a layoff by starting with fundamentals: Grip. Stance. Alignment. After a session on the range, he and Harmon walked the course, which was closed to club members while the grounds crew prepped fairways and greens and construction crews put up bleachers and hospitality tents. Tiger enjoyed having the course to himself, with no crowds and no more than a few other pros playing practice rounds of their own. If he found a tricky position he might encounter at the PGA, he could drop a few balls and try as many shots as he wanted without holding anybody up.

The course was nothing special. In a year when the three other Grand Slam events returned to courses revered around the world, Valhalla was an outlier. "There is little to no classic design to the place," one Tour pro griped. "It's the opposite of the kind of course that should host a major."

The wallflower at the prom lacked history as well as classic design. Opened in 1986, Valhalla had hosted one previous major, the 1996 PGA Championship, which Mark Brooks won in a playoff over Kenny Perry. Neither player had won a tournament since. As Dan Jenkins, the seventy-one-year-old dean of golf writers, groused, "Anything is better than Valhalla."

David Duval was almost as dismissive. Duval, whose bad back would force him to withdraw from the PGA, called it "a perfectly nice golf course—for a Nike Tour event. But a major championship? You have to be kidding."

The PGA of America, which represented the country's twenty-eight thousand teaching professionals, did its reputation no favors by choosing Valhalla for the year's last major. But the course was a Nicklaus design, a fitting spot for the Golden Bear to host the last leg of his farewell tour of the majors. Another factor was cost. The PGA of America owned the course, so it saved millions of dollars in leasing fees it would have had to pay another venue.

The week after his scouting trip to Louisville, Tiger teed up a Tour Accuracy at the Buick Open in Grand Blanc, Michigan. He didn't often play Tour events the week before a major, preferring the more controlled environment of gated Isleworth, far from crowds of fans and reporters. Spending four days on the mediocre course at Grand Blanc's Warwick Hills Golf & Country Club would do little to help him prepare for a run at his third straight major, but the decision wasn't up to him. His $25 million endorsement deal with Buick called for him to keep the company's logo on his bag and appear in Buick events.

He told the press he was glad to be there. Asked if he was risking burnout by playing on a week he could have spent at home in Florida, he spoke from the heart: "I don't think I've ever seen anyone love a job and get burned out."

As at the Memorial Tournament and Western Open, his warm-ups for the U.S. Open and Open Championship earlier that year, he wasn't much concerned about his finish at the Buick. His goal was to peak a week later in Louisville. But once committed to play, his impact on the Tour was clear: Buick Open ticket sales doubled with the announcement that he would be in the field. Record crowds thronged every hole he played. Trailing the leaders by four shots during Saturday's third round, he paused between shots while fans took up the "Tiger! Tiger!" chant. He finished the day six shots off the lead and two behind his playing partner, Phil Mickelson, who marveled at the ruckus. "I really enjoy playing with Tiger," said Mickelson. "What he goes through every day—I don't know how he does it. It's so loud, there's so much hoopla, I can't even hear." At one hole, Mickelson hit into the gallery. "It took me five minutes to get all the people out of the way so they weren't in danger" before he tried his next shot. Phil's lesson of the day: "Keep it in play when you play with him."

Third-round leader Rocco Mediate, playing several holes behind Woods and Mickelson, called his pairing with Woody Austin "the weirdest final group I ever played in." Mediate and Austin finished after Tiger signed his card and headed for the parking lot. "Tiger took all the fans with him. It was eerie. We got to the seventeenth hole, and there was hardly anybody there."

Mediate won with a 66 on Sunday. Woods shot 68 to tie for eleventh and earned $57,240, which did little more than cover his expenses and his return flight to Orlando, where he spent the following day drilling balls off the range at Isleworth. Even after missing the top ten at the Buick, he had won thirteen of the last twenty-four tournaments he had entered.

During Monday's practice session at Isleworth, Tiger focused on the opposite of his prep for the Open Championship. He practiced hitting the ball high to suit the green complexes at Valhalla instead of working on the stingers and bump-and-run chips that had worked at St. Andrews. The next morning he woke early and flew back to Louisville, where Muhammad Ali welcomed him at the airport. At fifty-eight, Louisville native Ali was suffering from Parkinson's disease, moving with difficulty after taking an estimated two hundred thousand punches in his boxing career. He plodded toward the younger man but brightened when they hugged.

Tiger made it to Valhalla Golf Club in time for a practice round with Mark O'Meara. He had his own reason for disliking the venue: the course's quirks were likely to give more players than usual a chance to win a major. But he sounded diplomatic during a pretournament press appearance. "Valhalla," he said, "is a typical Jack Nicklaus course. He gives you room off the tee but makes it a little more challenging around the greens. The course is obviously *different* from the caliber of major championship courses we've seen this year. You have Augusta, Pebble Beach, and St. Andrews, and I don't think anyone would say Valhalla is of the same caliber. But this golf course has a lot of rough."

A reporter asked if he could see himself breaking Nicklaus's record of eighteen majors. After all, he had won four so far and was favored to make it five that week. "Have I tried to chase him?" Tiger asked. "I don't think it's realistic to think about that until you get into the double digits" in majors. He had been talking privately for years about catching and passing Nicklaus's total but wasn't about to say so in public.

Bettors had enjoyed six-to-one odds on him before the 1999 PGA Championship, but a year later he was better than a two-to-one favorite, a nearly unprecedented occurrence in modern golf. Even those odds were a bit longer than they had been at the Open Championship a month before, when £100 wagers on Tiger Woods had returned profits of £100 to £150, depending on when they were placed. A $100 bet at the PGA Championship would bring a $160 profit if he won, a sign that bookmakers were factoring the venue into their calculations for the same reason that worried Tiger: lesser courses tend to favor the field against the favorites.

Some pundits were so confident that he would win at Valhalla that they were already looking ahead to the 2001 Masters. If Tiger won the PGA, he would have a chance to extend his streak to four majors in a row the next spring at Augusta. There hadn't been such a run at four straight since 1972, when Nicklaus had won the Masters and U.S. Open before finishing one shot behind Lee Trevino at the Open Championship. "I let it get away," the disappointed Nicklaus said that year, "but I know that the Grand Slam can be done." As the wire services reported at the time, "Trevino's triumph shattered Nicklaus's dream of a one-year sweep of the world's four major titles, an unprecedented feat that many players and observers have deemed impossible."

"It would have been good for golf for Jack to win the Grand Slam," Trevino said. "But we're all in this to win."

Twenty-eight summers later, Nicklaus listened to question after question about Tiger Woods. "Tiger is good for golf," he said, "but he needs challengers."

Nicklaus's fans claimed that the Golden Bear had faced down worthier rivals than Tiger had: not just Palmer, Player, and Trevino but Tom Watson, Billy Casper, Johnny Miller, and Tom Weiskopf, all of them major champions. It remained to be seen how Els, Mickelson, Singh, and Duval would stack up against Jack's rivals and how Tiger's streak of winning majors—if it lasted—would compare to Bobby Jones's 1930 Grand Slam and Byron Nelson's eleven consecutive tournament wins in 1945.

Then there was the matter of the calendar. If Tiger were to top 148 other players that week at Valhalla and then go on to win the 2001 Masters the next spring, would that be the second Grand Slam in golf history—the first professional Grand Slam?

Tiger's father didn't think so. Describing himself as "old school," Earl Woods told *Golf Digest* that a Grand Slam needed to happen in a single calendar year. "I feel that records should be kept on an annual basis, like baseball and football."

Arnold Palmer agreed. Asked if four consecutive majors over two calendar years would constitute a Slam, the man who invented the idea of the modern Grand Slam said, "No way, José." But younger players, including three-time major winner Nick Price, dared to differ. "If you've got possession of all four trophies at one time, it's a Slam," said Price.

Pressed for his opinion, Tiger shrugged. "Four in a row is four in a row," he said. He was focused on four days, not four tournaments. Winning majors—one at a time—was a matter of "peaking at the right time," he said, "and that's something I'm getting better at."

Sports Illustrated had some fun with the issue, quoting a "new" Dr. Seuss book called *Grand Eggs and Slam*. "In this charming children's tale," *SI* reported, "cynical columnist Sam-I-Am rejects the idea that four straight majors over two years counts as a Grand Slam. 'I do not like your Slam,' says Sam. 'Your Slam's a sham,' says Sam-I-Am. Over breakfast, Sam asks the Cat in the Red Shirt to take his foot off Sam's throat."

He wore a gray shirt for Thursday's opening round with Nicklaus and Vijay Singh. Tiger was pleased to be part of the Golden Bear's ongoing farewell tour and knew how pleased his dad would be to see Jack and Tiger together on TV. At the same time, playing his first ever tournament round with Nicklaus added a distraction for a player with designs on the first-round lead. Steve Williams thought Tiger was "pressing a little" that morning, "really wanting to impress Jack." When Tiger missed a short putt, CBS announcer David Feherty wondered if someone had "slipped some kryptonite into his bag."

Golf's superman bogeyed the fifth hole. After that, he took a chance at Nicklaus's gimmicky seventh, one of the longest holes in major-championship history at 597 yards, where an optional "island fairway" to the left dared players to take a shortcut over water to the green. Most players ignored that tempting second fairway, where the landing area was only twenty-six yards wide, but Tiger asked Williams for his driver. He had been hitting 3-woods off the tees, sacrificing distance for precision. Now he whacked a tee ball that bounced and nearly ran through the island fairway into the drink but stopped safely. On one of the longest holes in major-championship history, he reached the green in two with a 7-iron and two-putted for the first of four straight birdies.

Play was slow and sweaty all day. A hundred thirty-one touring pros and twenty-five club professionals plodded through heat that

Tiger and Jack Nicklaus played two rounds together at the 2000 PGA Championship.

reached 96 degrees, making August 17 Louisville's hottest day of the year. Brent Geiberger teed off at 2:00 p.m., then waited while the groups ahead of him got so stacked up that it was almost an hour before he could hit his second shot. Tiger went on to birdie all four of Valhalla's par-5 holes, reaching one in two shots with a 4-iron, the other three with 7-irons, firing a first-round 66 while averaging 329.5 yards off the tee. "My gosh, he hits the ball a long way," Nicklaus said. Tiger called it "an honor to play with Jack" and meant it, but added, "To be honest, I could care less who I am playing with. I'm trying to put myself in position to win a major championship."

His 66 left him tied for the lead with Scott Dunlap, a thirty-seven-year-old journeyman with no Tour victories in his fifteen years as a pro. Darren Clarke and Davis Love III stood two strokes back, with Mickelson and eleven others within four shots of the lead.

Co-leader Dunlap was realistic about his chances. "Tiger has won more majors than I've made cuts," he said. The 1981 valedictorian at Sarasota High School, Dunlap rivaled Tiger as one of the Tour's leading golf nerds. He could reel off the names and scores of major-championship winners dating back to the nineteenth century. "Tiger has won the last two majors by twenty-three shots combined," he noted that evening. "His presence is discouraging to everyone else in the field. All I can do is play another good round and take it from there."

A reporter asked Tiger about his golf heroes. Rather than answering "None" as he'd done on junior-golf questionnaires, he tried to give an honest answer. "When I was young," he said, "I looked up to a lot of different players for different reasons. Obviously, Jack Nicklaus was the greatest of all time. Ben Hogan was the greatest driver there ever was. Seve Ballesteros probably had the best short game. Ben Crenshaw putted the best. What I did was analyze every different player's game, try to pick the best out of each and every player, and try to look up to that."

That night a fast-moving thunderstorm dumped three inches of rain on the course Jack built. Torrential rains drenched the greens and filled some of the bunkers with water a foot deep. Gale-force winds toppled a fifty-foot sycamore beside the tenth fairway. The grounds crew chopped up the tree and carted it away, but Friday's second round was pushed back by an hour. The delay annoyed some of the golfers, while others figured that the storm would help their chances. A wet Valhalla would play longer, with drives checking up ten to fifteen yards shorter, but Friday's pins would be vulnerable on rain-softened greens.

FOURTEEN
JACK'S PACK

Friday brought another parade of five-and-a-half- and six-hour rounds. Some players were surprised by the glacial pace. Others had expected it, knowing that Valhalla was practically designed to slow a major championship to a standstill. All four of Nicklaus's par-5 holes were reachable in two, leaving one threesome on the green while another watched from the fairway, waiting for them to putt out, while the next three players cooled their heels in the tee box, waiting for the fairway to clear. There were also time-consuming hikes from one green to the next tee. Valhalla's members could zip along in carts, but the pros had to walk.

After the previous night's storm, a wetter and softer Valhalla played a stroke or two easier. Even John Daly had a chance to make the cut. The Wild Thing had plunged from number forty-eight in the world to number four hundred since winning the 1995 Open Championship at St. Andrews, but he was on the good side of the cut line through twelve holes. Then Daly double-bogeyed the thirteenth, bogeyed the fourteenth, and quit trying. He stomped through a triple-bogey 7 at the seventeenth and a triple-bogey 8 at the home hole to shoot 82. The antigrinder scrawled his name on his scorecard and stalked off the course.

The first-round co-leader, Scott Dunlap, looked certain to drop a stroke on Nicklaus's first hole, only to save par with a Hail Mary putt that seemed to give him a boost. At the third, he sank another long bomb. A twenty-five-footer at the tenth and a birdie at the eighteenth made him the leader in the clubhouse at ten under par.

Teeing off several groups after Dunlap, Tiger birdied the par-5 second hole for the second day in a row. With birdies at the seventh and eighth and a par at the ninth, he went out in 32. Well over an hour later, after another long delay, he and Nicklaus hit short irons at the thirteenth, where a narrow bridge leads from the fairway to an island green. They were approaching the bridge when Tiger waved his host forward: *After you.* Nicklaus returned the gesture: *No, after you.* Tiger smiled and led the way.

"He was taking it all in, walking a little slower than usual," Williams remembered. Accustomed to hearing galleries call out his name, Tiger enjoyed hearing this one chant, "Jack, Jack," pulling for Nicklaus to make the thirty-six-hole cut. It had been forty years since Nicklaus began a testy relationship with Arnold Palmer's adoring fans, who were known as Arnie's Army. A decade later, in the seventies, Nicklaus's loyal galleries were called "Jack's Pack," while "Lee's Fleas" swarmed Trevino. By 2000, most golf fans were pulling for Tiger. His galleries didn't need a nickname because practically every crowd was a Tiger crowd.

Jack's Pack was out in force that Friday, but the outlook wasn't brilliant. After a first-round 77, Nicklaus needed to shoot a two-under-par 70 to make the cut. By the time they reached the eighteenth tee, he was even par for the day. It would take an eagle 3 at his 542-yard finishing hole to get him to the weekend.

Tiger knew that a miracle finish by Nicklaus would blow the roof off Kentucky and be the lead story on *SportsCenter* that night. He was pulling for the once golden Bear, whose swing was a relic of the powerful move that had broken rivals' spirits thirty years before. But, in the moment, he was in no mood to celebrate anyone's legacy. Few golfers have ever been as laser focused on their games as Jack Nicklaus and Tiger Woods, and Tiger felt like kicking something after three-putting the seventeenth green for his first bogey of the day. Still, he had been thinking of something he wanted to say. He made a point of walking beside Nicklaus as they left the last tee.

"It's been an honor and a privilege playing with you," Tiger said. "Now let's finish it off the right way." *With birdies*, he meant.

Nicklaus said, "You got it. Let's go."

Nicklaus knew he had no chance to reach the green in two. A year after hip replacement surgery, he was fifty yards shorter off the tee than his twenty-four-year-old playing partner, with almost as great a gap between their fairway-wood distances. He laid up. Tiger then hammered a 3-wood that arrowed toward the flagstick. He liked few things better than closing a round in crowd-pleasing style. Watching the ball with the tunnel vision he brought to shots he liked, he thought it looked perfect. He blinked when it plugged into the face of a bunker just short of the green. "Great," he told Williams, his voice dripping with sarcasm. This wasn't the way he'd pictured closing his last major-championship round with Nicklaus.

All eyes turned to Nicklaus. The crowd was already roaring. Seventy-two yards from a pin just past the bunker that had swallowed Tiger's ball, Jack would make the cut only if he holed out his third shot.

With one swing, the most accomplished golfer in history summoned some of the old magic he had called on at Augusta, St. Andrews, Pebble Beach, Baltusrol, Birkdale, Oakmont, Oak Hill, and just about everywhere else championship golf was played. Even with a sand wedge, his swing was creakier and wristier now. He pivoted on his ceramic hip and brought the wedge down to crisp contact, sending up a thin green divot as the ball climbed over the bunker and over the top of the flag, bit the green, and began backing up, rolling like a short putt. Had he holed it? Almost. With Jack's whooping Pack urging the ball toward the cup, it slipped just past the edge. There was a collective groan, followed by cries of "We love you, Jack!" and "You're still the greatest!" Nicklaus waved to acknowledge what may have been the loudest ovation ever for a player who had just missed the cut.

Tiger would file that moment in his memory. "Pretty cool" he called it. But for now he had his own predicament to think about. A bogey from the bunker could cost him more than a chance to match Jack's birdie and finish on the correct note; it could cost him the second-round lead.

Golf's contingencies, from the rub of the green to the way a three-piece urethane-covered ball reacts to a sudden breath of wind, can drive even the best players to distraction. What if Tiger hadn't been playing a new Nike ball made in Japan by Bridgestone? Would his old Titleist Professional have ballooned a little, cleared the bunker, and given him an eagle putt? There was no point in wondering. He was plugged and short-sided, with a ridge between him and the green and the flagstick less than twenty feet away. It would be easy to make bogey from there, but he was still thinking birdie. One advantage he had on the field was a memory bank full of successes. Not even the young Nicklaus had ever made it so far with so few disappointments. Looking over his buried lie in Jack's bunker, Tiger remembered dueling Els down the stretch in Hawaii in 1997. That day, looking over an even worse lie in a greenside bunker, he'd thought the one thing no golfer should ever think: "I'm a dead man." With no realistic hope of getting the ball close, he had tried a more desperate version of his recent escape on the Road Hole at St. Andrews: swinging hard, he had smacked an intentional one-hopper that rifled out of the bunker, struck an embankment, popped straight up, fell back, and rolled onto the green close enough for him to sink the putt for a Houdini par.

Now he opened his clubface and stance. Again he swung hard, aiming for a spot two inches behind the buried ball, planning to dig deep into the sand. As he once described his approach to explosion shots in a *Golf Digest* tip, "I want to take a divot that is deep enough to bury a small animal in." His wedge sliced under the ball, wafting it over the ridge to the green.

Explosion shots don't spin much. Rather than hopping and stopping like most bunker shots, they float like knuckleballs and skitter away when they land. This one came down beside the flagstick and ran fifteen feet past. Birdie range.

Butch Harmon, standing behind the green, knew what a finely calibrated shot he'd just seen. According to Harmon, "When he first turned pro, Tiger had an average short game by Tour standards and a poor bunker game for a top-level player. Through sheer determination and an unquenchable quest for new information, he built the best short game in the world."

Tiger's downhill fifteen-footer was for more than the second-round lead. It meant holding up his end of his bargain with Nicklaus: "Let's finish it off the right way."

"You're going to make it," Williams told him. "We're going to get out of here with birdie."

Tiger ran the putt into the dark heart of the cup. He clenched his fist and nodded to Williams. "You were right."

Nicklaus's one-under-par 71 left him fifteen strokes behind the leader, one over the cut line. Tiger's 67 gave him the eighty-four-year-old tournament's thirty-six-hole scoring record and his third straight lead at the midpoint of a major. They were leaving the green when Nicklaus gave Williams a piece of advice: "Make sure you stick with that fella."

After the round, Nicklaus told reporters that he wished he could have made the cut at his thirty-seventh PGA Championship but had enjoyed a close look at the second-round leader's "phenomenal control" and "phenomenal concentration." He remembered playing with one of his own illustrious elders, Gene Sarazen, at the 1971 PGA. "He was sixty-six or sixty-seven years old at the time," Nicklaus said. (In fact, Sarazen was sixty-nine.) "It was a privilege to play with him, and it was fun. He had the opportunity to watch me in the prime of my career, and now I'm getting the opportunity to watch Tiger in his prime. I don't mind the shoe being on the other foot."

It had been only nine years since his 1991 clinic at Bel-Air, where he'd joked about the fifteen-year-old Tiger's talent, saying "When I grow up, I hope my swing is as pretty as yours." More than a few golf writers considered Nicklaus an egocentric know-it-all. Behind his back they called him Carnac, a reference to a swami Johnny Carson played in *Tonight Show* skits who knew the answer to any question before it was asked. He had never been as warm toward Tiger as Arnold Palmer was, but that was the difference between Palmer, a hugger, and the more reserved Nicklaus, who had been gracious to Tiger since the day they'd met. It may have been a case of like knows like. Twenty years after the young Tiger taped a list of Jack's achievements on his bedroom wall, Nicklaus recognized a worthy successor, praising Tiger with the same words Bobby Jones had used to describe the twenty-five-year-old Jack Nicklaus: "He plays a game with which I am not familiar."

"Of course, *I'm* playing a game with which I'm not familiar, either," Nicklaus said of his creaky joints and short, looping drives. Moments later, addressing a question that would still be debated twenty-five years later, he said, "I think he's a better player than I was."

Bob Gaus, a club pro from St. Louis, played in the last group that Friday. While the grounds crew waited to prep the course for Saturday's third round, he tapped in for a 77, missing the cut by half a dozen shots. He had missed too many putts. A boy waiting behind the green asked, "Can I have your golf ball?" Gaus said, "No, but you can have my putter," and gave it to him.

With two rounds left to play, there were fourteen players within sight of the lead. It may have been a sign of Valhalla's shortcomings that only two of them, Woods and Davis Love III, had ever won a major. But the result was still in doubt. Dunlap was hanging tough at ten under par, a shot behind Tiger, with Love, Fred Funk, and J. P. Hayes four behind at –7. Tiger's Stanford teammate Notah Begay and Tour journeyman Bob May were five back with thirty-six holes to play.

ESPN's Billy Andrade predicted an all-Tiger weekend. "He's totally in control of this championship," Andrade said. "He's short-sided himself one time in this championship. When he misses, he misses in the right places. He's totally in control of his emotions, he's patient when he has to be, and he's aggressive when he has to be."

Funk, a forty-four-year-old Tour veteran who'd shot 68 to stay close, told reporters he was up for a battle with the best player golf had ever seen. "I don't think we're scared of Tiger," he said. "We're amazed at Tiger. He has taken the game to a whole new level nobody has ever seen."

Dunlap was looking forward to playing in the final group the next day. "Tiger will be extremely difficult to beat," he said. "This is what he lives for. I don't think there'll be many bookies taking bets on Scott Dunlap."

Tiger said he'd "had a blast" coming down the home stretch with Nicklaus. "Everybody was yelling for Jack, not me. Nobody even noticed what I was doing."

Everybody would notice on Saturday, when he was the one struggling to break par.

FIFTEEN
GRINDING

Saturday is moving day, when players who make the second-round cut can improve their positions going into Sunday's final round. There were eighty of them that week, all with thoughts of making up ground on Tiger Woods. He had led by six after two rounds at the halfway point of the U.S. Open and by three at the Open Championship, but now had only a one-shot edge on Scott Dunlap.

Scott Van Pelt asked the leader about his mindset: "Are you confident going into the weekend?"

Tiger gave his widest smile. "Nah, I feel real terrible!"

He would be paired with Dunlap, an amiable Georgian, on Saturday. When Dunlap was asked whether that knowledge had weighed on him the night before, he said he'd slept like a baby, with "nothing to dread." Playing in the last twosome in a major was "the carrot that's been dangling in front of me all these years." Looking forward to the third round, he said, "I was just anxious to see how I'd do. I'm thirty-seven, and I'm still getting better. That's a great thing about golf—if I were a tennis player, I'd be teaching old ladies how to hit backhands."

Both men birdied Nicklaus's par-5 second hole, Tiger for the third day in a row. Both birdied the 597-yard seventh, but by then Dunlap had missed several of the sorts of putts that can keep a golfer up at night. "I've got some bad history with the putter," he admitted later. At the uphill ninth, after Tiger sank a fifteen-footer to make the turn in 33, Dunlap misfired from ten feet. Now the challenger was two behind. He missed an eight-footer at the tenth while Tiger birdied again to reach fifteen under par. His lead was up to three.

The twelfth at Valhalla, named Sting Like a Bee in a nod to Muhammad Ali, is the toughest hole on the course, a 467-yard par 4 to an elevated green between a thicket of bluegrass and a bunker so deep that club members compared it to a crater on the moon. Tiger's drive veered left—not quite a snap hook, more of a Hogan garter snake, but bad enough. A tree blocked his way to the green. Looking for options, he saw a ten-foot gap between the tree and a stand of woods to its right, and chose the riskiest option. Steve Williams nodded. Of course Tiger would try to hook an 8-iron shot through the gap.

He set up with the ball back in his stance, clubface tilted to the left. As any of the teaching pros in the field could attest, this is how to hit an intentional hook, with the stance aligned toward the trajectory and the clubface angled to the left, toward the spot where you want the ball to land. He was picturing a recovery like a shot movie star Jack Nicholson had watched him hit at the 1997 Masters. "I try to see the bigtime sporting events," Nicholson remembered, "and I had a feeling he was going to win that Masters. On the front nine Saturday, Tiger blocks a drive, and the only shot he's got is around a tree. I'm up by the green, watching the ball curve to the flag. He must have drawn that ball twenty or thirty yards."

This one worked, at least at first. Tiger's delofted 8-iron threaded the gap between trees and began curling left, hurtling through the gap, spinning hard from right to left, and nestled just short of the green. A mediocre pitch shot left him lying three, fifteen feet from the cup. He ran the putt a foot and a half past, marked his ball, and stepped aside while Dunlap sized up a delicate sidehill six-footer, the biggest putt of his fifteen-year pro career. With Tiger about to make bogey, a birdie could pull Dunlap back within a stroke of him.

Despite his "bad history" with the putter, Dunlap was enough of a golf nerd to know that the majors often turn on unlikely events. One shot can change the name on the trophy. He gave his putt a tap. Losing speed all the way, it slid toward the cup and fell in. He was thirteen under par for the tournament, with Tiger sure to bogey and fall to –14. Until Tiger didn't.

The leader stepped up to finish off his bogey putt. And pushed it. An eighteen-incher! The crowd gasped at the sight of Tiger Woods's first double bogey in 153 holes of major-championship golf.

Combined with Dunlap's birdie, Tiger's three-putt double had erased his three-shot lead in a single hole. With twenty-four holes left to play, they were tied. There were cries of "Go, Scott!" and "C'mon, Scotty!"

Dunlap had honors at the fourteenth, a 217-yard par 3. That distance left him wondering which club to hit. "I was between a four and a five," he recalled. Ultimately, he chose wrong. A near-pure 5-iron shot struck the top of a bank just short of the green and dripped back into a bunker.

Tiger was a club and a half longer than Dunlap. He asked caddie Williams for a 6-iron and knocked it into the same bunker. He nearly holed his bunker shot from there, leaving a tap-in for par, while Dunlap blasted out and two-putted for bogey. Advantage Tiger. Now he had a chance to step on the other guy's throat, but he was fighting his swing, fidgeting during his setup, uncomfortable over the ball. From the middle of the fairway at the fifteenth, he made his worst full swing of the tournament so far, yanking a 6-iron into dense rough thirty yards left of the green. Five minutes later, for the second time in four holes, he followed a crooked shot with a minor miracle, a surgical pitch that crept to within nine feet of the flag. He circled the putt as usual, took two smooth practice strokes, eyed the hole, took a breath—and missed. Dunlap's par left them tied again. As Williams put it later, Tiger "clearly didn't have his best stuff. He was grinding hard."

But he was keeping it together. Composure, Earl Woods recalled in his memoir *Training a Tiger: A Father's Guide to Raising a Winner in Both Golf and Life*, had been a cornerstone of Tiger's training since the Orange Bowl Junior International Golf Tournament in 1990, when he fell behind and decided to quit. "I could see it in his body language," Earl wrote. "He threw away a few strokes, got down on himself and blew the tournament in a funk." Fourteen-year-old Tiger wasn't the first phenom to get out of sorts on the course. Tommy Morris had learned his lesson when his father told him, "You throw a club, you lose the hole." Bobby Jones was nineteen, playing the Old Course for the first time, when he took four swings trying to escape a cavernous bunker, tore up his scorecard, and quit. Sixty-nine years later, Earl Woods gave his teen son a lecture. "I really let him have it. 'Who do you think you are? How dare you not try your best? You embarrassed yourself and shamed me.'" In Earl's telling, "Tiger never quit on a golf course again."

Ten summers after that father-son lecture, Tiger parred the next two holes while Dunlap bogeyed the seventeenth. Clinging to a one-shot lead, Tiger mashed a drive at Valhalla's par-5 eighteenth, the hole Nicklaus had nicknamed "Photo Finish." During a third round in which birdies were almost as common as divots—more than half the field broke par, with José María Olazábal firing a 63 to match Johnny Miller's famous 63 at Oakmont almost thirty years before as the best ever score in a major—Tiger was two over par on the back nine, fretting about his position on the leaderboard. He needed a finishing birdie to be sure of a spot in the final pairing the next day. That meant more than prestige to him. Sunday's last twosome has the advantage of seeing how everyone else is doing and knowing what score will win. He wanted that edge.

Dunlap's second shot at the eighteenth dropped into the bunker that guarded the green. Tiger's soaring three-wood approach cleared the bunker and left him a long putt for eagle. After marking his ball, he watched Dunlap pull off one of the sand saves of the week, blasting a floater that stopped inches from the pin. Tiger nodded his approval while the crowd roared, then hit his forty-five-foot eagle putt forty-four feet. Both men tapped in, finishing on the correct note, birdie-birdie. Tiger doffed his cap and shook Dunlap's hand. He would be taking a one-shot lead into Sunday's final round, but a two-under-par 70 had left him at −13 and let a dozen other players into the picture. If not for his mastery of the par-5 holes, he might have been three or four off the lead, but he had made eleven birdies in twelve tries on Nicklaus's par 5s. "You can't go out there every day and hit the ball well," he said. "To shoot a seventy as poorly as I struck it, as badly as I played—I'll take it." As for his double bogey at the twelfth, he joked, "I hit a good third putt." Soon he headed for the range to work with Harmon on tightening his hip turn, seeking the rhythm he'd been missing. He was the last player on the range that evening, still pounding balls as darkness fell.

CBS announcer Jim Nantz stuck around long enough to catch an off-camera moment. "If you win tomorrow," Nantz asked, "and you win at Augusta next year, holding all four titles at once, would you consider that the Grand Slam?"

"I would think that would have to count," Tiger said.

The best major venues often winnow the field down to the world's best players. It did nothing for Valhalla's reputation that the third-round leader's four closest pursuers—Dunlap, plus PGA Tour journeymen Bob May, J. P. Hayes, and Greg Chalmers—had combined for a single Tour victory in their total of forty pro seasons, Hayes's win at the 1998 Buick Classic. As a headline in the Louisville *Courier Journal* would put it, THESE TIGER HUNTERS AREN'T EXACTLY BIG GUNS. Dunlap, who had matched Tiger's 70 to stay within a shot of the lead, reminded reporters that he wasn't the only one with something to prove on Sunday. "There's going to be pressure on everyone," he said. "Tiger's pressure is going for a place in the record books. The pressure on Bob and myself will be the pressure of getting a first win on tour, let alone a major." He was talking about May, whose second-round 66 had vaulted him into a tie for second place.

If Nicklaus was right that Tiger Woods needed challengers, Bob May was one of the least likely.

May was another golf legend from Orange County. Seven years older than Tiger, he had grown up in La Habra, a twenty-minute drive from the Woods family's bungalow in Cypress. Or an hour, depending on traffic. Like Tiger, May was no country club kid. His father ran a Unocal gas station. But after trying the game with borrowed clubs, he proved so precocious that Eddie Merrins, the diminutive "Little Pro" at Los Angeles' posh Bel-Air Country Club, took him on when May was in the sixth grade. Every Sunday, Bob's dad woke before dawn and drove his son forty miles to Bel-Air for a 7:00 a.m. lesson with Merrins, who tutored Tour pros as well as celebrities including Bing Crosby, Fred Astaire, Sean Connery, and future Tiger fan Jack Nicholson.

Merrins had been a world-class player in his time, a three-time All-American at LSU who won a couple pro tournaments but was always a teacher at heart. He had served as an assistant pro under Claude Harmon, Butch's father, at Thunderbird Country Club in

Palm Springs before taking the top job at Bel-Air. In his spare time he coached UCLA's golf team to the 1988 NCAA title. Over the years the genial Merrins mentored Tour pros including Corey Pavin, Steve Pate, and Duffy Waldorf, all UCLA golfers, as well as Vijay Singh and Rickie Fowler.

In 1980, Merrins made eleven-year-old Bob May his littlest student. "Bobby loved to compete, and he loved to work. If he didn't play well," he recalled, "he'd practice until he beat those golf balls into submission." There was no driving range at Bel-Air, so young Bob would hit ball after ball at a tall palm tree on the seventeenth hole. At first he'd aim low, then higher. "The top of the palm's where the coconuts are," Merrins told him, and that tree became a symbol of May's ambitions. "Can you get to the top?" the Little Pro asked. Meaning: Can you max out your talent? Can you hit your best shot when it counts? After that, May could hear Merrins's voice whenever he faced a tough shot: "Can you get the coconuts?"

Two years older than San Diego phenom Phil Mickelson, May set amateur records that Phil and Tiger dreamed of matching. "When I was growing up, Bob May dominated," Mickelson said. "He was everybody's idol."

Tiger's dad knew all about him. "There was a junior player Tiger looked up to for a long, long time," Earl remembered. "This kid was winning every junior championship in Southern California going away. His name was Bob May."

Tiger was seven when he met May at a junior event. "He was seven years younger than me, but he was already a big deal," May recalled. "Phil was a year and a half younger than I was, and Phil and I were always pushing each other. Then here comes this kid everybody's talking about."

In those days, May and Mickelson towered over the new kid. "I looked up to him," Tiger said of May. "I just wanted to hopefully one day win as many tournaments as he did."

At fifteen, May was the youngest-ever qualifier for the U.S. Amateur Championship. He won All-America honors three times at Oklahoma State, leading the Cowboys to the NCAA title in 1991. That was the year he joined Mickelson and David Duval on a star-studded US roster that won the Walker Cup over a Great Britain & Ireland team led by Pádraig Harrington and Paul McGinley.

But May turned out to be one of those precocious athletes who top out early. After looming over Mickelson and Tiger in the junior ranks, he entered college standing five feet, six and a half inches. Four years later, he had grown half an inch. But he could drive the ball 270 yards and hit flag-hunting 6- and 7-irons the way other players hit wedges. With financial backing from Merrins and Bel-Air members including actor Joe Pesci and radio disc jockey Rick "Disco Duck" Dees, May turned pro in 1991. He disappointed his backers by washing out of the dreaded PGA Tour Q-School and spent a decade bouncing around minor-league circuits, making four aces on the Web.com Tour but not much money.

Like Duval, May had back trouble. An X-ray showed that his spinal nerve canal was half the normal size. He endured long rounds of physical therapy that helped him regain the swing Phil and Tiger once envied, but while Mickelson grew to six foot three and Tiger to six foot one, May still stood five foot seven in his spikes. He was long off the tee for a player his size but thirty yards short of Tiger long.

In 1999, he dueled Scotland's Colin Montgomerie down the stretch at the European Tour's British Masters. After twenty-two second-place finishes on pro tours, May edged Monty for his first professional victory. Later that year he made it through Q-School, earning Tour playing privileges for 2000, an achievement that came with a gold money clip embossed with his name and the PGA Tour logo.

Still, he had less name recognition than Scott Dunlap. Balding and sun-splotched after ten years of chasing the sun on half a dozen major and minor tours, May was now making his first ever appearance in the

PGA Championship. The seventy-eight-year-old Merrins had flown in from California to join his smallish galleries. By May's own estimation, "I was pretty much unknown." Yet he outplayed his playing partner Davis Love III on Saturday. The six-foot, three-inch Love drove the ball farther but not a lot farther, averaging 289 yards to May's 276. "I wasn't short off the tee for my size," said May. "I had a strong angle of attack and was long with mid- and short irons." While Love shot a third-round 72 to fall out of contention, May birdied seven of the last dozen holes to card his second straight 66.

"I birdied the eighteenth to come in at twelve under," he remembers. "That's when I thought, 'Wow, I might be in the last group tomorrow.'" Dunlap had also come in at –12, but May had precedence because he'd posted the same score before Dunlap finished. "When he came in at twelve under, I knew I'd be playing with Tiger on Sunday."

By then golf fans knew that Tiger had taped a list of Jack Nicklaus's records to his bedroom wall when he was growing up. But hardly anyone knew that he had done the same with a list of Bob May's achievements. "When I heard about that, it bothered me a little," May said. "I was like 'Dude, do your own thing.' Later on, I started to think of it as an honor."

Asked about playing in the final group with Tiger on Sunday, he sounded like Dunlap the day before. "I'm not supposed to win tomorrow," May said. "He is, and if everyone wants to say I'm just some guy playing with Tiger Woods, that's fine. Maybe everyone will know me a little better tomorrow night."

May enjoyed a big dinner with friends on Saturday night. "I was staying with a friend of a friend, and a bunch of my buddies flew out from Vegas." For the fourth night in a row they ate at Rafferty's, a Louisville steakhouse. May had the marinated rib eye, a Rafferty's specialty sizzled with soy sauce and pineapple juice, the same meal he'd enjoyed every night that week, "because it seemed to be working so far."

He slept soundly that night. "I wasn't afraid," May remembered a quarter century later. "I told myself, 'He's the longest hitter in the world, so he'll be playing a totally different course than you. But it's not a slugfest.' I thought about all the guys who'd gone against him and they collapsed in the last round. I knew I couldn't match him off the tee, but I was a good ball striker. We all are, really—nobody gets to the Tour on luck. I think it's the mental part of the game that separates great players from the really good ones, and it was Tiger's mental game, on top of his physical game, that made him superior to everybody else. That's what I was up against."

SIXTEEN
MAYDAY

The leader arrived for Sunday's final round flanked by security guards, his eyes hidden behind white-framed sunglasses. Tiger was expressionless, getting into the mindset he called his "tournament armor." On his way to the practice range, he passed hundreds of fans reaching toward him and calling his name.

There were no crowds waiting for Bob May when he drove up to the clubhouse in his courtesy car. He hauled his own golf bag out of the trunk. The only sign of his co-starring role in the day's drama was a lone CBS cameraman shooting B-roll. May nodded to him and said, "Hello."

Most experts viewed him as another day's Dunlap. "At least for today, Bob May will be known as The Golfer Playing with Tiger," one newspaper reported. Jim Nantz opened Sunday's CBS telecast with a backhanded compliment for the underdog, recapping a third round that he said "featured some incredible golf by the likes of Bob May."

Swing coach Harmon and caddie Williams liked the way their man was striking the ball on the range. Even so, "Tigah," as Kiwi Stevie pronounced his name, "was incredibly nervous." Nicklaus and Hogan would never have admitted to feeling jittery before the last round of a major, but Tiger was forthright about it. "If you're not nervous on a day like this," he said, "you're not alive."

In a prerecorded talk with CBS's David Feherty, he had taken the long view. "I'm only twenty-four years old," he said. "Hopefully I can compete out here with the young boys for another twenty-six years" before qualifying for the senior tour in the far-off year of 2025. By then, he predicted, "Some of the guys will be a lot bigger and stronger. The equipment will be different, but hopefully I'll still hang in with my little craftiness."

May was modest in his own pre-round talks. "Tiger's obviously the favorite," he said. "I just want to go out there and have a respectable round of golf. If it's good enough, great. If not, I did my best."

Tiger strode to the first tee not in his usual bright Sunday red but in a burgundy shirt with a black collar. His tailored black slacks were perfectly pleated, his black spikes polished to their usual mirror sheen. In the four years since he began advising Nike on what he wanted to wear on the course, he had turned "golf fashion" from an oxymoron into a growth industry.

The challenger, six inches shorter and less streamlined, wore wrinkled tan slacks, a gray shirt, and a white PING cap. "TV announcers liked to say I looked drab," May recalled later. "Maybe they were right."

Tiger ate a protein bar while they waited to tee off. A blue-suited PGA executive introduced the last twosome's arrival: "From Windermere, Florida, the 1999 and defending champion, Tiger Woods!"

From the start, Tiger had no intention of playing safe off the tee as he had done at St. Andrews, where position mattered more than power. Valhalla's 446-yard first hole offered long hitters a chance to cut the dogleg by going over a stand of trees more than two hundred

Journeyman Bob May battled Tiger on Sunday.

yards from the tee. He aimed that way and swung hard, smoking a high drive at the highest branches.

"My first thought was *He's yanked it left*," May remembered. "My next thought was *Oh, my goodness*."

Tiger's drive carried over the trees and bounded onto the fairway 324 yards from the tee.

Now it was May's turn. His introduction was brief: "From Las Vegas, Nevada, Bob May."

He teed up a liquid-core Titleist Professional, the ball most Tour pros still played. Unlike his opponent, whose Nike balls came from the factory stamped with his name, May was still accustomed to placing an identifying mark on his: he circled the numeral 1 under the Titleist logo.

Despite his small stature, May was no plinker, averaging 272 yards off the tee. He had a loop at the top of his swing, a quirk that led one golf writer to report that his swing "at its apex resembles a man banging on the ceiling with a brush." Purists called the move unorthodox, even ugly, but Eddie Merrins had encouraged him to stick with it, saying "It works for you, Bobby." May remembered a day on the range when he sought a second opinion. "Butch Harmon was there, and I asked him to look at my swing. Should I lose the loop at the top? And Butch said, 'If you change that, you're stupid. That loop is your signature. It's who you are.'"

May swung hard at Valhalla, bringing the head of his driver down from the curlicue at the top and smacking his Titleist to the fairway sixty yards short of Tiger's drive. "My ball rolled past the tree he'd gone over. I had a seven-iron into the green. He had a little flip sand wedge."

Still, they both made 4 at the first. Earl Woods, standing behind the green, pursed his lips as his son's birdie try slipped past. No skin.

Earl was no more pleased by what he saw at the par-5 second, where his son overcooked a 239-yard 4-iron that bounced into greenside rough and took four to get down, missing a six-footer for par. It wasn't like Tiger to give strokes away. He hadn't parred the hole all week, having made three birdies and now a 6, while May birdied to jump from one shot behind to one ahead. TV viewers saw a reshuffled CBS leaderboard sponsored by Pfizer, with a blue pill above the players' names:

BOB MAY −13
TIGER WOODS −12

At the third, Tiger's seven-foot putt to tie swooshed over the lip. The most telegenic golfer since Palmer held his putting pose for almost ten seconds. He settled for another par. At the fourth, May muscled an approach from thick bluegrass to birdie range, a shot that took strength as well as pinpoint control. Despite his relative shortcomings off the tee, he was almost as long as Tiger with his irons, partly because he intentionally delofted them a little, partly because he attacked the ball with a steep slash. "That shot at the fourth hole helped me relax," he said later. "I thought, *My game's here today.*" Tiger grazed the hole with another birdie try. May holed his birdie putt to go two shots ahead.

CBS announcer Gary McCord, following the final twosome, had a novel thought: "Tiger's got his doubts now."

Both players parred the fifth. At the sixth, May pushed a short par putt for his first bogey since Thursday, leaving Tiger a four-footer to get back within a stroke. But the cups seemed to be shrinking on him. He lipped out his putt to make a bogey of his own. Three over par for the day, he spent a long moment glaring at the hole as if it owed him one. Earl Woods shook his head. Tiger was still two behind, tied for second at −11 with Olazábal, Bjørn, and Greg Chalmers, with Franklin Langham and Stuart Appleby another stroke back. Appleby, an Isleworth neighbor of Woods, O'Meara, and their fellow celebrities, hadn't counted on being within a shot of his friend's score with a dozen holes to play. Earlier in the week, when a writer asked what he'd need to shoot to win the PGA Championship, Appleby said, "Tiger Woods."

Valhalla's 597-yard seventh hole favored Tiger. His 360-yard drive, followed by a 4-iron from 237, gave him a tap-in birdie while May settled for par.

BOB MAY −13
TIGER WOODS −12

At the par-3 eighth, Tiger knocked in a fourteen-footer to get to −13. May settled over a birdie putt of his own. With a cross-handed grip, his left hand low, he took a couple of practice strokes, then started the putt on its way.

It slid past the hole. They were tied.

Standing on the ninth tee, looking uphill toward the green and Valhalla's clubhouse, Tiger and May waited for Dunlap and J. P. Hayes to move out of range. Dunlap's putter had gone AWOL again; he and Hayes would finish back in the pack. May applied lip balm while the minutes passed. Steve Williams pulled the cover off Tiger's driver. That furry black-and-orange-striped head cover was already the most popular accessory in golf history. Starting in 2003, it would co-star in a series of Nike commercials, with "Frank" the head cover voiced by a little-known actor named Paul Giamatti. (Larry David hadn't gotten the role after insisting that Tiger play a round of golf with him first.) Frank was literally frank in the ads, backtalking a young man so many others tiptoed around. In any case, Tiger's personal driver cover was unique. The words *Rák jak Mæ*, Thai for "Love from Mother," were hand embroidered inside.

When the fairway was clear, he smacked a 326-yard drive. May couldn't match that sort of power, but with the other ball sitting like a pearl in the distance, he stepped up and belted his Titleist 294 yards. "Good drive," Tiger told him.

TV viewers saw them walking to their tee shots under a graphic comparing winning margins in majors. Nicklaus had won his eighteen majors by a grand total of forty-four strokes. Tiger had won his first four by a total of thirty-six strokes, dominating almost everyone paired with him. During his victories at Pebble Beach and St. Andrews, he had drubbed his playing partners by an average of six shots per eighteen holes, leading *Sports Illustrated* to joke that being paired with him made other pros so nervous that a round with Tiger Woods could be "a good walk soiled." But May wasn't backing down. He matched Tiger's par at the ninth. They were tied with nine to play. "We'd been chitchatting quite a bit up until then, catching up on our junior days. 'Do you remember So-and-So?' 'Oh, you mean Harry from La Jolla?' Stuff like that," May remembered. "But the talk pretty much stopped on the back nine. It was business time."

At the par-5 tenth, Tiger hit a towering 2-iron off the tee. May couldn't help thinking, *That might be the best two-iron I ever saw.* His own 280-yard drive left him short of Tiger's ball. With 271 yards to the flag, he began his fidgety pre-shot routine, thinking, *Swing the handle*, his mentor Merrins's mantra. Choking up on his 3-wood, he placed the clubhead an inch behind the ball. He waggled once, twice, three times, and then swung, torquing from the loop at the top through a smooth hip turn on the way down, his wrists firing the clubface to contact, the ball taking off on a rising line toward the green.

It fell a yard short, hopping into one of the deepest bunkers on the course.

Tiger hit his approach into the same bunker but caught a better lie. May was still away, trying not to think of the rotten luck that had left Tiger with a fluffy lie and him with such a puzzler. With the ball below his feet, he would have to loft his Titleist just over the bunker's lip and land it on a downslope softly enough to keep it from running twenty feet past—all with twelve feet of green to work with. Par would be a decent play from where he was, but with Tiger likely to get up and down for birdie, a par would cost May the lead. As he recalled, "It wasn't the day to play conservative." He risked a delicate out that cleared the lip by inches, kissed the green, and rolled to a stop eight feet past the hole. Then he sank the putt to match Tiger's up-and-down birdie.

At the par-3 eleventh, Tiger's 8-iron shot flew the green. Williams would keep that in mind. It was a sign of how pumped up his player was getting. A touchy pitch to four feet looked like it would give Tiger a chance to save par and stay tied—until May's downhill twenty-five-footer tumbled into the cup. Tiger, no longer a co-leader, had to sink his nervy putt to prevent another two-shot swing.

BOB MAY −15
TIGER WOODS −14

The twelfth is the hardest par at Valhalla, an uphill par-4 to an elevated green where club members often wrote 7's and X's on their cards. Tiger had double-bogeyed it the day before. Now he stung a 2-iron to the fairway. May spent a moment imagining what a luxury it must be to hit an iron off the tee on a 467-yard par 4. He knocked a 286-yard drive five yards short of Tiger's ball.

They were leaving the twelfth tee when Tiger pulled his caddie aside. "Hey, Stevie, I want to tell you something," he said. "I know this guy. He won't back down."

A couple minutes later, May swatted a 181-yard 8-iron shot that dropped like a dart two feet from the flagstick. Tiger called over to him, "Good shot!" Then he stuck a 9-iron to birdie range. His fourth birdie in six holes left him a shot behind May, who tapped in for his third birdie in a row. With half a dozen holes to play, May was starting to like his chances of pulling off one of the biggest upsets in golf history.

Tiger's birdie try at the thirteenth slipped under the hole—his sixth near miss of the day. He flipped his putter into the air and caught the offending clubhead as it spun back to him. If even half his near misses had fallen, he'd have been two shots ahead instead of one behind. His concerns multiplied at the par-3 fourteenth, where May's 4-iron cleared a greenside bunker by a whisper. His ball nipped the fringe, began rolling like a putt, and gave the hole a look on its way past as the crowd's noise reached new decibels. Had his tee shot landed an inch to the right, it might have been an ace. As it was, it stopped five feet from the cup. Of the eighty shots hit at the par-3 fourteenth that day, May's was closest to the hole.

Tiger's tee shot looked like it might clang off the flagstick like Nicklaus's 1-iron at Pebble in 1972 and win closest to the pin for the day. It flew past, missing the flag by inches, then hopped and checked back to ten feet. As he and May headed to the green, waving to acknowledge the crowd, a leather-lunged fan yelled, "Tiger, Tiger!" Another one shouted, "What about Bob?"

Tiger rolled in a slider for deuce and gave Williams a fist bump. For the moment, the leaders were tied. May stepped up to his five-footer, aiming half a ball left of the cup. Too much—until his ball broke a hair to the right at the last, catching just enough cup to swirl around the lip until it was hanging on the right lip, where it finally gave up and fell in.

"It was birdie for birdie, shot for shot—as good as it gets," Tiger said later.

After a safe drive at the fifteenth, May had 168 yards into the wind to a tucked pin guarded by Valhalla's Brush Run Creek. A sucker pin, it appeared to be, but May felt so dialed in that he went right at it, risking bogey or worse. He took a skillet-sized divot and struck a 7-iron that would have splashed into the creek had it started a tenth of a degree farther right. Instead it almost landed in the cup, leaving a dent in the green eighteen inches away. The crowd whooped and cheered. May would have a four-foot putt for his fifth birdie in six holes.

"This guy only sees the flag!" Ken Venturi told CBS viewers.

Tiger pulled his approach. He hated the shot from the instant it left his club and hated it more as it drifted left of his target and bounced into a hollow behind the green. After conferring with Williams, he chose to putt from there. He banged his ball uphill through the fringe and hurried after it, climbing to the green in time to see his ball drift fifteen feet right of the hole. He was still away. He was about to fall two strokes behind with three holes to play. Or would it be three behind? Either way, he blocked out every thought but one: "I had to make that putt. If I miss that putt and he makes, he's three up with three to go. But if I make mine, it will make his putt a little bit longer."

He stroked it straight in.

May was still two ahead as he rolled his four-foot birdie putt toward paydirt. And yanked it to the left. It never had a chance. The latest make-miss changed everything.

BOB MAY −17
TIGER WOODS −16

Williams gave Tiger a look and said, "Ballgame's on!"

The par-4 sixteenth was Valhalla's second-toughest par that week, with the field averaging 4.24. May, who had been splitting fairways with medium-range missiles, hooked his drive into trouble. Was this going to be where he fell short like everyone else who went up against

Tiger Woods? May bit his lip and looked at the ground while Tiger fired a 2-iron that was shorter than May's ball. That was a tactic: Had he driven past May's ball, May would hit next. This way, with his ball farther from the hole, Tiger would hit his next shot before it was May's turn. He struck a 7-iron that checked up beside the pin, leaving May to figure out an escape from his latest rotten lie.

He could get an iron through the rough to his ball, but even a Tigerish shot might hit one of the trees blocking his line to the green. He decided to deloft an 8-iron and try a power hook like Tiger's curveball through the woods at the twelfth hole the day before. It was a daring play, trying to tame Hogan's rattlesnake on the sixteenth hole on the last day of a major. A near miss could leave him lying two behind a poplar 150 feet yards from the green, with a chance to make 5 at best, 6 or 7 at worst, while Tiger had a fifteen-foot putt for a 3.

Waggle, waggle, waggle, bang! May's delofted 8-iron swerved around the poplar toward the green. It caught the front edge and rolled to within twenty-five feet of the pin. One witness swore you could hear the crowd from Indiana.

Tiger two-putted for par. May two-putted for par. "He's still got a one-shot lead on the best golfer in the universe," announcer McCord said.

The uphill seventeenth measured 422 yards. May hooked another drive. A hook can be a sign of lower-body fatigue; was he running out of gas? "Maybe," he admitted years later. "It was a long round. I might have been tired. I got a little short and quick with that one." But he kept his chin up. "I'd been over there before and still made par."

Tiger lashed a drive of 325 yards, the day's longest at the seventeenth. His ball was sitting up in the fairway while May's nestled in heavy rough with the grain of the bluegrass against him. He was almost twice as far from the green as Tiger. Again he chose his 8-iron. This time, with a more upright swing than he'd used for his intentional hook on the previous hole, he slashed almost straight down through the spinach, launching a 171-yard flier that sailed over Tiger's head. Tiger looked up, following the ball's flight with a hint of a smile on his face, knowing a hell of a shot when he saw one.

May's latest miracle carried to the green and came to rest forty feet from the hole. Raising a hand to the clamoring crowd, he began walking toward Tiger's ball, far ahead in the fairway. It took him almost a minute to get there.

There would be some debate about how far Tiger had to the flag. According to press reports, the distance was 96 yards. His caddie agreed, more or less.

"What have we got here, Stevie?" Tiger asked.

Williams would return to this moment in his book *Out of the Rough*: "I'd measured it—95 yards—and I knew that if I told Tiger 95 he'd want a sand wedge, but I wanted him to opt for his lob wedge." He risked the tournament—and probably his job—by deciding to psych his player into the right club selection. Knowing how amped Tiger was, Williams gave him the wrong yardage. "'Ninety yards,' I said. 'Lob wedge.'" It was the first time he'd dared to try such a tactic. With a bunker waiting to gobble up an approach that fell a yard short, it could have been his last. If it went wrong, "I would have been fired. But if I'd given him the correct yardage, we would have ended up in a debate over the club. It was easier to lie."

With his heart in his throat, he watched Tiger's 60-degree wedge shot spin into the sky. It came down like a raindrop less than a yard from the pin. "He hit it to two feet!" The caddie's gamble had paid off.

Retelling the story in later years, Williams would remember different yardages. "I told him ninety-eight yards." Or was it ninety-two? Whatever the exact distance, the number on Tiger's scorecard would be 3.

May lagged to two feet to save his 4. Hundreds of fans hurried from the seventeenth green to join the crowd lining the last fairway, where the gallery was already twenty deep.

BOB MAY −17
TIGER WOODS −17

The eighteenth favored Tiger as much as any other hole at Valhalla. The Tour leader in scoring average on par 5s had birdied Nicklaus's 542-yard finisher on Thursday, Friday, and Saturday while May went par, par, par. Tiger's 3-wood off the tee was longer than May's 276-yard drive. They walked to their tee shots, nodding and waving to their record-setting gallery, then waited for Dunlap and Hayes to putt out ahead of them. The penultimate pairing had started the day two shots off the lead but soon fell off the leaderboard. Dunlap saved par at the eighteenth for a final-round 75, a tie for ninth place, and a paycheck of $112,500, while Hayes shot 76 to tie for fifteenth, worth $56,200.

At last the green was clear. May was away, holding a 3-wood with 266 yards to the flag. The crowd of thirty thousand hushed, then cheered as he knocked it to the front edge of the saddle-shaped green, becoming the second player all day to reach the final green in two. Still he was eighty feet from the pin, with a swale to putt over. That gave Tiger a chance to get his hands on the Wanamaker Trophy.

These were the moments he relished. It was crunch time with the world watching, Sunday in a major with the trophy at stake. It was a chance to go all in, shoot the works, empty the tank, and live up to the rest of the sports clichés he grew up with. Some of them were true to his experience. He still believed that if he prepared and worked and focused and thought and tried hard enough, the ball would do his bidding.

He had 233 yards uphill to a flagstick that looked like a toothpick at the top of the rise that led to the green. He swung all out. His 2-iron shot arrowed toward the yellow flag. Watching it in flight, he leaned left as if to pull the ball that way. A helpful hop off the mound near the hole could give him a kick-in eagle putt, making this shot one of the most famous anybody ever hit, the 2-iron that clinched a third straight major. It looked perfect . . .

Until the ball drifted a couple feet to the right. It carried 230 yards and came down on the wrong side of the mound, a yard from perfect. It kicked farther right and slid more than twenty-five feet away.

May was still alive. If they both two-putted, they would go to a playoff. May couldn't afford to baby his thirty-yard lag putt, not with a steep swale to climb on the way, a swale that was taller than he was. He looked over his line. He walked from his ball to the hole to see the putt from there. It took him twenty-eight steps. He returned to the ball and went into his pre-putt routine: smooth practice strokes, touching the face of his putter after the last one. Then he sent his putt up the rise.

He overcooked it. Cheers turned to groans as May's Titleist barreled past the hole, all the way off the top of the green. "I was thinking, *Oh, my gosh, I can't believe I hit that bad of a putt.* I was thinking the big hill would kill the speed, but I hit it so hard it just kept going." With the PGA Championship on the line, he had missed an eighty-foot putt by almost twenty feet.

Tiger shot Williams a smile. Unless May had another miracle up his sleeve, two putts would put Tiger's name on the Wanamaker Trophy for the second year in a row.

Tiger's putt was no bargain. It was technically for eagle, but from his position, three putts were more likely than one. All day, no one had sunk one from the side of the mound that guarded the hole. He would need to send his ball up to the crest of the rise, where it would start downhill and break hard to the left.

He gave the putt just enough speed to clear the mound and begin trickling down the other side while Williams waved it toward the hole.

Tiger's putt stopped six feet from the cup. Disadvantage May. With his ball off the green, he couldn't even mark and clean it. "I hadn't looked at the leaderboard all day," he recalled, "but now I did look." He saw two names at the top: WOODS and MAY. "We were five ahead of everybody. And I thought, *You got yourself to this moment. Just make sure you get the ball to the hole.*"

Tiger stood beside Williams, staring at the sky. He turned toward May in time to see him settle over the ball with his cross-handed grip, wipe the putter face with his left hand, and send his last-chance putt trundling downhill.

"I played it outside left," May remembered. "My first thought was *I didn't hit it hard enough.*"

"Not gonna be," Venturi told 13 million TV viewers.

"It kept going, though," said May. "It was about three feet from the hole when I thought, *It's gonna get there.*" He straightened up out of his putting stance, watching his putt curl half an inch to the left on its last roll. With the crowd roaring, it caught the edge of the cup and fell in.

He wasn't sure how to react to making the putt of his life. "I thought about running around the green like Hale Irwin at Medinah, high-fiving the fans," May recalled. "Maybe if I'd done that, Tiger would have to wait, and you never know what might happen. Maybe he'd miss his putt. But that would be gamesmanship. That would be fine for some guys, but it wasn't me."

Instead, he nodded thanks to the crowd's ovation. He picked his ball from the cup. He stepped back to watch Tiger try a putt to stay alive and send them to a playoff.

"And his putt wasn't easy. There was a second when I thought, *If he misses, I win.* Then I thought, *Don't think like that!*"

The left half of the cup was white in late-day sun, the right half in shadow. Tiger went through his pre-putt routine while his ailing sixty-eight-year-old father stood behind the green. "Trust it," Earl whispered. "Trust it, Tiger."

The line was just left of the sunny side of the hole. Tiger's putt was a tester, a slippery six-footer. It was a test of skill and courage—misplaced courage, it looked like at first, as his Nike ball stayed on the high side for an instant before it took the break, caught the edge, and disappeared.

The crowd erupted. Tiger punched the sky. He and May had both shot 31 on the back nine to tie for the championship at eighteen under par, a tournament record.

They doffed caps and shook hands. "Nice putt," Tiger told May. "You, too."

They reported to the scorer's table, where May got a surprise. "I didn't realize we were going to a three-hole playoff." That year, for the first time, the PGA had switched its overtime format from sudden death to aggregate scores on the sixteenth, seventeenth, and eighteenth, which happened to be three of the longest holes on the course.

May signed for his third consecutive 66. He nodded to the greatest golfer in the universe. "See you at sixteen," he said.

SEVENTEEN

THRILLA AT VALHALLA

The playoff would be three holes of "medal play," a term that dates to days when Scottish aristocrats vied for their golfing societies' gold and silver medals. As the game grew, their match play tourneys began dragging on for days. In 1759, the Society of St. Andrews Golfers introduced a faster way of keeping score: "Whoever puts in the ball at the fewest strokes over the field . . . shall be declared and sustained victor." In medal play, often called stroke play, the golfer's goal is not to win the most holes against a single opponent but to take fewer strokes overall.

Sudden death is pure pressure, but the PGA's new playoff format was more of an endurance test. Three holes of medal play would call for another hour's worth of staying power from players who had already hiked more than seven miles in 80-degree heat. May's two-shot lead and Tiger's back-nine PB&B sandwich were both distant memories. After five hours of bringing full focus to every shot, club choice, and putt, every *thought*, they had ten minutes to recharge and refocus.

Tournament officials drove the players back to the sixteenth hole. Riding behind Tiger in their cart, Williams asked about his do-or-die putt to force a playoff. "What were you thinking?"

Tiger thought that was funny. He said, "Steve, it's a six-footer down the hill. My mom could hole that putt. I'm Tiger Woods—I'm supposed to hole it."

At the sixteenth tee, the players shook hands again. To determine who would hit first, a tournament official tore a sheet of paper in half, wrote a 1 on one piece and a 2 on the other, folded them, and dropped them into a hat. Tiger reached into the hat and unfolded the piece with a 2 on it. May would have the honor in the playoff.

He considered that a good omen. He could match Tiger, he figured, in everything except sheer power off the tee and preferred to knock his middling-distance drive into the fairway before Tiger unloaded a tape-measure shot. May waggled. He reminded himself to "swing the handle." He began his swing, taking his driver back slowly before delivering the clubhead from the loop at the top along the same strong angle of attack that had gotten him into a playoff for the PGA Championship.

"And I hooked it. Again!" He watched his drive bounce into snaggly rough a few paces from the horrid lie he'd had on the same hole in regulation. Then he watched Tiger step up and outdrive him with a 2-iron.

With the sinking sun painting trees' shadows on the fairway, May visualized another unlikely escape. He could still make 4, possibly even 3, if he could draw his second shot two hundred yards from the rough and clear a greenside bunker. He waggled, picturing the low, curving trajectory he needed, and swung, but the grass got between the club and his Titleist. The ball fell thirty yards short of the green and hopped into more rough.

May trudged to the fairway and stood behind Tiger, who had 197 yards to the flag. When they'd played the hole an hour and a half before, he'd also had 197. Precision like that would remind history buffs of a century-old Harry Vardon story. Vardon was said to hate playing the same course twice in the same day because his second-round shots kept landing in the divots from his first.

Tiger's sky-scraping 7-iron shot came to a landing on the green's top tier, twenty feet from the pin. With May up to his ankles in the rough, it was the ideal approach, a calibrated blend of skill and caution that left him a birdie putt and a near-certain par, while May would need another highlight-reel escape to get up and down for his own par. Tiger's 7-iron shot was the golf equivalent of a grandmaster's saying "Check."

May's latest recovery shot came out of the rough on a humpbacked arc. "It came out perfect, without much spin," he remembered, "and the green was firm." His low pitch "started tracking toward the hole. *This might be good*, I thought. It kept going, and I thought, *This might be better than good*." The ball climbed two tiers of Nicklaus's green, curling closer to the hole. Two feet away, it looked sure to reach the flagstick, but it ran out of steam three inches short.

Tiger laughed out loud. "Great shot!" he called across the fairway. With a shy smile, May raised his right hand to the clamoring gallery. His recovery would keep Tiger from taking the lead with a cozy lag and tap-in for par. Now Tiger needed to sink his twenty-footer to gain a stroke.

He went into his pre-putt routine, taking a pair of practice strokes. Like his famous head cover, his putter was one of a kind. Per his instructions, the putter maker Scotty Cameron had drilled a pair of holes in the head of Tiger's Cameron Newport 2 GSS putter (GSS for German stainless steel) so that it weighed four grams less than other models. Four grams is the weight of a sheet of printer paper. Tiger tested the lighter version and liked it better. Now he eyed the cup on the first playoff hole. He pulled the putter back and accelerated it smoothly to impact with his slightly inside-to-square putting stroke.

The ball began breaking left—too far left, it appeared, until it bent back enough to give it a chance.

Tiger stalked it toward the hole. McCord, the mustachioed TV announcer, was watching from behind the green. He had been walking with the final group all afternoon, whispering into his CBS mic. A southern Californian, McCord remembered when May "used to beat everybody a long time ago." What impressed him at Valhalla was "May's sheer doggedness. And Tiger's, too! May was being what we'd sometimes call a nuisance in this David-and-Goliath spectacle that just kept getting better. It was like a prizefight. Bob May just won't go away. He's going toe to toe with Mike Tyson, and here comes the next uppercut."

Seeing Tiger start toward the hole while his ball was still rolling, McCord told TV viewers, "He's running after it!"

Tiger pointed at the ball as he chased it toward the cup. "He runs after the ball, pointing at it," McCord recalled. "I'd never seen that from Tiger." In fact, Tiger had pointed at big putts before, but never in a tournament. O'Meara had seen him do it in their sometimes-heated practice rounds, and to a player of O'Meara's generation, it looked a little bush. No one could picture Hogan or Nicklaus showing off like that. "But it sure made for good TV," McCord said. With Tiger chasing it, pointing his finger, the ball caught the left edge and fell for a birdie that topped May's miraculous par. "The crowd went nuts. But what struck me was what Tiger did next. He picks the ball out of the hole and practically sprints to the next tee. It was *Game on, let's go!*"

May would swear that Tiger's run-and-gun putt "didn't bother me. Was he showing me up? You could say that, but I wouldn't. It's not something I would do, but it's different if Tiger does it. He's a great player and a showman. He gets excited out there, and he shows it."

They stood on the tee at the second playoff hole with the crowd buzzing. Tiger held the lead for the first time in five hours—and promptly blocked his drive into the gallery. Advantage May—until he yanked yet another hook into trouble to the left. After their twin 31s during one of the best back-nine duels in major-championship history, the duelists were knocking balls sideways.

The crowd parted to make way for Tiger, fans patting his back as he and Williams passed through them to track down his ball. There was no conventional shot from the spot where they found it, not with several trees' overhanging branches blocking his way to the green. After conferring with Williams, he opted for what was becoming the unofficial trouble shot of the 2000 PGA, a punched 8-iron.

Marshals moved spectators out of the way. Williams waved at a straggler, calling "Move back, mate!"

Setting up with the ball back in his stance, Tiger smacked a low line drive—lower than he meant to—straight toward a patch of gnarly rough that could bring double bogey into play. Lucky for him, his ball skipped off a cart path and bounced over the rough, but it came in low and hot enough to run through the green to a hollow behind it. There was no easy up and down from there.

The crowd on May's side of the fairway urged him on. "Go, Bob!" "C'mon, Bobby!" His 9-iron shot rode a high line into a greenside bunker. The second playoff hole was looking more like a drunken bar fight than a heavyweight title bout. Tiger putted onto the green, his Nike ball sliding to a stop six feet from the cup. May's bunker shot checked up two feet closer. They both made knee-knockers to finish the hole with a pair of scrambling pars, and there was one hole left to play.

Tiger had the honor at their return to the long eighteenth. With a one-shot lead and a chance to assert his advantage, he proved once again that golf can be hard even if you're Tiger Woods. He got stuck on the downswing, his old swing flaw, busting a drive that might have made Hogan reach for the Pepto-Bismol. It started left and went farther left. Tiger couldn't watch. He shut his eyes. *Not now!*

His tee ball streaked over trees and bounced between spectators, so far left that it disappeared from CBS camera range only to pop up a moment later, hopping down a cart path.

For the moment, May was in the driver's seat. But he swerved again, hooking his tee ball for the third time in three playoff holes. He gave the tee-box turf a halfhearted kick. But Tiger's power may have given May an advantage. His drive wasn't nearly as far left as Tiger's, partly because he couldn't hit the ball as far. He thought that might give him an edge until he saw where his opponent had ended up.

Tiger's miles-left drive had somehow bounced and rolled down a cart path out of trouble to one of the luckiest lies of any year. Ken Venturi, watching Tiger's tee shot on a monitor in the CBS booth, narrated a replay. "It could have been someone hit it with their hand," he said. "It was going into deep, deep rough, and this kid kept it from going in there." The video shows a young fan in a white T-shirt and gray shorts running toward Tiger's ball just as it bounds out of view behind a stand of reeds. Suddenly the ball changes direction. The fan runs after it. Moments later, golf's version of a Zapruder film shows a Black spectator in a white shirt, a red package under his arm, pointing accusingly at the kid running after the ball.

Did the kid knock Tiger's ball out of trouble? As golf writer Bob Harig noted, "Conspiracy theorists believe it was thrown into play by a spectator." According to Steve Williams, "There was a lot of talk that the ball might have got some help from someone in the gallery. When you watch the replay, you can't tell."

A PGA official in the area saw no interference. Tiger walked through knee-high rough to find his ball sitting nicely on hardpan. If not the biggest break he got that summer, it was one of them. If his ball had wound up in the reeds, he would have had no shot. He would have been forced to declare his ball unplayable and take a one-stroke penalty, giving back his one-shot advantage in the playoff. But the rub of the green or the unseen hand of the fan had worked in his favor.

He knocked his second shot into light rough 150 yards short of the green—the right play with a one-shot lead.

May's lie was worse. His second shot bounced into heavy rough 130 yards short of the green. If this was a heavyweight title fight, he and Tiger were staggering through the fifteenth round. Two hours before, they had been the second and third players all day to reach the eighteenth green in two. Now they were both lying two, more than a hundred yards short.

I need a birdie to have a chance, May thought.

Tiger had a pitching wedge from 150 yards. He took a practice swing. For a few seconds, the only sound was the distant whir of the MetLife blimp's engines 1,500 feet above. His wedge shot—the clincher?—was on target until it fell a yard short of the green and kicked into the front bunker. He couldn't believe it. With two chances to win the tournament on Valhalla's finishing hole, both times with an iron in his hands, he had missed twice.

I'm still alive, May thought. With his ball below his feet in the rough, he wedged a high parabola toward the green. His ball was headed for the mound in the middle of the green that had sent Tiger's 2-iron sideways an hour before. If it landed on the uphill side of the mound, it would kick to the left, leaving May a short birdie putt while Tiger faced an up-and-down from the bunker for his par. If May birdied and Tiger bogeyed, the make-miss would make Bob May the PGA champion.

Instead his wedge shot missed his target by a yard. It caught the right-hand side of the mound and ran twenty feet downhill. May was left with a long birdie putt from the worst part of the green. If Tiger got up and down from the bunker, as he'd done three times that week, May would need to hole his twenty-five-footer to send their three-hole playoff into sudden death.

Tiger had a good lie in the bunker. May wasn't surprised to see him send a spray of sand onto the front edge of the green, followed closely by his Nike ball, which hopped and stopped eighteen inches from the pin.

The crowd howled. Tiger pumped his fist. He high-fived Williams.

May had one last chance, a long putt that would have to climb the mound and slip down the other side. Tiger had missed by six feet from a similar spot in regulation. No one had made a putt from that part of the green all day.

"I have to make it," May said out loud.

He went through his unvarying pre-putt routine, running his fingers across the face of his putter after his last practice stroke. He took a breath. He started his ball up the hill. He watched it clear the mound and start bending left. A foot away, it was headed for the heart of the hole. Six inches away, it bent left and died an inch short of sudden death.

It was over. May tapped in, getting out of Tiger's way. Tiger tapped in. He hugged Williams, then turned to May, who doffed his cap and offered the customary handshake, only to be surprised to get a hug instead.

"Great playing!" Tiger told him. They left the green to chants of "Tiger, Tiger."

The winner lifted the sterling silver Wanamaker Trophy, showing it to the crowd, and gave it a smooch. The first PGA champion to successfully defend his title since Denny Shute in 1937, Tiger Woods had won three majors in nine weeks, all with record-breaking scores. No golfer since Hogan in 1953 had won three professional majors in a year. No one since Tommy Morris, who swung hickory sticks at the dawn of the modern game in the 1860s, had won four out of five.

"We're seeing a guy play at a level we have never seen," Ernie Els said. "And he's only twenty-four."

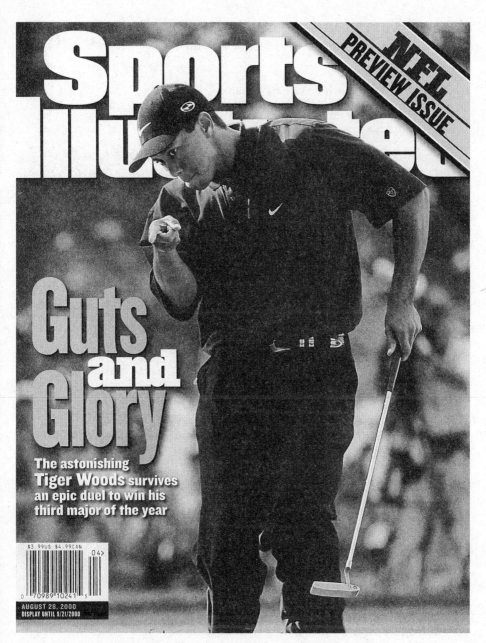

Sports Illustrated

Guts and Glory

The astonishing
Tiger Woods survives
an epic duel to win his
third major of the year

$3.99US $4.99CAN

0 70989 10241 5

04>

AUGUST 28, 2000
DISPLAY UNTIL 9/21/2000

The champion's putt in the playoff kept the Tiger Slam alive.

"I've played like that once in my life," said Nick Price, recalling his six-shot victory at the 1994 PGA Championship. "Tiger plays like that in every major. I feel sorry for the young guys. They'll have to play almost perfect golf to ever win a major."

Butch Harmon had a word of warning for Tour pros: "Tiger thinks he can get better, and I think he's right."

The tournament's host had his own view of Tiger's latest triumph. "He's better than the other players by a greater margin than I was," Nicklaus told reporters.

Sports Illustrated's Dan Jenkins wrote, "I never thought I'd see the day when a *golfer* would be the world's most famous athlete."

Tiger called Sunday's twenty-one holes "incredible. Hats off to Bob—he played his heart out."

May felt drained. "I put up a good fight," he said. He and Tiger had both taken 79 strokes over twenty-one holes in one of the best battles in modern memory. "The moral, I guess, is that if you're up against the greatest player in the world, spotting him more than twenty yards on every drive, don't give him a one-shot lead going into the day."

Tiger left the course in a stretch limousine. May went looking for Eddie Merrins, who hugged his prize pupil. "Great job. What a day!" the Little Pro said. "You almost got the coconuts."

EIGHTEEN
WHAT SLUMP?

Tiger's run-and-gun putt in the PGA playoff was the golf photo of the year. It became the cover of that week's *Sports Illustrated*. "This was golf to raise the dead," wrote *SI*'s Alan Shipnuck. ". . . It's time to put into words what Woods has said so eloquently with his clubs: He has wrought the greatest season in golf history."

Team Tiger didn't stick around Louisville to celebrate. As Earl Woods put it, "We came, we saw, we won, we got the fuck out of town."

The next day, Monday, July 21, Notah Begay phoned his old Stanford teammate to say congratulations. Begay, too, had something to celebrate: he had come in eighth at the PGA, eight shots behind Tiger, for his first top-ten finish in a major. That meant $145,000 and exemptions into years' worth of Tour events. "Where are you?" he asked.

"On the range." Tiger was back at Isleworth, tinkering with his grip, stance, and alignment. The 2001 Masters was nine months away, but he was already thinking about shots that would suit Augusta National: the high fade off the first tee; the big sling-shot draw at the thirteenth. He also needed to break in a new set of irons. His Titleist blades had served him well, but the clubfaces now had pea-sized smudges where he had worn away the sweet spots.

"All the talk in the golf world was whether he could be the first person to hold all four major trophies," Williams recalled. Everyone was talking about Tiger's streak in the majors except Tiger, who kept his thinking to himself. "Drawing a curtain around his thoughts was his way of dealing with unrelenting media speculation about this supposedly impossible goal."

Asked once again if his winning the 2001 Masters would constitute a Grand Slam, Tiger shrugged. "If you could put all four trophies on your coffee table, you could make a pretty good case."

Nicklaus said, "I don't care what you call it. If he does it, it will be the most amazing feat in the history of golf. If he lines up all those trophies on one table, it'll be better than anything I've ever seen."

The week after the PGA, Tiger defended one of his 1999 titles at the WGC-NEC Invitational at Firestone Country Club in Akron, Ohio. A second-round 61 gave him a seven-shot lead there. His big mistake of the day was moving a loose impediment: a wasp that had landed in his putting line. "I tried to pick him up, and he whipped his tail around and got me," he said after the round. It was the first time a stinger had ever hit him. The *Chicago Tribune*'s Rick Morrissey quipped that Tiger Woods's success had already annoyed plenty of WASPs. Lamenting the lack of drama in reporting another Woods victory, he wrote, "There are only so many ways to say that Tiger is a god, and his father, Earl, already has said most of them."

The sun had set over central Ohio as Tiger reached the last hole on Sunday. By then he was leading by ten. Playing with the ring finger on his left hand swollen after his wasp encounter, he squinted uphill. He could barely see the green and clubhouse, much less the flag. He could have walked in and finished the next morning, but he preferred to close out another victory and get out of Akron. He and Williams were trying to pick out a target line when a spectator behind the green sparked a cigarette lighter and held it in the air. Others did the same, and the green was lit by flickering lighters, giving the moment a rock concert vibe. Tiger's "Shot in the Dark," an 8-iron that fell out of the darkness to tap-in birdie distance, earned the ovation of the week.

Asked if he felt satisfied by his fifth win in seven events including two majors, he said, "No. I'm trying to get better."

Two nights later he faced off against Sergio García in a $1.5 million made-for-TV match at Bighorn Golf Club in Palm Desert, California. Played under stadium lights in prime time, the "Battle at Bighorn" ended with García sinking a birdie putt to win by a stroke, pumping his fist and celebrating as if he'd won a major. Tiger wouldn't forget that.

When Team Tiger announced that he would enter September's Canadian Open, tickets sold out in two hours. His record in Canada's national championship was nothing special. He had missed the cut there in 1997, his lone missed cut in four years as a pro. In the first round at Glen Abbey Golf Club near Toronto, he sprayed tee balls right and left and wound up in a tie for forty-fifth place. "Ugly" he called his round. A day later, he seemed headed for another unsightly score, only to rally with a Tigerish finish, going birdie, eagle, birdie, eagle to move into contention.

He and Grant Waite dueled down the stretch on Sunday. A thirty-six-year-old Kiwi with a toothy smile and a balky putter, Waite had a single Tour title to show for his thirteen years as a pro. He was the same age as Steve Williams and had grown up an hour's drive from Stevie's home turf at New Zealand's Paraparaumu Beach Golf Club, a biographical detail that didn't interest Tiger. Waite trailed him by a stroke as they teed off at the par-5 eighteenth, where Tiger drove into a fairway bunker. Waite split the fairway with his tee ball and smoothed a 5-iron shot to the green. Disadvantage Tiger.

With his ball in the bunker 218 yards from a tucked pin, with a stand of spruce bushes blocking his view of the flag, the sensible play was to the left. He could punch his bunker shot to the safe side of the fairway, pitch on, and two-putt for par. But with Waite on the green in two, that would probably mean a playoff. To win in regulation, Tiger needed a birdie of his own.

Recalling the shot, he said, "Two hundred and eighteen yards is a long way to hit a six-iron from a perfect lie in the fairway." It was a reckless distance for a 6-iron from wet sand in spitting rain, with bushes blocking the way and a left-to-right wind blowing toward the six-acre pond guarding the green. But he had been working on just such a shot, flattening his swing plane to "shallow out my approach to the ball and provide a little more margin for error." He had been pleased with the results in practice at Isleworth, "but practice and competition are two different things. Eventually you have to put techniques to the fire."

Aiming left of the spruces, he opened his stance an inch to promote a slight fade. "I also weakened my left-hand grip to make sure the clubface wouldn't turn over through impact. Then I just ripped it." He caught the ball flush, but it started a few degrees to the right of the line he intended.

Waite watched the 6-iron in flight. *He's hit it in the water*, he thought.

Instead, the three-piece Nike ball tunneled through the wind, holding its line long enough to clear the pond and carry past the top of the flagstick. It checked up on the back fringe. After a chip and a putt to match Waite's birdie, he had his ninth victory of the year, topping his total of eight the year before. It was the most since Sam Snead won eleven times in 1950.

Like Bob May two weeks before, Waite had broken a tournament record only to come in second. Thinking back on Tiger's bunker shot at the eighteenth, he said, "One grain of sand between the clubface and the ball could have changed my life forever. But it didn't." Part of the winner's genius, he said, was that he was "willing to try any shot."

Tiger's agent, Mark Steinberg, called his client's future "limitless." Tiger told Steinberg, "I need some downtime."

He took six weeks off, sleeping late, working out whenever he chose, tooling around Orlando in his white Porsche while blasting tunes by Prince, Shaggy, and Nickelback. Butch Harmon joked that the worst thing about coaching the world's best player was "hearing his quote-unquote music." In the evenings, America's most famous athlete binge-watched *South Park* and *The Simpsons*. He spent hours playing *Halo* and *Need for Speed* and claimed that playing video games helped his golf by building strength in his thumbs. Like millions of gamers of his generation, he had grown up with an Atari 2600. He graduated to a PlayStation he packed with the gear he took on the PGA Tour and now had one of the first PlayStation 2s. Meanwhile he was earning $6 million a year for his own franchise, *Tiger Woods PGA Tour*, by far the most popular golf game. Each summer he spent intensive sessions in an Orlando studio, wearing reflective motion-capture stickers while banks of cameras recorded his ever-evolving swing. The graphics got a little less cartoonish every year, and *Tiger Woods PGA Tour* went on to generate more than $700 million in sales.

He relaxed and recharged until the end of October, rarely going a day without practicing. He would barrel to the range at Isleworth, where the highest speed limit is twenty-five miles per hour, in a souped-up golf cart that topped out at almost forty miles an hour and had a sound system you could hear half a mile away. For Tiger, a staycation included hitting thousands of range balls, picturing shots he might need at Augusta.

As it turned out, the game changed forever during his six-week break from tournament play. Over that month and a half in the fall of 2000, the Titleist Professional—the ball that most Tour pros teed up every week—became obsolete.

In October, four months after Phil Mickelson buttonholed Acushnet CEO Wally Uihlein at the U.S. Open to ask if Titleist had anything in the works that might help him keep up with Tiger, several Titleist reps arrived at the Invensys Classic in Las Vegas. They came bearing gifts: four hundred plain white boxes. Each box held a dozen three-piece golf balls fresh off the assembly line. Rolling out a new design hadn't been a priority for a brand that already had the number one ball in golf, but now that Tiger was setting records with his new Nike ball, Titleist had no choice but to ramp up development of a "laboratory test ball" tentatively called the Pro V1. Mickelson loved it. "The harder you hit it, the less it spins," he said. Forty-seven Titleist pros liked the new ball enough to put it in play that week in Las Vegas.

Stewart Cink was one of the holdouts. Cink, who had won that year's MCI Classic with a Titleist Professional, was paired with Mickelson at the Invensys Classic. Mickelson raved about his new ball's blend of driving distance and short-game spin, saying "Man, you have to switch. This is the future." Cink tied for third that week, while Mickelson came in second behind another Pro V1 convert, Billy Andrade. Soon Cink and every other Titleist pro joined the crowd playing Titleist's new multilayered ball. With the pros raving about it and every golf publication touting it, Titleist shifted the ball's release to the public from spring 2001 to December 2000, just in time for Christmas. The Pro V1 was on its way to becoming what it still is today, the best-selling product in golf history.

Tiger's Tour Accuracy went on to make millions for Nike, but he was the only Tour star playing it until Duval followed Tiger to Nike in

2001. In terms of market share there would be no comparison, with Titleist keeping the upper hand as its Tour players and millions of civilians switched to the Pro V1. In the end, Vijay Singh's victory at the 2000 Masters—the only major Tiger didn't win that year—would be the last major won with a ball filled with rubber bands. In April 2000, most of the field at Augusta had teed up old-fashioned Titleist Professionals. Two years later, the number of golfers playing that ball at the Masters would be zero.

Two weeks after the Pro V1's Las Vegas debut, Tiger rejoined the Tour at the National Car Rental Classic at Disney World. He came in third behind Pro V1 player Duffy Waldorf. A week later, he finished second to Mickelson at the Tour Championship. In November, he flew to Bangkok, Thailand, for the Johnnie Walker Classic, shuttling from the roof of his hotel to the course by helicopter. His three-shot win over Geoff Ogilvy didn't count as a PGA Tour victory, but it delighted his mother. In between events, Tiger honored his father by showing up at junior clinics that Earl arranged, hitting a few shots and saying a few words. He liked spending time with kids and listened closely to their questions. When a grade schooler asked him how it felt to be a hero, he said, "A hero? Well, thank you. But what do I do that's heroic? I chase a little white ball around."

He had spent the year 2000 chasing it as well as anyone before or since. Twelve months after ringing in a new millennium in Scottsdale, Woods held three of the four major trophies. At twenty-five years old, he was the leading money winner in golf history. He had entered twenty tournaments that year and won nine, with seventeen top-five finishes. His $9.2 million in tournament winnings almost doubled second-place finisher Mickelson's $4.7 million. He won the Vardon Trophy with a scoring average of 67.79, a stroke and a half better than anyone else, setting a record that still stands. His average driving distance of 298 yards ranked second to John Daly's 301, but Daly, who cared as much about the driving distance title as about winning, almost always gripped and ripped a driver, while Tiger opted for the occasional 3-wood or 2-iron. The gap between Tiger's power and everyone else's had been clearest during the Open Championship at St. Andrews, where he averaged 320 yards off the tee to top the field's average by thirty-four yards. He had also led the 2000 PGA Tour in Greens in Regulation. According to Tour pro Paul Goydos, "Everyone was awed by his power" off the tee, "but he was the greatest iron player who ever lived."

Tom Watson, who had eight majors to his credit, twice as many as Tiger, said, "Someday I'll tell my grandkids I played in the same tournaments with Tiger Woods."

In December, *Sports Illustrated* named Tiger Woods its Sportsman of the Year for 2000. He was the first two-time winner in the award's fifty-five-year history, which put him one up on Palmer, Nicklaus, Ali, and his basketball friend Jordan. Ever more wary of the press since his embarrassing 1997 *GQ* interview, he usually got along with *SI*'s respected writers and photographers. Posing with a white tiger three times his size for a 1998 *SI* cover, he'd kept his cool when the 650-pound beast started growling. (An animal trainer holding a bucket of meat joked that it was "all that was left of Fuzzy Zoeller.")

One of the magazine's writers, John Garrity, had covered Tiger's career since his Tour debut as a sixteen-year-old amateur at the 1992 Los Angeles Open. "He struck me as a normal teenager," Garrity recalled years later. "Looking at his plain carry bag, I told him it wouldn't be long before he had a bag with his name on it. He said, 'That would be cool!'" Once Tiger turned pro and began to dominate the game, said Garrity, "It was thrilling to follow him around. It was like covering baseball in the time of Babe Ruth. But he changed."

Sports Illustrated's Jaime Diaz went back even further in the story. The first national reporter to focus on Tiger, Diaz had introduced Eldrick Woods to golf fans when he was still unknown outside southern

California. During Tiger's ascent through the amateur ranks, he and Diaz agreed to co-author two books, a memoir, and an instructional volume after Tiger turned pro. "We had an excerpt of the first book all teed up," recalled Jim Herre, *Sports Illustrated*'s longtime golf editor. "Then Tiger turned his back on Jaime. He shut it down at the eleventh hour."

Tiger was proud of his nine *SI* covers. Getting the cover was one of the sports world's benchmarks of fame and success. But by 2000, said Garrity, "He didn't need us anymore. He knew it, and we knew it. He'd look through you as if you weren't there."

That December, *SI* boss Bill Colson flew to the Williams World Challenge in Thousand Oaks, California, to introduce the Sportsman of the Year to the golf press. To mark the occasion, Colson arranged to have a copy of *Tiger Woods: The Making of a Champion*, a collection of *SI* stories on Tiger's achievements, placed on every reporter's chair in the press room. He and his PR team saw the gesture as a tribute— until Tiger's agent, Mark Steinberg, threw what one witness called "a real hissy."

"Steinberg made it clear that Tiger wouldn't participate in any *SI*-related activities," said Herre. Why? Because *SI* wasn't paying him. "Colson was so pissed, he called Mark McCormack," Steinberg's boss at International Management Group. McCormack, who had founded sports' most powerful agency with his client Arnold Palmer in 1960, was now IMG's chairman. "McCormack apologized about Steinberg's being an ass. He patched him in on the phone call. Steinberg whimpered and whined a bit and okayed Tiger's receiving the award."

Steinberg agreed that Tiger would fly to New York later that week to receive the Sportsman of the Year award from Jim Nantz on national TV. Then, after the conference call ended, he insisted that every copy of Garrity's book be removed from the press room. According to Herre, "That was his way of getting back at us. And it wasn't just Steinie being a dick. He was doing his master's bidding."

"Tiger's choice of the people around him wasn't an accident," said

Garrity. "He was building walls, starting to treat writers the way he treated other golfers. He wanted to intimidate us, to keep us on the defensive."

The next week's *Sports Illustrated* showed a smiling Sportsman of the Year beside the headline TIGER WOODS, ONE COOL CAT. According to Frank Deford's write-around cover story (the subject wasn't talking), his tale was that of a "myth aborning." Tiger was making the game "more luminous in the galaxy of sport. . . . With athletic majesty and utter excellence—and with a certain youthful panache—Woods not only is the consummate champion of this time but also is a popular sovereign who rules over a giddy and grateful links dominion."

Days later, the best-paid athlete on Earth re-upped with Nike for $100 million over the next five years, more than doubling the five-year, $40 million deal he'd signed in 1996. David Letterman devoted several of his *Late Night*'s popular "Top Ten Lists" to a rundown of "Tiger Woods' Pet Peeves" featuring:

- PGA's pointless insistence I complete all 18 holes before they fork over cash.
- Have to hire three maids for the trophy polishing.
- At press conferences, not allowed to admit, "I kicked everyone's ass because I'm much, much better than they are."

Another *Late Night* list counted down "Signs You've Had a Lame Summer," topped by "You're a pro golfer and your name ain't Tiger."

Golf was more popular than ever. In the wake of Tigermania a record 2.4 million Americans had taken up the game in 2000, a year sportswriters dubbed "The Year of the Tiger." He displayed his many trophies in his Isleworth mansion, but the mantel over the fireplace was reserved for the U.S. Open Trophy, the PGA Championship's Wanamaker Trophy, and the oldest prize in professional golf, the Claret Jug.

He had three more months to prepare for his chance to put the Masters Trophy, a sterling silver model of the stately clubhouse at Augusta, on his mantel with the other three. "Put one more up there," he said, "and it would look pretty good."

During those months, he broke up with his girlfriend Joanna Jagoda. She returned to California, where she would go on to graduate with honors from the University of California, Santa Barbara. As 2001 began, her ex-boyfriend finished eighth at the season-opening Mercedes Championships and fifth at the Phoenix Open, where Andrew Magee made the screwiest hole in one in PGA Tour history. Hitting downwind at the TPC of Scottsdale's 332-yard seventeenth hole, Magee clobbered a Pro V1 that bounced to the green, where Tom Byrum was lining up an eight-foot putt. Magee's drive rolled past Steve Pate, Byrum's playing partner, caromed off Byrum's putter, and rolled straight into the hole. After a moment's confusion, a Tour official ruled—correctly—that Magee's carom shot was the first (and still only) ace ever recorded on a par 4 in a Tour event.

Pate pointed to Byrum and said, "That's the only putt you made all day."

Magee would finish tied for forty-fourth, ten shots behind Woods, who finished fifth and was no more displeased with his game than usual. He told reporters, as always, that he was trying to improve. But after he came in thirteenth at the AT&T Pebble Beach Pro-Am and fourth at the Buick Invitational, the same reporters who had spent a year singing his praises coined a term he didn't like at all: "the Tiger Slump."

He said he wasn't worried about going winless in his first four events of the year. "I focus on four things," he said. The four majors. And the Masters was still six weeks off.

During a month of slump talk, some experts floated a new idea: Woods was losing his edge. Some pointed to his peers' use of the Pro V1, a ball that was as good as or better than Tiger's Nike Tour

Accuracy. "The standard of play has become so high that guys are playing more aggressively," said David Leadbetter, Harmon's rival as the Tour's leading swing guru. With Tiger in the field, Leadbetter argued, "They can't afford *not* to. We're reaching a point where you have world-class athletes trying to birdie every hole. They see Tiger pull off spectacular shots and think, *If I'm going to beat him, I've got to step up.*"

"He's basically standing still," Johnny Miller said of Tiger, "and other guys are leapfrogging up to him."

Earl Woods agreed with Miller. "Tiger's God-given advantage of length is being reduced. He must improve his overall game."

In March, the month before the Masters, Tiger accepted $2 million in appearance money to play in the 2001 Dubai Desert Classic, a European Tour event that had nicked its name from Bob Hope's old Tour stop in Palm Springs. On lush fairways reclaimed from lunar desert, Tiger took a one-shot lead over Thomas Bjørn into Sunday's final round. The two of them played all four rounds together that week, and Bjørn wasn't always sure he belonged. "Tiger hits shots nobody else in the world can hit," he said. On the long holes, "I was going in with a three-wood on which my feet came off the ground, and he's going in with a five-iron."

Tiger was a born closer, practically uncatchable when he led a tournament on Sunday. Only twice in his five years as a pro had he failed to turn a third-round lead into a trophy. But that Sunday in Dubai he threw up on his shoes, as golfers say. Tied with Bjørn on the eighteenth tee at Emirates Golf Club, he blocked his drive to the right, punched back to the fairway, and knocked his third shot into an artificial lake. He double-bogeyed to lose by two strokes. The winner, Bjørn, said what others were thinking: "The intimidation factor is disappearing. He's still the best player in the world by far, but he's going to lose tournaments."

With Tiger's winless streak at nine, there was more slump talk than Slam talk. A *Golf World* cover asked, WHAT'S WRONG WITH TIGER? Colin Montgomerie, ranked sixth in the world, said, "There is certainly a feeling of being less afraid of Tiger. People have beaten him, so the thinking is 'Why can't I?'"

Two weeks after his debacle in Dubai, Tiger defended his 2000 title at Arnold Palmer's Bay Hill Invitational. His presence doubled attendance, a favor to Arnie, as well as television ratings—a favor to NBC, which racked up higher ratings than CBS's coverage of the NCAA basketball tournament despite airing the golf tournament on tape delay. He shot 66-69 on the weekend to hold off Mickelson for his twenty-fourth title in the ninety-six Tour events he had played since turning pro. Discussing his "slump" after Palmer handed him the trophy, the winner said, "My bad shots this year have been worse than last year, but my good ones have been really good. It comes in spurts."

A week later, he charged from eighth place to the front of the pack at the Players Championship on Sunday, knocking in a triple breaker of a sixty-foot putt at the island-green seventeenth at TPC Sawgrass. A cautious bogey at the eighteenth led to his second one-shot victory in two weeks. His oversized winner's check read "$1,080,000 dollars and 00 cents," the richest first prize in golf history.

NBC Sports' Jimmy Roberts was waiting for a pre-arranged moment with the winner as Tiger came off the last green. Roberts, who had jokingly compared Tiger's early-season slump to "the few weeks that the Beatles didn't have a number-one song," was expecting the usual post-round blather, with the champion smiling and describing a few key shots. Instead, Tiger blew him off. He said, "Nice slump, huh, Jimmy?" and kept walking.

During his mandatory press conference that evening, he said he was tired of hearing about his "so-called slump." Roberts wasn't the only media member who had annoyed him, he said, "and I know who they are. They suggested it and said it. Obviously, they don't understand the game that well. It wasn't like I was missing cuts every week.

It's just that I had not won. The game is very fickle. Now I've won twice in a row, and they'll write about something else."

With two weeks left until the Masters, he skipped the next week's BellSouth Classic to hit balls at Isleworth. He was looking forward to having more time for snorkeling and scuba diving. The best thing about being underwater, he said, was that "the fish don't know who I am."

NINETEEN
RETURN TO AUGUSTA

Tiger was a self-described "sports junkie" who hated missing any news of his beloved Lakers, led by Kobe Bryant and Shaquille O'Neal. The NBA champion Lakers were on their way to a second straight Pacific Division title and the league playoffs, but he cut back on watching sports on his mansion's many widescreen TVs in the weeks before the 2001 Masters, making a special point of avoiding ESPN's *SportsCenter* and the Golf Channel. After seven months, he was tired of the drumbeat building up to the task ahead of him.

He liked to say that golf gave him two of his favorite things, "solitude and self-reliance." With Grand Slam talk dominating golf, Augusta National in the first week of April would bring only one of the two. "I know there's going to be a lot of talk and a lot of attention," he said, "but no matter what anybody says or thinks, there's not one single person who can hit a shot for me." His goal was simple: "Put myself in position coming down the back nine on Sunday. If I can do that, I'll have a chance to do something special."

"If Tiger Woods wins, it will be the greatest achievement in modern-day golf," Augusta National chairman William "Hootie" Johnson announced.

The favorite arrived in Augusta on Monday, April 2. The *Augusta Chronicle* welcomed him to town with more than the usual fanfare, declaring "Tiger Woods and his quest for the debatable Grand Slam have elevated the 2001 Masters to supernova status." *Golf Digest* called the upcoming tournament "golf's most eagerly awaited event since late September 1930," when Bobby Jones prevailed over 150 other nonprofessionals to complete his Grand Slam at the U.S. Amateur. Tiger settled into a rented house with Mark O'Meara and his wife, Alicia, who cooked for them. In the evenings, they relaxed and watched TV. By day, Tiger went on six-mile runs, worked out in the gym, and played practice rounds that drew bigger galleries than some of the world's top players would attract once the Masters began. Bookmakers made him a better than two-to-one favorite at record-setting odds—a $100 bet on him would return only $150 if he won. Mickelson was the oddsmakers' second choice at 8 to 1, with Vijay Singh at 12 to 1, Els at 15 to 1, and Duval at 20 to 1. O'Meara, the 1998 Masters champion, was at 100 to 1, which amused Tiger.

On a rainy Masters Tuesday, O'Meara and Tiger joined dozens of other Masters winners in the clubhouse for the lavish Champions Dinner. Defending champ Singh treated them to a menu of chicken curry and sea bass flown in from Thailand, filet mignon, and a 1982 Château Lafite Rothschild that retailed for $1,000 a bottle. Tiger, who had impressed nobody with his 1998 Champions Dinner featuring cheeseburgers, fries, and milkshakes, took note. He planned to do better if and when he got another chance.

He and O'Meara spent the evening schmoozing with Arnold Palmer, Jack Nicklaus, Gary Player, Tom Watson, Seve Ballesteros, and eighty-nine-year-old Byron Nelson, who cleaned his plate and asked for seconds. "There really is a special mystique to the Masters,"

O'Meara said later. Thinking back to his final-round duel with Fred Couples in 1998, he called it the one time he ever felt he was in what some players call "the Zone," a Zen state in which time slows down and golf seems simple. "I hit a good drive at seventeen, and Freddie said, 'Good shot, M.O.' At that point you're not hearing the crowd or smelling the flowers. You're trying to slow down your adrenaline. So I get to my ball. It's uphill to the green, and there's a moment when I look up and see the edge of the bunker in front of the green, the white sand in the bunker, and a cool, calming feeling comes over me. It's the only time that ever happened. I spent a moment just standing there, thinking *It's beautiful out here!*" Moments later he struck a picture-perfect 9-iron over the bunker, setting up a birdie that gave the forty-one-year-old O'Meara a tie for the lead with Couples and David Duval. Another birdie at the eighteenth made him the oldest first-time winner in Masters history.

Tiger considered his buddy Marko's victory a Masters highlight along with Gene Sarazen's "Shot Heard 'Round the World" in 1935, Palmer's four victories at Augusta, the forty-six-year-old Nicklaus's stirring charge in 1986, and Tiger's own twelve-shot triumph in 1997 to win his first major. After hundreds of hours of watching grainy golf videos on the couch back in Cypress and re-watching some of the same footage at the Golf Channel's Orlando studios, he knew more about the game's history than most fans or TV commentators. Nobody had to tell him that his five major-championship wins so far—the 1997 Masters, the 1999 PGA, and the latest three—left him thirteen behind Nicklaus's total of eighteen. Nobody had to tell him that Augusta was the ideal setting for a run at his sixth major.

He appreciated the beauty of the course Bobby Jones and Alister MacKenzie had built on what had been an orchard called Fruitland Nurseries before they transformed it into an American showplace for the old Scottish game. When Jones first walked the property, he marveled at it. "And to think this ground has been lying here all these years," he said, "waiting for someone to come along and lay a golf course upon it." In 1931, hoping to create "the perfect golf course," he and MacKenzie, a disciple of Old Tom Morris, laid out an inland version of the Old Course at St. Andrews, a thinking player's venue that rewards local knowledge above all else. As Tiger put it, the course "represents strategic golf at its most sophisticated. The genius of Augusta National is that it allows you to be so imaginative around the greens." Along with the Old Course and Pebble Beach, he considered it one of the world's best tests of a golfer's skill and spirit. After winning his first major at the 1997 Masters, he took the green jacket to bed with him and fell asleep hugging it.

Four years later, he played practice rounds with O'Meara and hit balls at the range while his father settled into a house Team Tiger had rented nearby. Earl liked few things more than holding court under the 150-year-old live oak between the clubhouse and the eighteenth green, where golf's influencers gather every April, but he was sixty-nine now, ailing with prostate cancer diagnosed two years before, unable to get around the way he used to. Still as opinionated as ever, he had toned down his rhetoric in public since 1995, when he invited the long-dead Bobby Jones to "kiss my son's Black ass." Picturing Augusta National's pristine fairways lined with azaleas, magnolias, pink dogwoods, and yellow jasmine, Earl echoed Jones: "It's like God designed it as a golf course. It's like a shrine."

What he didn't say was that he and his son could never celebrate the tournament's traditions with quite the same reverence many golfers and fans felt. They weren't as comfortable in Augusta as they were at Pebble Beach, St. Andrews, or even Louisville, because racism was baked into the tournament's history.

Earl had told his son about the notorious "Caucasian clause" that limited membership in the PGA to "golfers of the Caucasian race" until 1961, when Charlie Sifford broke pro golf's color line fourteen years after Jackie Robinson integrated Major League Baseball. Sifford went on to win the 1969 Los Angeles Open at the age of forty-six, which should have earned him an invitation to the Masters. It didn't. Lee Elder finally broke the Masters color line in 1975. That was the year Tiger was born, a fact he bore in mind as he marched to his first Masters victory twenty-two years later. Tiger Woods was only the fourth African American to compete in the Masters (after Elder, Jim Thorpe, and Calvin Peete). After winning the 1997 Masters, he embraced the tearful sixty-two-year-old Elder. As the *Chicago Defender* reported that week, "A man of color in a green jacket—for Elder, there was never a more beautiful sight."

By then Charlie Sifford had become a family friend and trusted adviser to Tiger, who said, "I called him Grandpa. He was like the grandpa I never had. I ended up becoming so close with him that I ended up naming my son, Charlie, after him." Yet Sifford always refused to set foot at Augusta National. He called the Masters "the most redneck tournament in the country."

Fred Hickman agreed. "The Masters isn't quite the same shiny tradition for us Black folks," said Hickman, who anchored CNN's *Sports Tonight* with Nick Charles. He was attuned to the less savory details of the club's history, like the fact that Rae's Creek had been named after a local slave owner. "The Caucasians-only clause might have been a thing of the past, but it wasn't exactly *Soul Train* at Augusta. The Black caddies and kitchen workers all came out to cheer for Tiger when he won, and then they went back to work. We covered it faithfully year after year, but the Masters was always a little Confederate for me."

The tournament's fraught history left Tiger between worlds, as he so often was. Defending his much-mocked description of himself as "Cablinasian," he explained again and again that he was "African American on my dad's side and Asian on my mom's side, and to think of me as an African American is to deny my mom's heritage. But I learned that to have one drop of Black blood in you in America meant that you were considered an African American." He remembered hitting balls at the Navy Course in Orange County, where Earl had taunted him to distract him and toughen him up. "It was 'motherfucker' or 'you little piece of shit,'" Tiger recalled, "or 'How do you feel, being a little n——?'"

During one of his first newspaper interviews, a reporter asked high school freshman Eldrick Woods which major championship he would most like to win. "The Masters," he said. "Because of the way Blacks have been treated—like they shouldn't be there. If I win that tournament, it would be really big for us." In those days, southern California's latest junior golf phenom graduated from the public courses where he learned the game to tournaments at exclusive country clubs where his was the only nonwhite face. "I could feel people staring at me." He claimed that "the Look" didn't bother him. "I stared right back. Racism was their problem, not mine." In his famous "Hello, World" commercial for Nike, he said, "There are still courses in the US I am not allowed to play because of the color of my skin." Later, reflecting on his breakthrough at the 1997 Masters, he returned to the topic: "It would have been naive of me to think my win would mean the end of 'the look' when a person from any minority walked into some golf clubs, especially the game's private clubs. I only hoped my win, and how I won, might put a dent in the way people perceived black people."

He was trying to have some fun while he did it. After winning the '97 Masters by a dozen shots, Tiger climbed into his white Cadillac courtesy car, rolled down the windows, punched a CD into the dash, and blasted his favorite Quad City DJ's tune, "C'mon n' Ride It" ("Girl, I wanna waller in the back of my Impala") all the way down Magnolia Lane.

•   •   •

He believed that one key to success at Augusta was to imagine playing each hole in reverse, "from the green back to the tee." That was something Earl had taught him. Earl emphasized putting first, then accurate iron shots that would lead to makeable putts, and finally driving to a part of the fairway that would provide the best angle for pinpoint approach shots. As Tiger explained after his first Masters victory, "It wasn't all that complicated. The majority of my putts were uphill because I was able to control my irons into the greens. Why? Because I had short irons into the greens, and why did I have those short iron shots? Because I drove the ball in the fairway."

Augusta National's green-jacketed officials had tweaked the course since then, lengthening the second and seventeenth holes, planting trees in strategic locations, and letting the rough grow to the immodest height of one and three-eighths inches (compared to five inches at the U.S. Open). Not that they deigned to call the rough "rough." Per the club's genteel customs, the high grass was called "the second cut," just as Masters spectators were not fans but "patrons." In a similar vein, the changes they'd made to Jones and MacKenzie's course were mere "modifications." Sportswriters coined a different term: they said the club was trying to "Tiger-proof" the course.

By any name, the new trees, higher rough, and added distance made Augusta National play about half a stroke harder. "You can't bomb away anymore like you used to," Tiger said at a pre-tournament press event. He had barely sat down when a reporter asked about the hype surrounding his pursuit of four straight majors. "Not many years ago, when Jack Nicklaus was the best player," the writer said, "he would win a major and maybe three other tournaments and we'd say, 'Another great year for Jack.' The expectations have changed with you. Who is to blame for the expectations getting a little bit out of hand? Was it us? Was it you?"

Tiger smiled. "Well, I know *that* answer. Don't look at me." After a moment he added, "You know, it's probably both. When you're playing well, the media blows it out of proportion. When you're not, they make it sound like you're terrible. I've had my successes the past couple years, and you guys have used your words to your advantage."

After a few more questions and routine answers, he stood up and left the media center. Half the press corps did the same, even though Phil Mickelson was waiting to speak next.

"It's going to be very difficult to beat Tiger," Mickelson told a half-empty room. "He seems to bring out his best game when he wants to. He's done it at four of the last five majors, and this golf course sets up very well for him." Asked if Tiger's streak in the majors was good or bad for the game, Mickelson took the high road. "Even though we are not too thrilled with the fact that somebody has won four out of five, it has brought a lot of attention, and we have all benefited indirectly. And it's not really that I want to stop his streak this week. It's that I would like to break through and win *my* first major."

He and Tiger both expected the 2001 Masters to be decided on the greens, like almost every other Masters, and the greens were likely to be lightning fast by Sunday. Tiger called the putting surfaces at Augusta "complicated," with "so many sneaky little undulations" to consider. In his college days he had practiced for his first Masters by putting on the gym floor at Stanford. If his knowledge of the tournament's history had taught him anything about Masters winners, it was this: "They kept the ball below the hole."

Thursday morning he felt strong on the driving range, which Masters officials insisted on calling the "tournament practice area." At the 2000 Masters a year before, fifty-nine of ninety-five players had teed up wound balls such as the Titleist Professional. That number was now four. Most touring pros were now playing Pro V1s that made them about ten to twelve yards longer off the tee. Tiger had gained even more yards by replacing his "archaic" Titleist with his three-piece Nike Tour Accuracy. After averaging 289 yards off the tee in the months before the switch, he had averaged 305 with the new ball. The difference was apparent at the practice area. With Tiger and Duval hitting Nike's new Tour Accuracy while Mickelson and other Titleist endorsers smacked the newer Pro V1, tournament officials raised the fence at the far end of the range from 95 feet to 105 feet to keep the pros from knocking balls over the fence. It didn't work. A few balls still cleared the fence and bounced into traffic on Washington Road.

As ever, Tiger left the range only after striking a satisfying drive—a rehearsal for his first tee ball that day. He and Williams had a routine for that moment: Tiger launched the last range ball and asked his caddie, "How's that, Stevie?"

Watching it fly, Williams said, "That will do."

Tiger got a pat on the back from Butch Harmon on his way to the first tee. "It's your time, pal," Harmon said.

Tiger said, "Butchie, I got this."

TWENTY
THURSDAY

At one in the afternoon on April 5, Tiger Woods teed up a Nike ball with his first name stamped on it. Byron Nelson and Sam Snead had poked ceremonial first drives hours before. Tiger wanted his tee shot to be as straight as theirs but about three times longer.

His run at a four-major Grand Slam began with his usual pre-shot ritual. He stepped behind the ball and eyed his target, a spot beyond the bunker at the dogleg on Augusta National's first hole. A high fade over the left-hand side of the bunker would give him a wedge to the green. He took his stance, settling his weight back and forth on his feet until he felt perfectly balanced. He took a breath. He leaned backward, then upward, and finally down to the ball, unleashing the most powerful swing the game had ever seen.

Patrons gasped. They had never expected to see Tiger Woods hit such a rotten shot.

"I overcut it," he recalled, admitting he'd felt "nervous" over the ball. Blocking a drive off the first tee wouldn't have been much of a problem before the "Tiger-proofing" modifications club officials had made the year before. As it was, his path to the green was blocked by three newly planted pines. He spent a minute conferring with Williams, who wasn't thrilled to be spending his afternoon in the all-white overalls Masters caddies were required to wear. That sartorial tradition dated back to the 1940s, when cofounder Clifford Roberts decided that the club's all-Black caddie corps should stand out more from Augusta National's green fairways. The custom had lasted through the transition to Tour caddies that began in 1983, when Bruce Edwards caddied for Tom Watson and Jack Nicklaus II carried his father's bag. Masters caddies' white overalls are almost identical to the yellow ones the club's trash collectors wear. "Ridiculous jumpsuits," Williams called them.

Tiger chose a 2-iron for his escape from the trees at the first hole. With his ball lying in pine straw, he punched a line drive under the pines' branches to a greenside bunker and settled for bogey. "I knew right away it was going to be a blue-collar day," he recalled.

Augusta's second hole, a 575-yard par 5 called Pink Dogwood, was a drive and a 4-iron for him. It was here that the twenty-year-old Tiger Woods, still an amateur, had once played a practice round with Raymond Floyd, Greg Norman, and Fred Couples before Tiger's first Masters in 1996. Steve Williams had been on Floyd's bag that morning. The weather was cold, the air so damp and heavy that none of the other players could reach the trap at the edge of the dogleg, three hundred yards off the tee. They rolled their eyes when the skinny kid asked, "Can I fly that bunker?" According to Williams, "We're all looking at each other with little smirks on our faces and sharing a look that says, 'He's got a lot to learn.'" Whereupon Tiger blasted one over the bunker. After the round, Williams got his autograph.

Five years later, Tiger pounded another drive past the same bunker but wound up missing a birdie putt, settling for a par that felt like bogey. One spectator carried a sign reading TIGER FOR PRESIDENT. A few were pulling against him. A golf writer heard a patron spit the N-word as Tiger passed by. The object of everyone's attention fought back with birdies at the third, seventh, and ninth holes to make the turn two under par. Good enough, he thought. With the course playing harder than expected, his main goal was to finish the day in red numbers. Tuesday's rain had softened the greens, so club officials had opted to protect their venue's virtue in the first round with hole locations that some players saw as more suitable for Saturday or Sunday. As Tiger put it, "The pins are touching some corners." He would lead the field in driving distance that day with an average of 304 yards, but his other clubs let him down. When he kept an iron shot below the pin, it was often too far below for a realistic birdie putt. When he left an approach above the hole, putts slid past. Augusta National's bentgrass greens were smoother than the bumpy *Poa* at Pebble Beach or the fescue at St. Andrews but more deceptive. Tiger's word was "grainier." Down-grain putts could run two or three feet farther than they looked like they would. Sidehill putts broke more. A ten-footer might break a yard and miss by a foot or two.

He bogeyed the difficult downhill tenth but got a stroke back at the fifteenth, where Gene Sarazen had hit his "Shot Heard 'Round the World" in the second-ever Masters, a 4-wood shot that barely carried the stream guarding the green, struck the far bank, and rolled into the cup for an albatross, a three-under-par deuce on a par 5. The patrons behind the green sent up a glad shout after Sarazen's miracle shot, but it wasn't the kind of roar that reached every corner of the course. There were only a dozen patrons—including Bobby Jones—on the fifteenth hole that day. Sixty-six years later, with a crowd of thousands cheering him on, Tiger hit a drive and a 6-iron. An even-par back nine left him signing his card for a two-under-par 70. He said he was "relatively satisfied. Anytime you shoot in red numbers the first day of a major championship, you're in an all-right position."

He was tied for fifteenth behind contenders including Phil Mickelson, who shot 67 to stand fourth after eighteen holes, and defending champion Vijay Singh, the last man not named Woods to win a major, described by the *Augusta Chronicle* as "the forgotten Masters champion."

Steve Stricker, a runner-up to Singh at the 1998 PGA Championship, shot 66 to stand in second place. Asked about the other leaders' chances, Stricker mentioned only the guy in fifteenth place. "It's fun to watch the history Tiger's been making," he said. "It's a great time to be part of the game, as a player and spectator. Nothing is unbelievable when it comes to him."

Chris DiMarco, the surprise first-round leader, was making his Masters debut. A thirty-two-year-old Floridian, he wore a green shirt because "green is synonymous with the Masters." Five years before, stricken with the yips, DiMarco had thought about quitting the game. While Tiger Woods won $790,594 in his three months as a Tour rookie in 1996, DiMarco had earned $18,678, nowhere near enough to cover his expenses. He could hit a 180-yard 7-iron onto a dime, then three-putt and wish for another line of work. "I can't make a putt from six inches," he told Tour veteran Skip Kendall that year. "I've completely lost it."

Kendall, a reformed yipper, showed him a "claw" grip that took the right hand almost entirely out of the putting stroke. "I tried it," DiMarco recalled. Placing the first and second fingers of his right hand on the grip of his putter as if he were playing a flute, he lined up a four-footer. "Lo and behold, it went straight in the middle. I was like 'Wow!' Reborn."

After winning the 2000 Pennsylvania Classic to qualify for the Masters, DiMarco now found himself with a one-stroke lead after a 65 that featured only twenty-seven putts. He told reporters he could hardly believe he was leading the Masters. As a kid of eight or nine, he said, he used to "play four balls. I would play my ball, and I'd have one that was Nicklaus, one was Palmer, one was Player, and I'd try to beat them. I always made them miss the four-footers."

He was looking forward to sleeping on the first-round lead. But first he was going to enjoy a Thursday-night dinner.

The restaurant in the Augusta National clubhouse was packed, as it usually is during Masters week. DiMarco found a table, where he sat by himself and spent several minutes trying in vain to get a waiter's attention.

TWENTY-ONE
UPS AND DOWNS

Friday brought cool weather without a breeze to stir the flags. Tiger opened his second round with a routine par. His game plan was to avoid mistakes on Augusta National's par 3s and par 4s and kill the par 5s the way Nicklaus used to do. One difference was that Nicklaus had hit mid-irons, long irons, and fairway woods into the par 5s. Tiger was so much longer off the tee that his second shot was often a short iron. After an opening par, he expected to make birdie at the par-5 second hole. Instead, a mediocre chip left him with another par that felt like a bogey.

He struck back with birdies at the third and fourth. Four under par for the tournament at the 180-yard sixth, with the course playing softer than usual, he sent a 7-iron soaring over the pin. His Nike ball spun backward to tap-in range while his six- and seven-deep gallery sent up a roar that carried all over the course. Two holes later, at the par-5 eighth, he chose strategy over firepower, purposely driving into the rough to gain a better angle to the green. That was a tactic he would never have tried at a U.S. Open, where the punishing rough grew five inches deep, but the second cut at Augusta was barely a slap on the wrist. He had 253 yards to the hole, no more than a three-quarters 3-wood shot, with the only trouble to the left of the green. He began his smooth swing, his left shoulder under his chin, torso torquing, and heard an unwelcome voice in his head. "Coming down on my downswing, I screamed at myself, *Don't hit it left!*" Any duffer could predict what happened next.

Butch Harmon, standing shoulder to shoulder with the crowd (Augusta National allows only players and caddies inside the ropes), winced as his star pupil raked his 3-wood across the target line, sending a low liner to the left. Then the ball began curling from left to right—an accidental bleeder that faded and skipped onto the green. His worst swing of the day had left Tiger with a fourteen-footer for eagle. All around Harmon, patrons cheered what appeared to be a sensational shot. Harmon just smiled and shook his head, knowing they had seen an illustration of one of the game's simple truths: sometimes even Tiger Woods got lucky.

Tiger's eagle putt slipped past the hole. He settled for his fourth birdie in half a dozen holes.

At the ninth, where a beveled green slopes from back to front, caddie Williams urged him to hit a sand wedge from 106 yards. Tiger said no. A sand wedge might bite, shift into reverse, and slide back off the green. He thought a pitching wedge with a little hook spin would have a better chance to stay close to the flag. He won the argument, as usual, but lost the shot over the flag. His approach checked up on the green's upper tier. His downhill, down-grain birdie putt rolled past the cup and kept going, he missed a comebacker, and that is how you turn a birdie into a bogey at Augusta.

Still he made the turn in 33. He was watching the leaderboard and gaining ground on the leaders until several missed putts left him gritting his teeth. It was Winston Churchill who described golf as "a game played with weapons ill suited to the purpose." A century later, Tiger was starting to feel that way about his Scotty Cameron putter. He missed a twelve-footer at the tenth. He three-putted the sixteenth, running a birdie putt past the cup and blowing another comebacker. He owed both of his three-putts to leaving iron shots above the pin. He hoped to strike back at the eighteenth, where the hole location offered a perfect target, an upslope just beyond the flag. "I could use the backstop behind the hole as a little friend," he recalled.

The next few minutes went according to plan. Sand wedge to the ridge a few feet past the pin. Backspin, birdie putt. Chants of "Tiger, Tiger, Tiger!" He signed for a second-round 66 that put his name on top of the leaderboard.

For the moment. First-round leader DiMarco was just making his way through Amen Corner. By the time he finished with a second-round 69, DiMarco was two up on Tiger and the rest of the field. The *Augusta Chronicle* paid him a compliment of sorts: "He could be this weekend's Bob May."

The second-round cut eliminated forty-four golfers including former champions Nicklaus, Watson, Floyd, Ballesteros, and Zoeller as well as Greg Norman, who shot a birdie-free 82 and was described by the *Chronicle* as one of "Augusta's walking dead."

David Toms made the cut despite a stomach flu that left him thinking about withdrawing. Like Tiger and most of the other pros, Toms was sharing a rented house with friends that week. "I have a doctor staying with me, but he's an anesthesiologist. He knows nothing about the stomach."

Mickelson's second-round 69 left him tied with Tiger, two shots behind DiMarco. He had raised his game in 2001, winning the Buick Invitational in February to move past Ernie Els into second place in the World Golf Ranking while evangelizing for Titleist's Pro V1. The

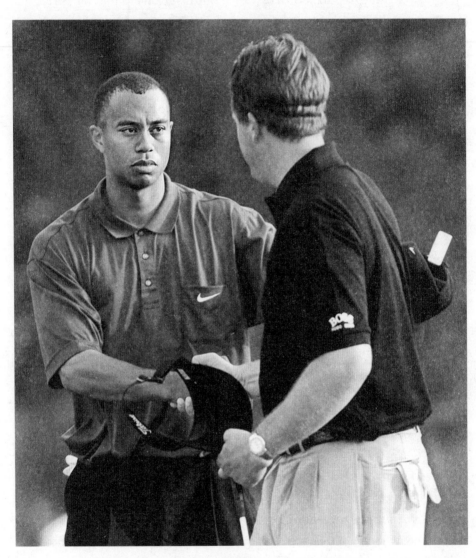

He stared down Phil Mickelson at the 2001 Masters.

new ball's "drop-and-stop" made it ideal for Augusta National, he said. "It launches higher and comes into the greens more vertically." Despite his eighteen Tour victories, the world's second-best golfer was still zero for thirty-four in majors, still chafing at the unofficial title of "Best Player Never to Have Won a Major," a distinction familiar enough among the press corps to be known by the world's clumsiest acronym, BPNTHWAM. The *Augusta Chronicle* singled him out for a question: "Mickelson: Best player without a major or choke artist . . . or both?" He considered the 2001 Masters "by far" his best chance yet. "Chipping and putting is the biggest part of this tournament, as well as driving the ball a good distance." Nobody had a better short game than Mickelson, who had four wedges in his bag that week. He was a match for anyone including Tiger, at least on his best day, but his best day hadn't come on Sunday at a major. He could be disarmingly honest. "I try not to think about how bad I would dearly love to win one," he said. And he had heard that Team Tiger saw him as a threat to go low at the drop of a flop wedge, even if Kultida Woods privately called "Lefty" Mickelson, who was chubby compared to her son, "Hefty."

The year 2001 was shaping up as a difficult time to be the second or third or fourth best golfer on Earth. Duval, top ranked as recently as 1999, had fought through his lower-back woes and a sore right wrist that had kept him off the Tour for a month. He often looked grim on the course, but his rigid expression hid a competitive fire to match Tiger's or anyone else's. After a cortisone shot and four weeks off, Duval shot a second-round 66 to move into contention, one shot behind Woods and Mickelson, three behind DiMarco. "I'm as jacked as I can be," he said. But he couldn't get a break from the press. As soon as he took his seat at the front of Augusta National's vast media center for his mandatory post-round appearance, a writer asked if he minded being called "a dullard."

"A what?" Duval had been expecting to talk about shooting 66 after breaking in a new set of irons. "Are you referring to my game or my personality?" He said his injured wrist was pain-free. He called himself a golf fan, said he was "jacked" to be part of a big-name leaderboard, and left the media center without looking back.

Ernie Els, tied for tenth halfway through the tournament, was another generational talent whose career coincided with what was shaping up to be a better career. He had won two U.S. Opens, but, like Mickelson and Duval, he was still trying to prove he could stand up to Tiger Woods. Steve Williams liked to say that Woods and Els had "had a lot of great battles. Tiger won them all."

"Ernie was kind of puzzled," said John Garrity of *Sports Illustrated*. "He'd look at Tiger and think, 'What does it take for me to beat this guy?' What he needed was to beat the guy *someplace*." *SI* joked that Els could write a bestseller called *How to Play Almost Like Tiger*, sharing his "semi-amazing secrets, from 299-yard drives to pretty darn good iron shots." Garrity saw "how dejected Ernie was." Like Duval and Mickelson, he would find his career defined by how he came up short against Tiger. Els was golf's Joe Frazier.

Argentina's Ángel Cabrera was another contender, tied with Duval and four others for fourth place, three strokes off the lead. Nicknamed "El Pato" for his ducklike gait, Cabrera was not accustomed to being surrounded by reporters after a round. Peppered with questions about Tiger, he brightened, recalling a match he and his countryman Eduardo Romero had played against a US team of Woods and Duval at the 2000 EMC World Cup in Buenos Aires. "Just to be near Tiger, to play against Tiger and be competitive with Tiger, is important," he said. "You learn from it."

For his part, Tiger was pleased to be "right there in the ballgame. There's so much golf to be played. Come Sunday afternoon, that's when it will be challenging and when it will be fun." He and Masters rookie DiMarco would be paired in the last group on Saturday. Would that give Tiger an advantage? He was honest enough to say yes. "I've been there before. I've won majors and lost majors. I know how to control my emotions. I know what to expect and what I'll probably experience coming down the stretch."

When it was the second-round leader's turn to face the press, he was quickly asked if he had much business leading the Masters: "Woods, Duval, DiMarco—do you belong in that group?"

The clean-cut Tour veteran smiled. "I guess I do this week! I'm excited. I think I've gained a lot of fans over the last few days. The bottom line is, Tiger's got to play the course, too, and he's got a lot going on this week. The pressure on him is amazing. That's all anybody talks about—four majors to get the Slam."

Would he be nervous, teeing it up with Tiger in the third round of the Masters?

"If anyone says they don't get nervous, they're not telling the truth." DiMarco calmed his nerves, he said, by focusing on the home front: his wife, Amy; their children, four-year-old Cristian and two-year-old Amanda; and the family cat, Titleist. "When I'm in a nervous situation, I'll close my eyes and think about my daughter or my son running around, just to get out of the moment, out of negative things." His plans for Friday evening: "Play with the kids, watch a little *SportsCenter*, go to bed."

The forecast called for hotter weather over the weekend, hot enough to bake the greens and make downhill putts run like quicksilver. The Stimpmeter, a metal ramp used to measure green speed, gave modest readings of around 10 for the Old Course at St. Andrews during Open Championship week. Fast PGA Tour greens stimp at 12, lightning-fast ones at 13. Augusta National keeps its Stimpmeter readings secret, but on a hot, breezy Masters weekend they might push 15.

TWENTY-TWO
CHALLENGERS

Saturday brought morning temperatures in the seventies, ten degrees higher than normal for April in Georgia. By the time the leaders reached the second nine that afternoon, the thermometer near the main scoreboard read 86 degrees. Club officials banned helicopters from the airspace over the course, the better to keep aerial photography under their control, but a crow flying over Amen Corner would have seen flags at the eleventh, twelfth, and thirteenth holes flapping in different directions at ten to fifteen miles an hour. The greens were forgiving enough for players who started early but got firmer and faster, making the course more difficult by the hour.

Chris DiMarco took a two-shot lead to the first tee. He had slept with his caddie the night before. Amy DiMarco, the junior high sweetheart who became Chris's wife in 1991, carried his bag when family duties allowed it. The DiMarcos seldom bickered over club selection the way Tiger and Stevie sometimes did. As Chris recalled of their rounds together, "I'd say to her, 'Do you think it's a four-iron or a five-iron?' And she'd say, 'I don't know.' And if I was acting up, she'd say, 'Stop being a baby.'" Steve Stricker, tied for fourth with Duval and Cabrera, also had his wife, Nicki, on the bag that week. When the Strickers teamed up, they often discussed which club Steve should hit, he said, along with "what we're going to have for dinner."

Like Bob May at Valhalla, DiMarco would get used to being outdriven all day. After he and Tiger matched pars at the first hole, DiMarco bogeyed the long second hole to drop a stroke but stood to get one back at the short par-4 third, where Tiger's offline tee ball rolled to a spot beside a tree. The rub of the green got worse for Tiger: he found the ball nestled against a pine cone. Loose impediments such as pine cones can be moved without penalty, but only if doing so won't cause the ball to move, and his Tour Accuracy with its half-inch black swoosh had practically plugged itself into this particular pine cone. With eighty yards to the green, he asked Williams for a pitching wedge. With his left leg pinned against the tree trunk, Tiger slapped at the ball with his wedge, trying "to kind of half fat it up there." The pine cone shot sideways, his ball looped forward and rolled to the green. He saved par while DiMarco birdied to restore his two-shot lead.

While the greens weren't yet as fast as they would be, swirling breezes were playing tricks with approach shots. Tiger was determined to avoid any choice that could bring a 6 or 7 into play. Saturday afternoon at the Masters is no time to guess about the wind. He and DiMarco matched pars at the fourth, fifth, and sixth. This was precisely the way he had opened his final rounds in the PGA at Valhalla and the U.S. Open at Pebble Beach, with six consecutive pars, playing more cautiously than he had to. With so much golf left to play, he was minimizing risk.

He was cordial, telling DiMarco "Nice shot" and "Good putt," as he did with most of his playing partners—nowhere near as tight-lipped as he might be with Phil Mickelson or Sergio García. Still, he knew the effect his power could have on shorter hitters, particularly those with less experience in the spotlight. "Tiger felt that when you're playing with a guy who hasn't been in contention in a major, you like to stamp your authority on him," Williams recalled. DiMarco had qualified for four majors in his eleven years as a pro and hadn't finished better than fifteenth. He was swinging hard at 7-iron approach shots, hoping they would stay below the hole, while his playing partner spun sand wedges that nipped upslopes and settled under flagsticks. Still he matched Tiger's birdie at the tight par-4 seventh. They both made the turn in 35.

CHRIS DIMARCO −11
TIGER WOODS −9

Other players were taking more chances. According to *SI*'s Alan Shipnuck, Mickelson was "dancing on a knife's edge" as he so often did. Playing in the group ahead of Woods and DiMarco, Mickelson had been poised to go four under par for the day with a six-foot birdie putt at the eighth. With the greens drying out and speeding up, "I tried to just trickle it in," he remembered. The putt slipped past—not a foot past, as it might have a few hours earlier, but three feet. He botched the comebacker and walked off with a bogey after three-putting from six feet. Mickelson charged back with birdies at the ninth and thirteenth only to stumble again at the fourteenth, where he fluffed a flop shot, his specialty, and missed a four-foot par putt. He would need to do better than that to have a chance of playing in the last group on Sunday.

As the leaders moved toward Amen Corner, DiMarco marveled at the throng following them. His father and brother were in the gallery somewhere, but there were so many faces in the festive crowd of more than ten thousand following the last twosome that he could never pick them out, despite looking for them all afternoon. Walking down the tenth fairway, he called over to Tiger, "You go through this every day?"

Tiger said, "Yep. How do you like it?"

DiMarco laughed. "You can have it, partner. It's all yours."

Ernie Els, playing an hour ahead of them, finished off a third-round 68 to vault from twelfth place into the top five. He had finished second to Singh at the 2000 Masters, the last major Tiger hadn't won. He had finished second behind Tiger at the 2000 U.S. Open and 2000 Open Championship, keeping his chin up and praising the winner each time, but he was ready to win again. Els had made one of the best pars of his life on Thursday, escaping a scrape that had made Tiger's run-in with a pine cone look ordinary. With his ball in a miserable lie under a tree at the tenth hole, he had considered a penalty drop. But he was already two over par. "I thought, *I'll go in there and play it.*" So he knelt beside the ball. He turned a sand wedge upside down and swung left-handed, slashing a shot that popped to the fairway and hopped all the way to the edge of the green. A fifteen-foot par saver "kept me in the tournament," and from there to the end of the third round, he went eleven under par—better than Woods, DiMarco, or anyone else. His only regret about his left-handed recovery shot was that there were no TV cameras to capture it for *SportsCenter*. Augusta National wouldn't allow eighteen-hole coverage until 2002.

Mark Calcavecchia, a little thick around the middle after he turned forty, charged into contention with a back-nine 33. A talkative veteran of twenty Tour seasons whose high fades suited the course, he was known for epic ups and downs. On the range at one Tour event, Calcavecchia dead-shanked a 5-iron shot that would have embarrassed a 20 handicapper. He laughed, then went out and shot 66. Fans remembered his collapse at the 1991 Ryder Cup as vividly as his 5-iron shot to win the 1989 Open Championship at Royal Troon. Since then he had endured a long winless streak, a divorce, and a career-threatening case of the yips. "It's hard to play when your head's in the crapper," he said. "My putting was horrific. Anything outside eighteen inches was fifty-fifty. Even when I putted good, I knew I was going to start putting bad eventually." Then one day, playing in a group behind DiMarco's, he saw DiMarco using the claw grip. He tried a modified version of the claw. After that, "I had this big old grin on my face." At the 2001 Phoenix Open, he sank putts from near and far to set a Tour scoring record of twenty-eight under par.

Two months later, Calc fired a third-round 68 that put him near the top of the scoreboard. "I'm going to have to play a great round tomorrow," he said, "but I have a chance."

Tiger spent most of his afternoon "plodding," as he put it. At the long par-4 eleventh, Amen Corner's front gate, his cautious approach stopped ten yards from the pin. With the greens quickening, he had to guard against three-putting, but he still gave his long, curling putt what he called "a *hit*." As a kid growing up on woolly public courses in Orange County, he had had to accelerate the putter through the ball. "The greens at Augusta were superfast, but I still wanted that *hit*," he said. On Augusta National's glassy greens, as anywhere else, "It was important to be decisive." This one rolled thirty feet, curling, straightening out, dropping in to pull him within a stroke of DiMarco.

The unpredictable winds in Amen Corner make the treacherous twelfth hole one of the trickiest par 3s in golf. In past years, Tiger had hit as much as a 6-iron. With 141 yards to the pin and a breeze in his face, he and Williams agreed that an 8-iron to the back of the green was the percentage play. He was starting his swing when the wind died. From the corner of his eye, he saw the flag go limp. "I should have backed off," he remembered, "but I went ahead and hit the eight-iron." Hit it over the flag and over the green. The lie wasn't bad, but there was a sprinkler head in the way, so he couldn't putt onto the green. He chipped over the sprinkler and bogeyed. He was two behind again.

It was time to get a little more aggressive. At the par-5 thirteenth, which favors a long draw off the tee, his 3-wood carried and rolled precisely 300 yards. From there he smoked a 185-yard 8-iron, barely missed an eagle putt, and tapped in to gain a stroke on DiMarco. He birdied the fourteenth to pull even, then faced a ticklish chip at the fifteenth. DiMarco, who bogeyed the hole, recalled seeing "Tiger's eyes getting a little bigger" at the chance to get up and down for a third straight birdie. Tiger put a little hook spin on his chip. With Williams urging it toward the hole, the ball curled to the left and stopped two feet from the cup. With the tap-in, Tiger had gone without a par since they entered Amen Corner, going birdie, bogey, birdie, birdie, birdie.

TIGER WOODS −12
CHRIS DIMARCO −10

They finished the round that way. Tiger's 68 gave him the third-round lead while DiMarco's even-par 72 kept him close. But Chris and Amy DiMarco wouldn't be rejoining Tiger and Williams for the final round. Sunday's last twosome was almost certain to be Woods and Calcavecchia—a pairing of the genial Calc and golf's most relentless calculator. Only Mickelson, still out on the course, had a chance to crash the party.

Mickelson was a leaderboard watcher. "I knew I needed to birdie seventeen and eighteen to get into the last group," he recalled. "I wanted to be playing with him." He didn't need to say who he meant by "him." But even after sinking a fifteen-footer for birdie at the seventeenth, Phil had a mountain to climb on the uphill finishing hole. Of all the leaders, only Els had played the last two holes even one under par that day, much less birdie them both. Mickelson surprised his fans by playing for position with an iron off the eighteenth tee but crushed a 2-iron and followed it with an 8-iron to birdie range. A ten-foot putt would get him into Sunday's final twosome.

He looked the putt over from every angle. He rolled it in.

"I have a lot of respect for Tiger," Mickelson said minutes later. "With that being said, I've been able to go head-to-head with him and come out on top a few times." Earlier, asked again and again how it felt to play with Tiger Woods, he had joked, "It's soooo groovy!" Then he'd added, "No, it's enjoyable. I like playing with the best." Now the world's top two golfers would tee off together the next day, with Phil's first major and Tiger's Slam on the line.

"I like my chances," Mickelson said.

How much did he want to win? "Desperately."

Mickelson's birdie-birdie finish would leave DiMarco and Calcavecchia, a pair of reformed yippers, in Sunday's next-to-last pairing. "We've got a couple of funky grips," Calcavecchia said. "We'll be clawing it together all day." As for the leader, "Tiger is a human being, and he's going to be nervous. However, he *is* the best in the world. He has that going for him!"

Els and Duval were three shots off the pace at –9. "Tiger's not going to back down. He's the danger man out there," Els said. "But there's a lot of talent on that leaderboard. Even if you're three or four behind going to the final nine, you've got a chance. It all happens on the back nine on Sunday."

Duval swore that his back and wrist were sound, and he had three subpar rounds to prove it. After just missing a playoff with O'Meara at the 1998 Masters, after six top-ten finishes in the next ten majors, he was in the mix again. Reporting for another mandatory press conference, a task he enjoyed about as much as a two-stroke penalty, he looked around a half-empty room. Duval's galleries had been about half the size of Tiger's. So was the crowd in the media center. "I thought I played fairly well," he said, "but because of the turnout, I guess I didn't play all that well."

Like Mickelson, he was dying to win his first major, though he would never admit to being desperate to do so. Like Mickelson, Duval was a rival Team Tiger saw as a threat to go low enough on Sunday to spoil the Slam. Did he think he could do it?

"There's a lot of people that have a chance," he said. "I think I'm one of them."

When it was Tiger's turn in the media center, he faced a standing-room-only crowd of reporters. His first comments were typically bland: "There are a lot of good players at the top of the board who have a wonderful chance. I'm going to go out there with the intent of trying to keep the ball in play and put it on the green so I have, hopefully, some uphill putts."

Reporters pressed him for his thoughts on what one called "the historical implications of tomorrow. Are you thinking about that or just totally shutting it out?"

"I'm thinking about my swing," he said. "Going to the range to work on it. Sorry."

The questions kept coming. "Give us something better than that. This is something a lot of us may never see again in our lifetime—if you win. Has that entered your mind?"

"I hope you live a little longer, then." The writers laughed. A few applauded. When there were no more questions, he stood up and headed for the practice putting green, where he met Butch Harmon for an hour's work before dinner.

TWENTY-THREE
THE BACK NINE ON SUNDAY

Augusta National's back nine was originally the front nine. Horton Smith played the course that way when he held off Craig Wood at the first Augusta National Golf Club Annual Invitation Tournament in 1934 to win $1,500, worth about $35,000 today. The Augusta lawyer and businessman Bobby Jones, thirty-two, tied for thirteenth and earned $0. He was still and always an amateur.

During the club's first years, the members struggled on the front nine, where their brassie and niblick shots kept bouncing into Rae's Creek. In their day, the holes now known as Amen Corner—Augusta's eleventh, twelfth, and thirteenth—were the second, third, and fourth. And the golfers thought the other nine was easier. As a mercy to the members, Jones and the other club officers reversed the nines in 1935, giving their friends a better chance to warm up. The legendary sportswriter Grantland Rice, a founding member of the club, blessed the switch and dubbed their annual invitational "the Masters."

Then as now, club officials never refer to a front side or back side in order to avoid reminding anyone of a person's backside. At Augusta, there is the "first nine," where the world's best golfers vie for position on Masters Sunday, and the "second nine," where the drama plays out.

Tiger Woods arrived with hours to spare on Sunday, his eyes hidden behind his white-framed sunglasses, dressed in a Sunday-red shirt with black slacks and a black cap with a Nike swoosh. Fighting a late-morning case of nerves, he calmed down by controlling his breathing. After hitting balls on the range and practice putting green, he walked to the first tee flanked by the usual pair of security guards. On the way he passed a crowd of supporters including Nike CEO Phil Knight, who was paying him $20 million a year, and Tida Woods, who called out, "Good luck, Tiger!" He ignored them.

He wasn't being rude. "He was *focused*," Butch Harmon recalled. "He was thinking about his tee shot on the first hole."

By then the *Augusta Chronicle*, seeking Black voices for a story on the weekend's action, had found a bunch of them—not at the Masters but at a public course nearby, where "about a dozen black men at Augusta Municipal Golf Course" were watching on TV, pulling for Tiger. So was Augusta resident James Brown, who told the *Chronicle* that Tiger Woods was "good for the country," comparing him to Joe Louis, boxing's "Brown Bomber."

At 2:55 p.m., Tiger joined Mickelson on the first tee. Skies were clear, the weather still warm at 85 degrees but not as hot as the day before. Was he still jittery? Over the past eight months he had practiced this very shot several hundred times, picturing a high fade over the bunker at the corner of the gentle dogleg to the right, executing it perfectly before he left the range. This time he pulled it to the wrong side of the fairway and beyond—into trouble in the pines to the left. He punched out, chipped on, and two-putted for bogey while Mickelson made a routine par. Now they were tied.

Tiger pummeled his tee ball at the 575-yard second, where he reached the green with a drive and a 4-iron, a pair of near-perfect shots. Two putts for birdie got him back to –12. Mickelson matched him to stay tied. An unruly patron whistled and shouted, "Go, Phil!" The final pairing dueled through the rest of the first nine, with Tiger carding four pars before stepping up his game with birdies at the seventh and eighth while Mickelson was his usual up-and-down self, playing the fourth through eighth holes bogey, birdie, bogey, birdie, birdie. Ahead of them, Ángel Cabrera and the red-hot Jim Furyk pulled closer while Ernie Els blew a three-foot putt to drop a stroke at the fifth. Els was on his way to another long day of watching his playing partner charge toward a major title, but this time the charger was Duval. Wearing a white shirt buttoned up to his Adam's apple and a black Nike cap identical to Tiger's, Duval reeled off six front-nine birdies without changing his deadpan expression. A leaderboard full of marquee names made his pre-round prediction ring true: "It's everything you want in a Masters Sunday." Duval parred the ninth to shoot 32 on the first nine. Minutes later, Woods and Mickelson made the turn in 34. The stage was set for a second nine to stir the ghosts in Amen Corner.

TIGER WOODS –14
DAVID DUVAL –14
PHIL MICKELSON –13

Television coverage didn't begin until well into the afternoon. It began with a sepia-toned tribute to Bobby Jones, followed by a sepia-toned tapestry of still photos and grainy clips featuring Palmer, Player, Nicklaus, Ballesteros, Faldo, and Woods. When the live feed began, CBS anchor Jim Nantz welcomed 40 million viewers to the climactic day of Tiger's run at four straight majors. "Today," he said, "golf takes a step into the future."

• • •

Tiger would remember the round as four and a half hours of "grinding, grinding, grinding." He had to deal with a rub of the brown at the par-4 tenth, where he and Williams looked down at his ball and saw that it had picked up a speck of mud. There is only one way to manage the flight of a mud-flecked golf ball: hit it and hope. Mud-flecked balls don't usually fly as far as clean ones, but this one sailed over the flag and bounced to a devilish lie behind the green. He saved his four with a jeweler's touch, getting up and down for par as Mickelson got lucky. While Tiger contended with a muddy ball, Phil was banging a sideways approach shot that struck the trunk of a pine tree and bounced to a safe lie, saving a four of his own.

The greens were speeding up, the wind quickening as they reached Amen Corner. Calcavecchia clawed his way into contention until he left an approach on the high side of the hole at the thirteenth, the wrong side. Aiming his putt twenty feet right of the cup, he rolled his Pro V1 up a slope and watched it pause ten feet above the hole. Then the ball turned over once more, picked up speed, and nearly ran off the green. Calcavecchia bogeyed and fell back.

At the par-4 eleventh, the most difficult par 4 on the course, where a pond guards the green, Tiger hit a 310-yard drive and had 145 yards to a tucked Sunday pin. Only two Masters winners had ever birdied the eleventh on their way to a green jacket: Jack Nicklaus in 1986 and Tiger Woods in 1997. Tiger could easily hit a wedge 145 yards, but a wedge shot might spin back off the green into the pond. He opted for what he called "a little chippy eight-iron" that flew lower and wouldn't spin as much. Tracking the shot in the air, he pursed his lips and narrowed his eyes. He liked it. "Yes," Williams said under his breath. The ball landed and began rolling like a putt. It stopped eighteen inches from the hole.

According to ESPN's Andy North, a two-time U.S. Open winner,

"What Woods did at the 11th hole was unreal. That's a scary shot. . . . You could stand there literally 50 times and you couldn't hit a ball as close as he hit that one."

Duval, two holes ahead, heard the Tiger roar behind him. The volunteers behind the Masters' manually operated scoreboard got busy switching names and scores.

TIGER WOODS −15

DAVID DUVAL −14

PHIL MICKELSON −12

The par-3 twelfth at Augusta National, named Golden Bell for the yellow-flowered shrubs behind the green, rings up more double and triple bogeys than any other hole on the course. With input from Bobby Jones, Alister MacKenzie designed it sideways, with a narrow green that would make for a more typical par 3 if the tee were in the woods to the left. Instead, golfers need to float tee shots to a neck of turf beyond Rae's Creek, with bunkers fore and aft and the grassy bank near the front fringe trimmed so tight that shots with a touch too much spin trickle backward into the creek. That was where Arnold Palmer, chasing a second straight green jacket, made a triple-bogey 6 and lost the 1959 Masters by two strokes. And the twelfth at Augusta wasn't finished with its victims.

On his way to victory at the 1980 Masters, Spain's Seve Ballesteros double-bogeyed the hole and was widely quoted calling himself a "son of a beech." That same year, Tom Weiskopf was even par as he stood on the twelfth tee. After his ball spun off the front fringe and rolled into the creek, he could still hope to save bogey. Weiskopf took a drop and swung a sand wedge. *Splash.* After two more tries and two more splashes, he stood in the drop zone near the creek, lying eight. Patrons couldn't help giggling. His next shot landed short of the creek but hopped in. His eleventh stroke stuck on the back of the green. From there he two-putted for a 13, the only ten-over-par "decuple bogey" in tournament history. Asked if his ordeal might help him identify with golf's struggling duffers, Weiskopf said, "I can't even identify with myself after that."

In 1996, Greg Norman rinsed his tee ball in Rae's Creek on the same hole and double-bogeyed to lose his lead over Nick Faldo. Later years would bring a disastrous double by Mickelson in 2009, a Rory McIlroy four-putt in 2011, a quadruple-bogey 7 to sink Jordan Spieth in 2016, and a 10 by a fellow named Woods in 2020.

Coming off his crowd-pleasing birdie at the eleventh, Woods had the honor. He had called the tee shot at the twelfth "one of the most demanding and confusing in golf, because of the wind and where the green is situated. You have to time your swing around the wind, and you have to get lucky." He had made 6 there the year before, when the wind had knocked down his 8-iron, which had crept back into the creek, a shot that had helped keep him from challenging Singh for the lead. If not for that 8-iron at the twelfth in 2000, he might have been going for his sixth straight major now.

There wasn't enough breeze to ruffle his shirt as he stood on the tee. But the wind could shift at any second. A sly gust through the trees could change a shot once it was in the air. He waited, watching the treetops. He took an 8-iron, the same club he hit in the creek the year before. The air was still as he started his swing. He went through with it, "but as soon as I made contact, I could feel the wind on the back of my neck." Thinking *Please don't affect the ball*, he looked up in time to see the wind carry it into the bunker behind the green. Then he watched Mickelson's near duplicate of his tee shot hang up in the breeze and drop short of the same bunker, safely on the green.

The two of them crossed the Hogan Bridge to the green. The bridge is made of gray stones to evoke the Swilcan Bridge at St. Andrews but carpeted with all-American AstroTurf. Tiger gentled his sand shot to a landing in the fringe behind the green, which took enough speed off the ball to bring it to a stop six feet from the hole.

Mickelson lagged to tap-in range.

A hole ahead of them, Duval unwrapped a protein bar. He was taking a bite when he heard a groan from Amen Corner. Tiger had missed his par putt.

TIGER WOODS −14
DAVID DUVAL −14
PHIL MICKELSON −12

Leaving the twelfth green, Woods and Mickelson crossed the green-carpeted Byron Nelson Bridge to the next tee and a drive Tiger had been waiting eight months to hit.

The par-5 thirteenth at Augusta National doglegs to another side-long green guarded by a creek. The ideal first shot would be a long, sweeping draw for Tiger, a fade for a lefty like Phil, who called the thirteenth "my favorite hole at Augusta. It sets up better for a lefty than for a right-handed golfer. It's much easier to hit a big fade around the dogleg corner than it is to try to hook it."

Mickelson had the honor. There was no doubt that he would hit driver. He leaned into a towering fade that wowed the crowd, splitting the fairway less than two hundred yards from the green.

For Tiger, there was risk as well as potential reward at the thirteenth. He was so long off the tee that he didn't dare hit driver. He reached for his 15-degree Titleist 3-wood, the club he had swung a thousand times in practice while thinking of Sunday at the Masters. "In every practice session in those eight months, he would nominate shots," Williams recalled. "In particular, that big draw at thirteen. I would say, 'Let's see the tee shot on the thirteenth at Augusta.' Every time, he would have a three-wood in his hand." But even a 3-wood would sail into the trees to the right if it didn't draw at a severe enough angle. In practice he sometimes blocked the shot to the right or pull-hooked it dead left. He had struck the ideal sweeper often enough to "see that specific shot in my mind's eye," but as he set up over the ball, he still wondered, "Will it hold up under pressure?"

Looking back later, he would remember his tee shot at the thirteenth in the present tense. "My last thought before I take the club back is *Draw*." He seldom swung all out, preferring control to maximum power. This time was different. He launched a sweeping draw that slingshotted around the dogleg and kept going. If this wasn't the perfect golf shot he'd said was his ultimate goal, it would do for now. The ball flew past Mickelson's drive, bounced, and rolled fifteen more yards.

Mickelson had studiously avoided watching Tiger's swing all day. Now, hearing the patrons hoot and holler, he looked up in time to see Tiger's ball settle into the fairway well past his drive. As they were leaving the tee box he asked, "Do you always hit your three-wood that far?"

"No," Tiger said, laying it on thick. "Sometimes farther."

That was a bit of a mind game, Williams remembered. "He wanted to humiliate Phil," who had no idea how many times Tiger had tried that big slinger and knocked it to parts unknown. After hundreds of rehearsals, "that was the best one Tiger ever hit," Williams said. "He looked over and gave me a little wink."

Just as he'd done at the eleventh, Tiger had set up a birdie or possible eagle by picturing the hole in reverse, the way his father had taught him: from the green to the ideal position in the fairway, and from there back to the tee. He and Mickelson matched second shots, hitting irons safely left of Sunday's sucker pin. Both men two-putted for birdie.

Duval, playing ahead with Els, was swinging like a well-oiled machine while showing as much emotion as the USGA's golf ball–testing robot, Iron Byron. After barely missing an eagle chip at the par-5 fifteenth, he tapped in for a share of the lead.

Woods and Mickelson's next hole, the par-4 fourteenth, was

bunkerless but not defenseless. The green featured a false front below an upper tier that could send unsuspecting putts downhill like luge racers. Ben Crenshaw called it "the most three-puttable green in America." Tiger described the margin for error there as "infinitesimal." He and Mickelson waited in the fairway as Calcavecchia, playing in the group ahead of them, miscalculated a birdie putt, easing his ball toward the hole and watching it run almost twenty feet past. Now at –9 after consecutive bogeys, he was out of the running as the Masters came down to the world's three best players.

When the green was clear, Tiger flew a wedge over the flagstick. "Perfect," said Williams. "Absolutely perfect." They expected Tiger's Nike Tour Accuracy, spinning to his exacting specifications, to check and creep back. Instead, the ball stuck twenty-five feet above the hole. He yawped at it: "Aw, come on!"

Mickelson's wedge shot landed in nearly the same spot and spun back, leaving him a twelve-footer for birdie. Tiger sputtered "God" out loud and "Damn it" under his breath, slapping his wedge to the turf.

His birdie putt tracked a similar line to the one that had sent Calcavecchia to a three-putt bogey, but Tiger started his a bit higher. It stayed that way before coiling leftward in the last few feet as the crowd's voice rose, cheering it toward the cup as it slid down from the high side, the "pro side," with every chance to fall in.

It whispered past the lip. He was still grinding, tapping in for his par, still tied with Duval while Mickelson looked over his twelve-footer to pull within a shot of them.

Mickelson's birdie putt was harder than it looked, and he knew it. Tiger Woods wasn't the only player who watched tapes of old majors. "In 1986, Tom Kite had basically the same putt and left it short," Mickelson said later. The putt also had a subtle break to the left. He read the break with precision but repeated Kite's mistake. "I got so into the line that I forgot to make an aggressive stroke. Left it right in the heart, too."

TIGER WOODS −15
DAVID DUVAL −15
PHIL MICKELSON −13

Tiger had gained no ground on the second nine. That gave Duval a chance to take the lead alone at the par-3 sixteenth. With the temperature still hovering between 80 and 85, he toweled off his face, arms, hands, and the face of his 7-iron. "I can't pull out an eight," he recalled. Not with 176 yards to carry the front bunker, 183 to the pin. With an 8-iron, anything less than fully flush contact was likely to fall short. He took two practice swings, then fired a 7-iron that he thought "might be the best golf shot I ever hit." It easily cleared the bunker, arrowing toward the flag. "I thought I might have made a one."

A patron yelled, "In the hole! Go in the hole!"

Duval watched with mounting concern as his ball seemed to defy gravity. It flew over the flag and over the green, kicking to the collar of the rough. For an instant his chin dropped. Had his protein bar plus adrenaline plus too-pure contact turned his 7-iron into a 6? At the worst possible time? He would have a cruel downhill chip to the green.

At the hole behind him, the par-5 fifteenth, Tiger was at the top of his backswing. Shifting his weight into a 120-mile-an-hour downswing, he suddenly stopped in midswing—a feat of strength, particularly in his wrists, and split-second timing.

He glared at one of the fans crowding the tee, a man whose camera had audibly clicked. Williams pointed at the offender. "Cameras are not allowed!"

Tiger stepped out of the tee box. He said, "Put the cameras away, will ya?" He snapped the towel off his bag, wiped his face and the grip of his driver. "The gallery goes so quiet when I'm preparing to hit," he once recalled, "that when someone does speak or a camera clicks, it can sound like a bomb going off." After a minute he steadied his breathing. "I controlled my heart rate through my breathing. I was able to get into an almost meditative state on the course." He took his stance again and thumped a 312-yard drive down the middle.

Duval was standing over his ball at the sixteenth. After a moment he chose the same club he had hit from the tee, a 7-iron, to chip to the glassy green sloping away from him. The shot skipped through the fringe, picked up speed, and ran six feet past the hole—an exquisite play from a devilish lie. He cracked a smile for once.

Meanwhile, Mickelson was in trouble at the fifteenth. With a sturdy pine blocking his way, he hit a long, looping second shot that left him with a fluffy lie in a greenside bunker. From there, an up-and-down birdie by a player famous for his short game would be an odds-on proposition. Tiger's second shot checked up safely below the pin, earning a cheer that carried the two hundred yards to Duval on the sixteenth green. Tiger would have an uphill twenty-two-footer for eagle. He gave Williams a fist bump.

Duval took his time over his six-foot par putt. It could keep him tied with Tiger, at least for the moment. It was the sort of putt he would make three times out of four. It never had a chance, leaking to the right and dropping him to –14 with two challenging par 4s ahead.

Mickelson, too, could match that score with an up-and-down birdie. When his aggressive bunker shot ran twelve feet past, Tiger had a chance to take command of the tournament. Sinking his makeable eagle putt would give him a two-shot lead with three holes to play if Phil holed his putt, a three-shot edge if Phil missed. He gave his eagle try a firm rap and watched it slip by the hole.

Mickelson stayed close by knocking his putt to the heart of the cup. Woods stepped up to finish off his three-footer for birdie. And looked startled when he lipped it out. He tapped in for a three-putt par on a hole he had birdied Thursday, Friday, and Saturday, knowing he'd had his pursuers on the ropes and letting them stay on their feet. He stared down at the cup while Williams replaced the flagstick. Mickelson, his throat unstepped on, headed for the next tee.

TIGER WOODS −15
DAVID DUVAL −14
PHIL MICKELSON −14

The leader muttered on his way to the sixteenth tee but was calm by the time he got there. He remembered something Harmon liked to say, a truism that traced back from Nicklaus and Hogan to Jones: "Your last shot has nothing to do with your next shot." As he said later, "I kept my head down the entire time I was walking to the tee. *Forget that hole. You have three holes to play. You have a one-shot lead. Let's go ahead and make one more birdie coming in.*"

Mickelson had honors at the par-3 sixteenth. Like Duval, he hit a 7-iron, but he pulled it. His Pro V1 drifted to the right and stopped on the green's top tier, forty feet above the hole. From there he had next to no shot at birdie and major worries about saving par. The two best players without a major win had given Tiger all the battle he wanted through sixty-nine holes only to misfire from the tee where Nicklaus had drilled a 5-iron shot to three feet in 1986 on the way to the last and most celebrated of his eighteen major victories. That was a highlight Tiger could picture as he teed up his ball. He made a point of re-watching Nicklaus's 1986 Masters triumph every year before the tournament started. He could quote Jack's caddie—his son Jackie— who had watched the ball in flight and said, "Be good." Tiger knew that the Golden Bear hadn't bothered to watch the ball. Jack was leaning down to pick up his tee when he said, "It is."

Unlike the other leaders, Tiger hit an 8-iron. His ball dropped a foot from Mickelson's, bit the green, and spun back to two-putt territory. Advantage Tiger.

Mickelson's long lag stopped six feet below the hole. He was marking his ball while Duval missed a ten-footer for birdie at the seventeenth. Didn't anybody want to stop Tiger's Slam?

Phil did, desperately. After Tiger cozied his putt to twelve inches, ensuring his 3 to stay at fifteen under, Mickelson lined up his six-footer to stay within a stroke. Like Duval and most other Tour pros, he made almost 75 percent of his six-foot putts. Like Duval, he missed that one, pushing it past the cup.

Patrons groaned. Tiger was two up on Mickelson, one up on Duval.

But Duval wasn't finished yet. A near-perfect approach at the eighteenth gave him a six-foot putt to tie Tiger.

Mickelson wasn't done, either. He attacked the uphill seventeenth, firing his approach to ten feet. Tiger's more cautious approach landed twenty-five feet right of the pin, in safe two-putt range. Then came another "Aw, come on!" moment. His ball came down in a perfect position, hesitated, and rolled back off the green. That left him a touchy up-and-down for par while Mickelson was looking at birdie.

The short game was the last facet of the game that Tiger Woods mastered. "When he first turned pro, he had an average short game by Tour player standards," Butch Harmon remembered. "Through sheer determination and an unquenchable quest for new information, Tiger built the best short game in the world." During practice rounds with one of his mentors, Raymond Floyd, Tiger had learned to use different clubs around the green. "When I first came to work with him," said Williams, who had caddied for Floyd, "Tiger would chip with only one club. I shared some of Raymond's tricks with him. Raymond could chip with a three-iron, five-iron, seven-iron, you name it. Tiger's chipping improved, and he'd often say, when he wanted to hole a chip, 'Okay, Stevie, time for a Raymondo here.'"

Tiger settled over his chip on the brink of the seventeenth green.

His bump-and-run Raymondo threatened the hole but slipped past. He leaned back on his heels, amazed that it hadn't gone in.

Duval settled over his short birdie putt at the eighteenth. Tiger remembered listening for news from the crowd. "There isn't a leaderboard on every hole," he said, but he was familiar enough with Augusta on a Masters weekend "to decipher generally what's happening by the roars around me, or the lack of them." Moments after his ball spun back off the green at the seventeenth, he heard one. *David's stuffed it at eighteen*, he thought. But after Tiger chipped onto the seventeenth green, there was no roar from the same direction. "When I didn't hear anything after my chip, I said to myself, *David missed it*."

Duval, crushed after missing three short putts at the sixteenth, seventeenth, and eighteenth, strode past CBS Sports' Bill Macatee, refusing to talk.

Tiger saved par at the seventeenth. Mickelson missed his birdie putt.

TIGER WOODS –15
DAVID DUVAL –14
PHIL MICKELSON –13

Barring an eagle deuce by Mickelson, a par at the last hole would seal the Slam for Tiger.

He lashed a 330-yard drive up the chute to the last fairway. It was the longest drive of the day at the uphill eighteenth, increasing his average distance for the week to a record 305.5.

Mickelson yanked his tee ball into the pines. It popped out safely but left him sixty yards short of Tiger's ball. From there, he stuck his approach fifteen feet behind the flagstick. After all his adventures, Phil was still alive. If he sank his birdie putt and Tiger bogeyed, they would go to a playoff.

Tiger's seventy-five-yard flip wedge shot dropped over the flag and spun back, his ball settling inches from Phil's Pro V1. For all practical purposes, that sealed it. Even a make-miss in Phil's favor would leave him a stroke behind.

But Tiger wasn't letting his guard down. Still focused on playing the hole, he marched uphill between greenside bunkers, unsmiling. His parents were waiting behind the green—Earl in a Titleist cap Acushnet paid him to wear and Tida dressed in Sunday red, smiling under her trademark red visor. For most of the day they had been two of only a few people of color in a gallery of thousands, but now many of the club's daily workers—busboys, waiters, cooks, cleaners, trash collectors, and parking attendants, most of them Black—came out to watch.

Tiger studied his eighteen-foot putt with his customary care. He wanted to end on the correct note. The putt would be quick. He started it on its way. It was a foot from the cup when he raised his fist, watching it fall.

In the CBS booth above the green, Jim Nantz spoke the line he'd been saving for this moment. "There it is," he said. "As grand as it gets!"

Earl wagged a finger at Tida as if to say, "I told you!"

Their son stepped aside to let Mickelson finish. Tiger blinked. He took a long breath. He took off his cap and hid his face behind it. "I started thinking, *I don't have any shots left to play*. I was in such a zone. When you're focused so hard on each and every shot, you kind of forget everything else. Realizing you have no shots left takes you a little by surprise. It's weird. *Finished*. I started losing it, getting a little emotional. That's why I put the cap over my face, to pull it together so that when Phil made his putt I was able to shake his hand."

Phil didn't make his putt. He two-putted to finish third, then doffed his black visor and shook Tiger's hand. Mickelson had made twenty-five birdies that week, topping everyone else, including Tiger, who had made twenty-two. He and Duval had both birdied the fifteenth, where Tiger had three-putted, only to miss chances at the

Overcome by emotion when he completed the Slam, Tiger hid his face behind his cap.

sixteenth, seventeenth, and eighteenth. The conventional wisdom says that he who putts best on Sunday wins the Masters. Mickelson had taken seven putts on the last three holes, Duval six, Tiger five.

Tiger followed him off the green. Still carrying his putter, Tiger embraced Earl and pulled Tida into a family hug. Butch Harmon, holding back tears, got a quick hug as the champion ducked into the scorer's hut.

Fourth-place finisher Calcavecchia stood nearby with Fred Couples, waiting to congratulate the winner. "It's a Grand Slam," said Calc. "I know some historians feel differently. They think you need to win all four in one year." According to Couples, "Maybe it's not if you're a historian. But it will never get done again."

Mickelson spoke to CBS Sports' Macatee after signing his card. "I missed some crucial putts," he said. "I'm throwing shots away left and right, and to compete against Tiger—that's not cutting it."

Brad Faxon said, "I've heard people say Tiger doesn't have the players to play against like Jack did when he had Player and Palmer and Watson. That's such a crock. Sure, David and Phil haven't won majors yet. But there are more good players now. If Tiger wasn't here, you'd see a lot more trophies on the mantles of Els, Duval and Mickelson."

Duval looked out at a standing-room-only crowd at his mandatory news conference. An hour after finishing second, he had collected himself.

"The first thing I'd like to say is congratulations to Tiger. He's a friend of mine." Still puzzled at the 7-iron shot that flew the green at sixteen, he lamented one of golf's ironies: "I don't want to say it was untimely, but if I had missed it a little bit, it would have turned out well." Asked to put his friend's four straight majors into perspective, he said, "I probably can't. I don't know what to compare it with because I'm not sure there's something you *could* compare it with in modern golf."

Within minutes of sinking his last putt to win by two, Tiger fielded a call from George W. Bush, the latest golfing president. "There is no greater honor than to represent your country and to wear the green jacket," Bush told him.

When it was Tiger's turn to face the press, he spoke about luck. "When I won here in '97, I hadn't been a pro for a full year. I've witnessed a lot since that first year. I have a better appreciation of winning a major championship. To win four of them in succession is hard to believe. You have to peak at the right time. On top of that, you have to have some luck. To have it happen four straight times—some of the golfing gods must be looking down on me."

A reporter asked, "If you were to meet Bobby Jones in the clubhouse tonight, what would you say to him?"

Tiger said, "Wow." He gave the question some thought. Jones, who still had a locker in the Champions Locker Room, had died in 1971. "Well, how he came back is what I'd want to know. I'd probably ask him, 'What the heck are you doing here?'" That got a laugh from the jam-packed media center. "And then probably ask if he'd want to sit down and have a beer."

Earl Woods, who had claimed that a true Grand Slam needed to take place in a calendar year, changed his mind. Maybe four majors over two years was just as good. "It's like when a scientist discovers a star," he said. "He discovers it, he gets his name on it. Nobody's ever done this before, so Tiger should get his name on it."

Butch Harmon thought Earl had it right. "People said it wasn't a real Grand Slam," said Harmon. "Tiger heard that. We all did. Well, Bobby Jones won a Grand Slam with two amateur events in it. And here's something I can tell you about Tiger Woods: the good Lord gave him great talent, but his greatest strength was what you couldn't see. He outworked everybody. He was smarter than everybody. I think

Tiger was put on the planet Earth to do what he did: to play the game better than anyone before or since, and that's Slam enough for me."

Tiger Woods would go on to win nine more major championships. He would become pro golf's first billionaire. He would endure injuries that traced back to a lifetime of swinging golf clubs with unprecedented force hundreds of thousands of times. He would suffer scandals of his own making. He would win the 2019 Masters at the age of forty-three after eleven years without winning a major, running his total to fifteen, three short of Nicklaus. But for all the injuries and tabloid headlines to come, he could always look back on the spring of 2001, when he flew home from Augusta and put the Masters Trophy on his coffee table along with the sterling silver U.S. Open Championship Trophy, the Claret Jug, and the PGA's Wanamaker Trophy. He was twenty-five years old.

"I wasn't in the game for the trophies," he said. He was in it for what they represented: "The Tiger Slam, as people call it—the Grand Slam to me, because I won four majors in a row."

EPILOGUE
LEGACIES

Wincing, he punched a wedge out of thick U.S. Open rough. His knee was killing him. Drives hurt the most. It was June 15, 2008, seven years after the Tiger Slam. The weather was mild during the U.S. Open at Torrey Pines Golf Course in San Diego, with colorful hang gliders riding updrafts over the beach while fans climbed rocks near seaside holes to get a look at Tiger Woods. But he was miserable.

Two months after surgery on his left knee, he had trudged through four days of five-hour rounds on the longest course in major-championship history. A right-handed golfer pivots on his left leg. No one else knew it yet, but he had a torn ACL and two stress fractures in his left tibia, the bone between the knee and the ankle. Dressed in a bright Sunday-red shirt and black Nike cap, he was grinding as never before, walking gingerly between swings, going all-out on drives that left him gnashing his teeth in pain.

He reached the final green tied for second behind Rocco Mediate, facing a do-or-die putt to force a playoff. The putt was twice as long as the six-footer he had holed to make the playoff with Bob May at the 2000 PGA. Since then, he had won the 2002 Masters and U.S. Open, the 2005 Masters and Open Championship, the 2006 Open Championship, and the 2007 PGA, running his career total to thirteen majors. A third U.S. Open title would get him a step closer to Nicklaus's eighteen.

Mediate, watching on a locker room TV, was on the brink of winning his first major at the age of forty-five. A bubbly Tour veteran, he was a Tiger Woods fan. After a limping Tiger closed his third round with a rush featuring a birdie and two eagles, Mediate had hugged him and said, "Are you completely out of your mind? Jeez-oh, man!"

Mediate expected Tiger to sink his twelve-footer to force a playoff between them. "That's what he *does*."

Tiger agreed with Steve Williams that the putt would break seven inches to the left. He started it on its way. It broke six and a half inches, barely enough to catch the right lip, then spun to the back of the cup and dropped in.

He won the next day's playoff in sudden death. At the time, that was simply what he did. "With his 14 career majors," *Sports Illustrated* reported, "Woods has crept ever closer to Nicklaus's epic total of 18, and it is mind-boggling to think that at 32 he is potentially one great calendar year away from attaining the unattainable."

Instead, he was almost finished winning majors. Within a year, his life unraveled. Sex scandals and his first car crash turned his name into a punch line. David Letterman's "Top Ten Tiger Woods Text Messages" included "I'm sorry, which mistress is this?" as well as "I was dreaming about you when I was passed out on the street" and "You're breaking up with me for Lee Trevino?" Jay Leno asked, "What's the difference between Santa Claus and Tiger Woods? Santa quits after three ho's!"

A chastened Woods apologized to his family, his wife, and his fans. At thirty-three, he looked finished. But he had enough left in him

Proud dad Tiger joined son, Charlie, on the course.

for an encore. More than a decade later, after going winless in twenty-eight majors, he came from behind to win the 2019 Masters.

"Overwhelming," he called it. "My dad was here in 1997. My mom's here—she was there in '97 as well. And now I'm the dad." His children with Elin Nordegren, daughter Sam and son Charlie—named for Charlie Sifford—were there to see him win his fifteenth major. "It means the world," he said. "It's come full circle."

Nicklaus's record of eighteen majors is safe, but Tiger's influence on the game has been far greater. In 1995, the year before he turned professional, there were 25 million golf fans in America. Today, due in large part to Tigermania, which made golf more popular than ever, there are 40 million. While becoming the pro tour's first billionaire, he also enriched other players. Darren Clarke joked that Tiger shouldn't do anything as dangerous as skiing or scuba diving "because he's making us all so much money." In 1995, total purses on the PGA Tour amounted to $56 million, equal to about $110 million in 2024 dollars. Today they total more than $500 million. Greg Norman led the 1995 PGA Tour with $1.65 million in winnings. Wyndham Clark, Brian Harman, and Xander Schauffele all earned more than that by tying for second at the 2024 Players Championship. Scottie Scheffler won that tournament while running his 2024 earnings to $27.6 million before the Fourth of July.

More lasting than fandom and money is the fact that at his peak, Tiger Woods played golf better than anyone else, before or since.

Tiger Woods holds the record for consecutive weeks as the top-ranked player in the world, 281, which he set from 2005 to 2010. He also ranks second, with another run of 264 weeks from 1999 to 2004. Greg Norman stands third on the all-time list with 96 consecutive weeks. In all, Woods spent 683 weeks ranked number one in the world. That's thirteen years. To match that record, Scottie Scheffler would need to maintain his number one ranking every week until 2035.

Jack Nicklaus called Tiger the best player ever. Gary Player considered the Tiger Slam the greatest achievement in sports history. "One of the first things I noticed about Tiger," Player said, "was his strong belief in his own destiny." Nick Faldo agreed, saying "Tiger knew he was different. Special. Nobody could drive it like him. Nobody could hit long irons like him. The wedges, the putter—there wasn't anybody ever who was that good in every department."

According to Justin Ray, who analyzes the game for the Golf Channel and The Athletic, "Woods had an incomprehensible run of twenty wins in forty official PGA Tour starts from the 1999 Memorial through the 2001 Memorial. Then he did it again in a forty-start span from late 2005 through the 2008 U.S. Open." Ray was just getting warmed up. "In the last sixty years, there are three instances of a player winning five or more PGA Tour starts in a row. They belong to Tiger Woods with seven straight, Tiger Woods with six straight, and Tiger Woods with five straight—all separate streaks. He is the only player since 1950 to win the same PGA Tour event four years in a row, and he did it twice, at Bay Hill from 2000 through 2003 and Torrey Pines from 2005 through 2008."

From 1999 through 2007, Woods played in seventeen WGC stroke-play tournaments, the nonmajors with the strongest fields, and won twelve times. He was a combined 188 under par in those events. That was 131 strokes better than any other player, with Jim Furyk second best at 57 under.

Tiger's dominance was never more dramatic than during the ten-month span in which he won all four majors. Since then, four players have won two consecutive majors. Phil Mickelson won the 2005 PGA Championship and 2006 Masters back to back; Pádraig Harrington won the 2008 Open Championship and PGA; Rory McIlroy won the 2014 Open Championship and PGA; Jordan Spieth won the 2015

Masters and U.S. Open. They all fell short of three in a row, much less four. No golfer since Tiger has held three of the four major titles at the same time. Only Brooks Koepka, who won three out of five in 2018–2019, came close.

Other metrics attest to his brilliance. After rebuilding his swing in 1997–1998 and switching golf balls in 2000, Woods didn't merely lead the world's best players in driving distance during his Grand Slam; he blew them away, averaging 307.4 yards off the tee while the rest of four elite fields averaged 277. He never played a round over par—and all sixteen of his Grand Slam rounds would have been under par if Pebble Beach hadn't lowered its par to 71 for the 2000 U.S. Open. While playing three classic courses and a pretty good one in major-championship conditions, he won four times with a total score of sixty-five under par, with Phil Mickelson and Ernie Els second best at twenty under.

Flashbacks to the Tiger Slam often leave out the fact that it was part of a run of five majors out of six. From his victory at the 1999 PGA through his fifth-place finish at the 2000 Masters to his win at the 2001 Masters, he won five majors while all the other golfers in the world combined to win one.

"He's often compared to Michael Jordan," says statistician Ray, "but to me the comparison is Wilt Chamberlain. Chamberlain had a season where he averaged fifty points and thirty rebounds per game. That's the class Woods was in at his peak. He was doing things relative to his peers that don't even make sense when you read them in retrospect. It will take decades to fully appreciate the level of golf Woods was playing at his best. It will never be equaled."

Today, Tiger often caddies for his son, fifteen-year-old Charlie, in junior events. "I don't know what the future holds in the game of golf for him," he says, "but I can tell you this: we're going to have a lot of fun along the way."

When Charlie lost his temper after a bad shot, Tiger told him, "Son, I don't care how mad you get, as long as you're a hundred percent committed to the next shot." On the range, he would cough, jangle his keys, or toss a ball to distract his son in midswing, the way his father used to do to him. He was also teaching Charlie to think of playing a hole in reverse, from the green back to the tee.

POSTSCRIPTS

Three months after finishing second at the 2001 Masters, **DAVID DUVAL** won the Open Championship at Royal Lytham & St. Annes Golf Club, holding off Sweden's Niclas Fasth by three strokes. The Claret Jug he'd sipped champagne from after Tiger's victory in 2000 was his. But Duval's first and only major was also his last tour win. After decades of fighting injuries, he is now a TV analyst and competitor on the PGA Tour Champions circuit for players fifty and over.

ERNIE ELS went on to win the 2002 Open Championship at Muirfield. At age thirty-two, he came from behind to edge Adam Scott at Royal Lytham & St. Annes Golf Club for his second Open Championship and fourth major. But like Duval, he never escaped Tiger's shadow. "Growing up as a winner and then running into a guy like Tiger—there was some frustration," he acknowledged. After his and his wife, Liezl's, son, Ben, was diagnosed with autism in 2006, he devoted much of his time to Ben and to helping others with autism. In July 2024, the fifty-four-year-old Els won one of the senior tour's majors, the Kaulig Companies Championship. He announced that he would donate his $525,000 winnings to charities including the Els for Autism Foundation.

In 2002, **BUTCH HARMON** and Tiger Woods parted ways after eight major victories and ten years of working together. Since then, Harmon has tutored Phil

Mickelson, Dustin Johnson, Rickie Fowler, and many other Tour pros. Still active at eighty-one, he runs the Butch Harmon School of Golf in Henderson, Nevada. His office wall still features the photo of Ben Hogan he showed Tiger in 1997. "People ask me who was the best golfer ever," he says. "I tell them Jack Nicklaus was the greatest champion. Fans talk about his eighteen majors, and some know about his nineteen second-place finishes, but he also had another nineteen top fives! Nicklaus was golf's greatest champion, but Tiger was the greatest player ever."

JOANNA JAGODA, Tiger's girlfriend in the late 1990s and 2000, graduated from the University of California, Santa Barbara, and earned her law degree at Pepperdine Law School. Today, Joanna Jagoda Roche is an executive director and assistant general counsel at JPMorgan Chase.

BOBBY JONES died in 1971. Before retiring from competitive golf at the age of twenty-eight, he won the U.S. Open four times and the Open Championship three times, as well as five U.S. Amateur Championships and one British Amateur Championship, which were considered majors in his day. By that reckoning, Jones won thirteen major championships, leaving him behind only Nicklaus, who would have twenty including his two U.S. Amateurs, and Woods, who would have eighteen including his three U.S. Amateurs.

Four years after the 2000 PGA Championship, **BOB MAY** could barely swing a club. In 2004, he underwent surgery on his spinal nerve canal and two herniated discs. May never won a PGA Tour event, but he is remembered by a generation of fans as the guy who dueled Tiger Woods a quarter century ago. "Tiger won, but I felt like there was no loser that day," he says. "People were waiting for somebody to stand up to him, and I took him to twenty-one holes." Now fifty-six, May runs the Bob May Golf Academy in Las Vegas, half an hour from Butch Harmon's more lavish facility. Friends and pro-am partners still tease him about the 2000 PGA Championship: when one of them sinks a putt to win a hole, they'll run and point at the cup the way Tiger did at Valhalla.

POSTSCRIPTS

By 2004, **PHIL MICKELSON** was zero for forty-six in the majors. But after sinking an eighteen-foot putt to win that year's Masters by a stroke over Ernie Els, he went on to claim five more major championships to rank twelfth on the all-time winners list (along with Nick Faldo and Lee Trevino). Like Els, Mickelson would have won more majors had his prime not coincided with Tiger's. "It was really frickin' hard to play Tiger back then," he said. "He hit it so far and so straight and was such a clutch putter, you felt like you had to play perfect golf to beat him."

ELIN NORDEGREN married Tiger Woods in 2004. She is the mother of their daughter, Sam, and son, Charlie. She divorced Woods in 2010 after his affairs with other women made worldwide news, and received a reported $100 million divorce settlement. They have co-parented their children since then. "I betrayed her," Tiger admitted in 2017. "My regret will last a lifetime." He said he'd told the children, "Daddy made some mistakes. . . . But look what happened at the end of it. Look at how great you are. You have two loving parents that love you no matter what." Nordegren went on to have three children with her partner, former NFL player Jordan Cameron, and work as a mental health counselor in Florida.

MARK O'MEARA credited his fierce practice rounds with Tiger for at least part of his late-career success. According to *Sports Illustrated*, "You can't see the two of them together without thinking that the older man looks like Woods's accountant." But O'Meara won the 1998 Masters and Open Championship at the age of forty-one. "I'm proud of myself," he said, "because I kept improving." He was inducted into the World Golf Hall of Fame in 2015.

The **TITLEIST PRO V1** is the best-selling product in golf history. Twenty-five years after its debut and eight years after Nike shut down its golf division in 2016, the Pro V1 is sold in pro shops and sporting goods outlets worldwide and dominates the PGA Tour. According to Tour veteran Stewart Cink, "We can talk about drivers and shafts and athleticism all day, but the golf ball was the big factor" in the game's recent evolution. "Before, a golfer had to decide which one of the holy grails of golf-ball performance he or she wanted: distance or feel. Now you had a ball that was both. It really unleashed the beast." The Pro V1 now accounts for the lion's share of the multibillion-dollar golf ball market.

253

In 2006, Tiger flew to New Zealand to serve as best man at **STEVE WILLIAMS**'s wedding. In 2011, after a dozen years together that included thirteen of Tiger's fifteen majors, Tiger fired him over a dispute about Williams's spending a week as Adam Scott's caddie. Two years later, Williams was on the bag when Scott won the 2013 Masters.

EARL WOODS died at age seventy-four in 2006, two months before that year's Open Championship at Royal Liverpool Golf Club. After winning the tournament, his eleventh major, Tiger burst into tears. "I miss my dad so much," he said. "I wish he could have seen this one last time."

KULTIDA WOODS, age eighty, joined her grandchildren, Sam and Charlie, at the 2024 U.S. Open at Pinehurst Resort in Pinehurst, North Carolina, where her son received the USGA's highest honor, the Bob Jones Award for "commitment to sportsmanship and respect for golf's time-honored traditions." Accepting the award, Tiger said, "I didn't do this alone. I had the greatest rock any child could possibly have, my mom. Thank you, Mommy."

Twenty-five years after saying that he hoped to "compete out here with the young boys" for another quarter century, **TIGER WOODS** will turn fifty and qualify for the senior tour on December 30, 2025.

LEADERBOARDS

100TH U.S. OPEN

Pebble Beach Golf Links, Pebble Beach, California

FIRST ROUND: THURSDAY AND FRIDAY, JUNE 15–16, 2000

Tiger Woods	65 (−6)
Miguel Ángel Jiménez	66 (−5)
John Huston	67 (−4)
Bobby Clampett	68 (−3)
Hale Irwin	68 (−3)
Loren Roberts	68 (−3)
Ángel Cabrera	69 (−2)
Nick Faldo	69 (−2)
Rocco Mediate	69 (−2)
Hal Sutton	69 (−2)

SECOND ROUND: FRIDAY AND SATURDAY, JUNE 16–17, 2000

Tiger Woods	65-69 = 134 (−8)
Thomas Bjørn	70-70 = 140 (−2)
Miguel Ángel Jiménez	66-74 = 140 (−2)
José María Olazábal	70-71 = 141 (−1)

Kirk Triplett	70-71 = 141 (−1)
John Huston	67-75 = 142 (E)
Hal Sutton	69-73 = 142 (E)
Lee Westwood	71-71 = 142 (E)
Nick Faldo	69-74 = 143 (+1)
Vijay Singh	70-73 = 143 (+1)

THIRD ROUND: SATURDAY, JUNE 17, 2000

Tiger Woods	65-69-71 = 205 (−8)
Ernie Els	74-73-68 = 215 (+2)
Pádraig Harrington	73-71-72 = 216 (+3)
Miguel Ángel Jiménez	66-74-76 = 216 (+3)
Phil Mickelson	71-73-73 = 217 (+4)
José María Olazábal	70-71-76 = 217 (+4)
John Huston	67-75-76 = 218 (+5)
Lee Westwood	71-71-76 = 218 (+5)
Michael Campbell	71-77-71 = 219 (+6)
Nick Faldo	69-74-76 = 219 (+6)
Loren Roberts	68-78-73 = 219 (+6)

FOURTH ROUND: SUNDAY, JUNE 18, 2000

Tiger Woods	65-69-71-67 = 272 (−12)
Ernie Els	74-73-68-72 = 287 (+3)
Miguel Ángel Jiménez	66-74-76-71 = 287 (+3)
John Huston	67-75-76-70 = 288 (+4)
Pádraig Harrington	73-71-72-73 = 289 (+5)
Lee Westwood	71-71-76-71 = 289 (+5)
Nick Faldo	69-74-76-71 = 290 (+6)
Stewart Cink	77-72-72-70 = 291 (+7)
David Duval	75-71-74-71 = 291 (+7)
Loren Roberts	68-78-73-72 = 291 (+7)
Vijay Singh	70-73-80-68 = 291 (+7)

129TH OPEN CHAMPIONSHIP

The Old Course, St. Andrews, Scotland

FIRST ROUND: THURSDAY, JULY 20, 2000

Ernie Els	66 (−6)
Steve Flesch	67 (−5)
Tiger Woods	67 (−5)
Scott Dunlap	68 (−4)
Ian Garbutt	68 (−4)
Sergio García	68 (−4)
Pádraig Harrington	68 (−4)
Tom Lehman	68 (−4)
Shigeki Maruyama	68 (−4)
Dennis Paulson	68 (−4)

SECOND ROUND: FRIDAY, JULY 21, 2000

Tiger Woods	67-66 = 133 (−11)
David Toms	69-67 = 136 (−8)
Steve Flesch	67-70 = 137 (−7)
Sergio García	68-69 = 137 (−7)
Loren Roberts	69-68 = 137 (−7)
Thomas Bjørn	69-69 = 138 (−6)
Fred Couples	70-68 = 138 (−6)
Ernie Els	66-72 = 138 (−6)
Tom Lehman	68-70 = 138 (−6)
Phil Mickelson	72-66 = 138 (−6)

THIRD ROUND: SATURDAY, JULY 22, 2000

Tiger Woods	67-66-67 = 200 (−16)
Thomas Bjørn	69-69-68 = 206 (−10)
David Duval	70-70-66 = 206 (−10)
Darren Clarke	70-69-68 = 207 (−9)
Loren Roberts	69-68-70 = 207 (−9)

David Toms	69-67-71 = 207 (−9)
Ernie Els	66-72-70 = 208 (−8)
Steve Flesch	67-70-71 = 208 (−8)
Tom Lehman	68-70-70 = 208 (−8)
Dennis Paulson	68-71-69 = 208 (−8)

FOURTH ROUND: SUNDAY, JULY 23, 2000

Tiger Woods	67-66-67-69 = 269 (−19)
Thomas Bjørn	69-69-68-71 = 277 (−11)
Ernie Els	66-72-70-69 = 277 (−11)
Tom Lehman	68-70-70-70 = 278 (−10)
David Toms	69-67-71-71 = 278 (−10)
Fred Couples	70-68-72-69 = 279 (−9)
Paul Azinger	69-72-72-67 = 280 (−8)
Darren Clarke	70-69-68-73 = 280 (−8)
Pierre Fulke	69-72-70-69 = 280 (−8)
Loren Roberts	69-68-70-73 = 280 (−8)

82ND PGA CHAMPIONSHIP

Valhalla Golf Club, Louisville, Kentucky

FIRST ROUND: THURSDAY, AUGUST 17, 2000

Scott Dunlap	66 (−6)
Tiger Woods	66 (−6)
Darren Clarke	68 (−4)
Davis Love III	68 (−4)
Stephen Ames	69 (−3)
Ed Fryatt	69 (−3)
Fred Funk	69 (−3)
J. P. Hayes	69 (−3)
Stuart Appleby	70 (−2)
Brian Henninger	70 (−2)

LEADERBOARDS

Miguel Ángel Jiménez	70 (−2)
Jonathan Kaye	70 (−2)
Tom Kite	70 (−2)
Phil Mickelson	70 (−2)
Jean van de Velde	70 (−2)

SECOND ROUND: FRIDAY, AUGUST 18, 2000

Tiger Woods	66-67 = 133 (−11)
Scott Dunlap	66-68 = 134 (−10)
Fred Funk	69-68 = 137 (−7)
J. P. Hayes	69-68 = 137 (−7)
Davis Love III	68-69 = 137 (−7)
Notah Begay III	72-68 = 138 (−6)
Bob May	72-66 = 138 (−6)
Stuart Appleby	70-69 = 139 (−5)
Stephen Ames	69-71 = 140 (−4)
Thomas Bjørn	72-68 = 140 (−4)
Greg Chalmers	71-69 = 140 (−4)
Darren Clarke	68-72 = 140 (−4)
Phil Mickelson	70-70 = 140 (−4)
David Toms	72-68 = 140 (−4)

THIRD ROUND: SATURDAY, AUGUST 19, 2000

Tiger Woods	66-67-70 = 203 (−13)
Scott Dunlap	66-68-70 = 204 (−12)
Bob May	72-66-66 = 204 (−12)
J. P. Hayes	69-68-68 = 205 (−11)
Greg Chalmers	71-69-66 = 206 (−10)
Stuart Appleby	70-69-68 = 207 (−9)
Thomas Bjørn	72-68-67 = 207 (−9)
José María Olazábal	76-68-63 = 207 (−9)
Notah Begay III	72-66-70 = 208 (−8)
Franklin Langham	72-71-65 = 208 (−8)

259

FOURTH ROUND: SUNDAY, AUGUST 20, 2000

Bob May	72-66-66-66 = 270 (−18)
Tiger Woods	66-67-70-67 = 270 (−18)
Thomas Bjørn	72-68-67-68 = 275 (−13)
Stuart Appleby	70-69-68-69 = 276 (−12)
Greg Chalmers	71-69-66-70 = 276 (−12)
José María Olazábal	76-68-63-69 = 276 (−12)
Franklin Langham	72-71-65-69 = 277 (−11)
Notah Begay III	72-66-70-70 = 278 (−10)
Darren Clarke	68-72-72-67 = 279 (−9)
Scott Dunlap	66-68-70-75 = 279 (−9)
Fred Funk	69-68-74-68 = 279 (−9)
Davis Love III	68-69-72-70 = 279 (−9)
Phil Mickelson	70-70-69-70 = 279 (−9)
Tom Watson	76-70-65-68 = 279 (−9)

THREE-HOLE PLAYOFF: SUNDAY, AUGUST 20, 2000

Tiger Woods	12 (−1)
Bob May	13 (E)

65TH MASTERS

Augusta National Golf Club, Augusta, Georgia

FIRST ROUND: THURSDAY, APRIL 5, 2001

Chris DiMarco	65 (−7)
Ángel Cabrera	66 (−6)
Steve Stricker	66 (−6)
John Huston	67 (−5)
Lee Janzen	67 (−5)
Phil Mickelson	67 (−5)
James Driscoll	68 (−4)
Miguel Ángel Jiménez	68 (−4)

Chris Perry   68 (−4)
Kirk Triplett   68 (−4)

SECOND ROUND: FRIDAY, APRIL 6, 2001

Chris DiMarco   65-69 = 134 (−10)
Phil Mickelson   67-69 = 136 (−8)
Tiger Woods   70-66 = 136 (−8)
Ángel Cabrera   66-71 = 137 (−7)
David Duval   71-66 = 137 (−7)
Toshimitsu Izawa   71-66 = 137 (−7)
Lee Janzen   67-70 = 137 (−7)
Steve Stricker   66-71 = 137 (−7)
Mark Calcavecchia   72-66 = 138 (−6)
José María Olazábal   70-68 = 138 (−6)
Kirk Triplett   68-70 = 138 (−6)

THIRD ROUND: SATURDAY, APRIL 7, 2001

Tiger Woods   70-66-68 = 204 (−12)
Phil Mickelson   67-69-69 = 205 (−11)
Mark Calcavecchia   72-66-68 = 206 (−10)
Chris DiMarco   65-69-72 = 206 (−10)
Ángel Cabrera   66-71-70 = 207 (−9)
David Duval   71-66-70 = 207 (−9)
Ernie Els   71-68-68 = 207 (−9)
Rocco Mediate   72-70-66 = 208 (−8)
Kirk Triplett   68-70-70 = 208 (−8)
Brad Faxon   73-68-68 = 209 (−7)
Lee Janzen   67-70-72 = 209 (−7)
José María Olazábal   70-68-71 = 209 (−7)
Steve Stricker   66-71-72 = 209 (−7)

FOURTH ROUND: SUNDAY, APRIL 8, 2001

Tiger Woods	70-66-68-68 = 272 (−16)
David Duval	71-66-70-67 = 274 (−14)
Phil Mickelson	67-69-69-70 = 275 (−13)
Mark Calcavecchia	72-66-68-72 = 278 (−10)
Toshimitsu Izawa	71-66-74-67 = 278 (−10)
Ernie Els	71-68-68-72 = 279 (−9)
Jim Furyk	69-71-70-69 = 279 (−9)
Bernhard Langer	73-69-68-69 = 279 (−9)
Kirk Triplett	68-70-70-71 = 279 (−9)
Ángel Cabrera	66-71-70-73 = 280 (−8)
Chris DiMarco	65-69-72-74 = 280 (−8)
Brad Faxon	73-68-68-71 = 280 (−8)
Miguel Ángel Jiménez	68-72-71-69 = 280 (−8)
Steve Stricker	66-71-72-71 = 280 (−8)

GOLFERS WITH THE MOST PROFESSIONAL MAJOR CHAMPIONSHIPS

	MASTERS	U.S. OPEN	OPEN CHAMPIONSHIP	PGA CHAMPIONSHIP	TOTAL
Jack Nicklaus	6	4	3	5	18
Tiger Woods	5	3	3	4	15
Walter Hagen	0	2	4	5	11
Ben Hogan	2	4	1	2	9
Gary Player	3	1	3	2	9
Tom Watson	2	1	5	2	9
Harry Vardon	0	1	6	0	7
Bobby Jones	0	4	3	0	7
Gene Sarazen	1	2	1	3	7
Sam Snead	3	0	1	3	7
Arnold Palmer	4	1	2	0	7
Lee Trevino	0	2	2	2	6
Nick Faldo	3	0	3	0	6
Phil Mickelson	3	0	1	2	6

A NOTE ON SOURCES

During a year and a half of research, I relied on interviews with people involved in the Tiger Slam, plus a stack of books and digital records that helped me reconstruct the ten months when Tiger Woods played the game better than anyone else before or since. Butch Harmon, Mark O'Meara, Bob May, and Gary McCord shared their in-the-moment experiences. Statistics guru Justin Ray, the Head of Content at Twenty First Group, helped put the Tiger Slam into historical perspective. Other go-to resources included *Training a Tiger: A Father's Guide to Raising a Winner in Both Golf and Life* by Earl Woods with Pete McDaniel (New York: HarperCollins, 1997); *How I Play Golf* by Tiger Woods with the editors of *Golf Digest* (New York: Warner Books, 2001); *Unprecedented: The Masters and Me* by Tiger Woods with Lorne Rubenstein (New York: Grand Central Publishing, 2017); Steve Williams and Hugh de Lacy's *Golf at the Top with Steve Williams: Tips & Techniques from the Caddy to Raymond Floyd, Greg Norman & Tiger Woods* (New York: Ulysses Press, 2006); Williams's *Out of the Rough: Inside the Ropes with the World's Greatest Golfers* with Michael Donaldson (New York: Viking, 2015); Butch Harmon's *The Pro: Lessons About Golf and Life from My Father, Claude Harmon, Sr.* (New York: Three Rivers Press, 2006); Jeff Benedict and Armen Keteyian's

Tiger Woods (New York: Simon & Schuster, 2018); and two books
by Tom Callahan, *In Search of Tiger: A Journey Through Golf with
Tiger Woods* (New York: Three Rivers Press, 2003) and *His Father's
Son: Earl and Tiger Woods* (New York: Penguin, 2010). I spent hours
locked in the Sports Illustrated Vault, the magazine's online library, re-
reading vivid coverage of the Tiger Slam by Alan Shipnuck, John Garrity, Rick Reilly, and a dozen other *SI* scribes, and enjoyed it almost as
much as researching a story the old-fashioned way in the eighteenth-
floor library in the Time & Life Building. Garrity and Jim Herre, *SI*'s
longtime golf editor, helped me understand what was going on behind
the scenes. CBS, NBC, ESPN, and Golf Channel archives provided
video. ASAP Sports provided transcripts of post-round press conferences with Woods and other players.

Some details came from sources including Bob Harig's *Tiger and
Phil: Golf's Most Fascinating Rivalry* (New York: St. Martin's Press,
2022), John Garrity's *Tiger 2.0 . . . and Other Great Stories from
the World of Golf* (New York: Sports Illustrated Books, 2008), Tim
Rosaforte's *Raising the Bar: The Championship Years of Tiger Woods*
(New York: Thomas Dunne Books, 2000), Michael Bamberger's *Men
in Green* (New York: Simon & Schuster, 2015), Hank Haney's *The
Big Miss: My Years Coaching Tiger Woods* (New York: Crown, 2012),
Theodore P. Jorgenson's *The Physics of Golf* (New York: Springer-
Verlag, 1994), Tom Callahan's *Arnie: The Life of Arnold Palmer* (New
York: HarperCollins, 2017), Phil Mickelson's *One Magical Sunday
(But Winning Isn't Everything)* with Donald T. Phillips (New York:
Warner Books, 2005), John Feinstein's *The Majors: In Pursuit of
Golf's Holy Grail* (New York: Little, Brown, 1999), Triumph Books
Publishing Staff's *Tiger Woods: The Grandest Slam* (Chicago: Tri-
umph Books, 2001), and Hughes Norton and George Peper's *Rain-
maker* (New York: Atria Books, 2024) as well as *Golf Magazine* and
Golf Digest archives and those of the *Augusta Chronicle*, Louisville

Courier Journal, St. Andrews Citizen, New York Times, Chicago Tribune, and *Los Angeles Times.*

Evin Priest's *Chasing Majors* podcast added many of Steve Williams's insights into his years on the bag with Tiger. The golf blogger Jay Flemma and Valhalla member Andy Vine had interesting things to say about Valhalla. Mark James Sharman's 2007 East Tennessee State University master's degree thesis, "A Study of How Four Black Newspapers Covered the U.S. Masters Tournament 1994 through 2001," helped me see the Tiger Slam through the eyes of reporters writing for Black readers.

ACKNOWLEDGMENTS

A book needs to be a labor of love, or it wouldn't be worth the work that goes into it. I had a fine time catching up with Butch Harmon, Bob May, Mark O'Meara, Gary McCord, and other key sources. Justin Ray helped me see the Tiger Slam from a fresh angle. My *Sports Illustrated* friends Jim Herre and John Garrity shared their experiences and deep knowledge of the game. Other *SI* colleagues who helped make me a little smarter about golf over the years include Michael Bamberger, Rick Reilly, Alan Shipnuck, Jaime Diaz, Gary Van Sickle, Steve Rushin, and Luis Fernando Llosa. I owe thanks to old colleagues at *Golf Magazine* and friends at *Golf Digest*, as well as Jeff Babineau and the Golf Writers Association of America.

Other sources of golf knowledge and inspiration include the late Dan Jenkins, the late Fred Hickman, David Leadbetter, Mark Mulvoy, John Paul Newport, the late Arnold Palmer, Doc Giffin, Mark Frost, and Jim Nantz. In Scotland, David Malcolm and David Joy were prized sources for earlier golf books who became friends.

David Halpern shepherded the book from an idea in a meeting to publication with his usual wisdom and aplomb. I'm glad to be a part of David Halpern Literary Management.

Until last year I knew Jofie Ferrari-Adler only by reputation. It's better to know him as the best ally any writer could have. Major thanks to Jofie and his colleagues at Avid Reader Press, Julianna Haubner, Carolyn Kelly, David Kass, Jonathan Evans, Lynn Anderson, Allison Green, Eva Kerins, Meredith Vilarello, Alison Forner, Clay Smith, Sydney Newman, and Ruth Lee-Mui.

My mother, Patricia Cook, took me to play golf for the first time when I was ten and saw me miss my first two-foot putt. Randy Phillips and I used to play Heather Hills (Pete and Alice Dye's first eighteen-holer!). Fifty years and a heart transplant later, Randy is an inspiration. Thanks also to Kathy Robbins, Janet Oshiro, Mark Risley, Helen Rosenberg, Michael Bardsley, Phil Sullivan, Alexis Johnson, Arthur Kretchmer, Ken Kubik, Doug Vogel, and Chris Carson.

Pamela Marin is my in-house editor and partner in all things. Our son, Cal Cook, is my golf partner and role model. Our daughter, Lily Lady, is my puzzle partner and role model.

I was lucky enough to see Tiger Woods at his best, from his early career (we both used to play Dad Miller Golf Course in Anaheim) through his championship years on PGA Tour ranges and courses, including the 2008 U.S. Open at Torrey Pines, where he limped to victory with no ACL and two stress fractures in his left leg. Whatever else you may think of him, when he was on the course there was no greater grinder.

INDEX

earnings, 9, 30, 81, 84, 86, 126, 179,
  181, 183, 188–89, 204, 241
endorsements, 20–22, 125, 186, 224
favorite color, 74
fitness of, 49, 55, 57
as gamer, 181
home in Isleworth, 88
Jack Nicklaus, vs., 44
later years, 241
legacy, 243–49
nickname, 37
PGA Tour winning streaks, 247
pre-putt routine, 59, 75–76, 78, 83–84,
  101–2, 164–65, 169, 174

pre-round practice sessions, 93
pre-shot routine, 101–2, 201
racial identity, 14, 80–81
teen years, 42
tournament winnings,
  183
TV tribute, 225
winless streak, 181–90
see also Tiger Slam
World Golf Ranking, 209

Z
Zoeller, Fuzzy, 12, 14, 55, 209

IMAGE CREDITS

ABOUT THE AUTHOR

A former *Sports Illustrated* senior editor and editor in chief of *Golf Magazine*, **KEVIN COOK** has written about golf for *Sports Illustrated*, *The Wall Street Journal*, and many other publications, and talked about the game on ESPN, CNN, and Fox News. His first book, *Tommy's Honor*, won the United States Golf Association's Herbert Warren Wind Award.